A Little Heaven Below

Worship at Early Methodist Quarterly Meetings

Lester Ruth

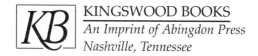

KINGSWOOD BOOKS
An Imprint of Abingdon Press
Nashville, Tennessee

A LITTLE HEAVEN BELOW:
WORSHIP AT EARLY METHODIST QUARTERLY MEETINGS

Cataloging-in-Publication Data is available
from the Library of Congress.

00 01 02 03 04 05 06 07 08 09—10 9 8 7 6 5 4 3 2 1

MANUFACTURED IN THE UNITED STATES OF AMERICA

In Memory of a Beloved Father
Charles K. Ruth
1920–1999

Contents

Abbreviations

AM	*The Arminian Magazine* (British edition)
Discipline/year	The official book of doctrine and discipline of The Methodist Episcopal Church. First edition was *Minutes of several conversations between the Rev. Thomas Coke, LL.D., the Rev. Francis Asbury, and others, at a Conference begun in Baltimore, in the State of Maryland, on Monday, the 27th of December, in the year 1784. Composing a Form of Discipline for the Ministers, Preachers and Other Members of the Methodist Episcopal Church in America* (Philadelphia: Cist, 1785). The 1786 edition is entitled *The General Minutes of the Conferences of the Methodist Episcopal Church in America, forming the Constitution of the said Church.* Editions from 1787–1791 are entitled *A Form of Discipline, for the Ministers, Preachers, and Members of the Methodist Episcopal Church in America.* After 1792 all editions are titled *The Doctrines and Discipline of the Methodist Episcopal Church in America.*
Hymns	*A Collection of Hymns for the Use of the People Called Methodists,* edited by Franz Hildebrandt & Oliver Beckerlegge (Nashville: Abingdon, 1983); volume 7 of *Works.*

9

HLS	*Hymns on the Lord's Supper,* by John Wesley and Charles Wesley (Bristol: Farley, 1745; facsimile reprint, Madison, NJ: Charles Wesley Society, 1995). These hymns also appended to J. Ernest Rattenbury, *The Eucharistic Hymns of John and Charles Wesley* (London: Epworth, 1948; reprint with updated grammar, Cleveland, OH: OSL Publications, 1990).
JLFA	*The Journal and Letters of Francis Asbury,* 3 vols.; edited by Elmer T. Clark (London: Epworth; Nashville: Abingdon, 1958).
JGC/year	Refers to the *Journal of the General Conference of the Methodist Episcopal Church* for the year indicated. Citations from *Journals of the General Conference of the Methodist Episcopal Church, 1796–1856,* 3 vols. (New York: Carlton & Phillips, 1856).
Minutes/year	Annual or General Minutes of The Methodist Episcopal Church; citing page numbers from collection in *Minutes of the Annual Conferences of the Methodist Episcopal Church for the Years 1773–1828* (New York: T. Mason and G. Lane, 1840).
MQR	Refers to quarterly theological journal of The Methodist Episcopal Church under its fluctuating names (*Methodist Magazine* [1818–1828], *Methodist Magazine and Quarterly Review* [1830–1840], etc.).
Works	*The Works of John Wesley;* begun as "The Oxford Edition of The Works of John Wesley" (Oxford: Clarendon Press, 1975–1983); continued as "The Bicentennial Edition of The Works of John Wesley" (Nashville: Abingdon, 1984–); 15 of 35 vols. published to date.
Works (Jackson)	*The Works of John Wesley,* 14 vols.; ed. Thomas Jackson (London: Wesleyan Methodist Book Room, 1872; Grand Rapids: Baker Book House, 1979).

Introduction

"People are the primary liturgical document." So begins *Protestant Worship: Traditions in Transition,* a book by the prominent liturgical historian James F. White.[1] In this study of Protestant worship's breadth, White sounds this particular note to balance what he sees as a common methodology brought to Protestant worship, namely using liturgical texts—particularly eucharistic texts—to tell the history of this worship. White's emphasis on the importance of identifying people as the central "text" for writing liturgical history thus provides a corrective to other studies. When written texts are emphasized over the examination of Protestant people, White states, the result can be a "distorted image."[2]

Unfortunately, the telling of American Methodist liturgical history has not been exempt from this malady. In many previous accounts of this history, the failure to treat—comprehensively and intentionally—the Methodist people as the "primary liturgical document" has led to not only a distorted image but even a gross caricature of their worship.

---

1. James F. White, *Protestant Worship: Traditions in Transition* (Louisville: Westminster/John Knox, 1989), 16.

2. Ibid., 13. White offers several reasons why written texts should not have primacy of place in Protestant liturgical historiography: 1) many Protestants speak extemporaneously, using liturgical texts seldom or never; 2) even if a written text does not change, changes in other liturgical spheres (architecture, music, liturgical rhythms, popular piety, etc.) can radically transform a group's worship; and 3) with regard to eucharistic texts, intense focus on these texts is misplaced since the Eucharist is an infrequent service for many Protestants.

11

Specifically, the first fifty years or so of American Methodism have been portrayed at times as a period of liturgical and sacramental poverty, during which the American Methodist people almost immediately squandered the rich liturgical heritage bequeathed to them by John Wesley, the movement's founder.[3]

According to this caricature promoted by many scholars, the nature of the liturgical impoverishment of early American Methodists was multifaceted. Their whole approach to worship is portrayed as driven by entirely practical and utilitarian concerns.[4] They are judged to be a people who felt "no need for ordered worship, however beautiful, however ancient, however sound it might be."[5] A bishop who supposedly was clearly antisacramental is accused of leading them away from the worship countenanced by John Wesley.[6] American preachers are dismissed as "lacking familiarity with the mind of Wesley, as indeed with any larger frame of reference."[7] In the absence of such reference a "human-centered revivalism, easy believism, and individualism" is asserted to characterize the period.[8]

Moreover, early American Methodists have been seen as erroneously believing that salvation was solely an individualistic, personal matter and thus little concerned with communal dimensions of religious experience such as tradition and liturgy.[9] They are lamented for missing the opportunity to become a good "liturgical" church, instead opting for lesser forms of worship.[10] They are censured for creating liturgically unorthodox anomalies, such as using the love feast as a kind of "sacramental substitute."[11] The infrequent sacra-

---

3. See, for example, approximately the same language in Earl Kent Brown, "Liturgy Today: Historical Perspective on Methodist Worship," *Religion in Life* 39 (spring 1970): 33.

4. Edwin E. Voigt, *Methodist Worship in the Church Universal* (Nashville: Graded Press, 1965), 71.

5. Paul S. Sanders, "An Appraisal of John Wesley's Sacramentalism in the Evolution of Early American Methodism" (Th.D. diss., Union Theological Seminary, 1954), 250.

6. William Nash Wade, "A History of Public Worship in The Methodist Episcopal Church and Methodist Episcopal Church, South, from 1784 to 1905" (Ph.D. diss., Notre Dame, 1981), 136-56, 183-88. The method that Wade employs in the dissertation should be seriously questioned, particularly in his use of Bishop Francis Asbury's published journal. Wade too sharply isolates Asbury as a liturgical influence, probably overestimating his liturgical power and underestimating the role of other Methodist people and preachers in the shaping of early Methodist worship.

7. Paul S. Sanders, "The Sacraments in Early American Methodism," *Church History* 26 (1957): 360.

8. Terril D. Littrel, "Holy Communion in the American Methodist Tradition," *Doxology* 12 (1995): 28.

9. Sanders, "Appraisal of Wesley's Sacramentalism," 250.

10. Kenneth B. Bedell, *Worship in the Methodist Tradition* (Nashville: Tidings, 1976), 52.

11. Robert Milton Winter, "American Churches and the Holy Communion: A Comparative Study in Sacramental Theology, Practice, and Piety in the Episcopal, Presbyterian, Methodist,

mental observance that resulted from the initial shortage of ministers is assumed to reflect a lack of appreciation for the Lord's Supper. In explicit contrast with the Wesleys, the Americans' sacramental practice and teaching is described as a form of sad "memorialism" where sacraments lack a decisive importance for Christian life or worship.[12] Hence the period is identified as the beginning of decline for the Lord's Supper in Methodism.[13] It is also commonly portrayed as the time when Methodism's heritage of good evangelical hymnody was "perverted" by revivalistic songs and the whole concept of the church year was lost.[14]

The cumulative result of such previous scholarly assessments is a very distorted image of early American Methodist worship. As White has suggested, the major reason for the distortion is the failure to consider the people themselves as the central liturgical text. One is struck by how little attention is paid to early American Methodists' own writings in much current liturgical historiography. Only a few individuals are included in most studies, and frequently only a fraction of their writings are examined.[15] This has been a grave methodological error not only in short treatments of Methodist liturgical history but also in the larger, more influential studies by William Wade and Paul Sanders.[16] The resulting imbalanced views have been adopted and circulated in several prominent general survey texts.[17]

When the writings of Methodist people themselves are explored in detail, with close attention paid to the wealth of their own reflections and a willingness to understand them on their own terms, a very different image emerges. Instead of liturgical shallowness, early American

---

and German Reformed Traditions, 1607–1875" (Ph.D. diss., Union Theological Seminary, 1988), 579. See also Doug Adams, *Meeting House to Camp Meeting: Toward a History of American Free Church Worship from 1620 to 1835* (Saratoga: Modern Liturgy-Resource Publications, 1981), 104.

12. John Bishop, *Methodist Worship in Relation to Free Church Worship* (New York: Scholars Studies Press, 1975), 73, 129.

13. Littrel, "Holy Communion," 25-28.

14. Sanders, "Appraisal of Wesley's Sacramentalism," 380, 425.

15. Among earlier studies, an example of how a more accurate, nuanced portrayal of early Methodist worship is possible by using primary sources more widely is Fred Hood, "Community and the Rhetoric of 'Freedom': Early American Methodist Worship," Methodist History 9/1 (October 1970): 13-25. Hood's history is not without its own problems, however, as in its portrayal of Francis Asbury.

16. See Wade, "History of Public Worship," and Sanders, "Appraisal of Wesley's Sacramentalism."

17. See, for instance, the use of Sanders's views in the well-known work of Bard Thompson: *Liturgies of the Western Church* (Philadelphia: Fortress, 1985), 410-11. Wade has been cited in influential books like Nathan Hatch's *The Democratization of American Christianity* (New Haven: Yale University Press, 1989), 267, and in promising new studies like Frank Senn's comprehensive history, *Christian Liturgy: Catholic and Evangelical* (Minneapolis: Fortress, 1997), 550.

Methodists practiced an amazing complexity of services and rituals. Instead of mere pragmatism and rabid individualism, they exulted in the communal dimension of their worship to the point where they struggled to find words adequate to describe their liturgical assembly. Instead of a sacramental depreciation, they exhibited a deep piety toward the Lord's Supper, a spirituality in continuity with Wesley in thought and practice. And instead of squandering their inheritance of hymnody and the Christian calendar, they supplemented and adapted what they received. In sum, early Methodists participated in what is now understood positively as inculturation.

Most important, in contrast to the reigning assertion that their worship was impoverished, early Methodists gloried in proclaiming as loud as they could, sometimes literally at the top of their voices,[18] that God was present in their worship, that in public prayer God bestowed grace upon the gathered community. If they were liturgically poor, the abiding sense of God's graciousness in their midst certainly fooled them.

A new portrayal of early American Methodists at worship, listening to their voices and accepting them on their own terms, is the goal of this book. To pursue this end, I will use a wealth of materials dating from before 1825: journals, diaries, letters, liturgical fragments, hymns, circuit records, histories, and autobiographies.[19] Much of this material is unpublished and has been little considered by liturgical historians.[20] I also give careful attention to distinctive elements of Methodist polity since it provides the flavor and context for other aspects of Methodist life, including worship. In the end, the reader must judge whether I succeed in giving voice to these early Methodists, for I believe people truly are the primary liturgical document.

The particular lens through which I will examine early American Methodist worship is an especially crucial liturgical setting: the quarterly meeting. While modern Methodists may know the descendants

---

18. See the section below on shouting.

19. One benefit of looking at these sorts of documents, rather than specifically liturgical texts, is that one can better assess the piety, time, place, prayer, preaching, and music of the early Methodists. According to White (*Protestant Worship,* 15-16), these are better categories than "texts" and "rubrics" to use in describing Protestant worship.

20. The holding sources for unpublished materials are identified in their listing in the Select Bibliography. I will use short titles for this material in the footnotes, as well as for published materials contained in the Select Bibliography after their first reference in each chapter. All quotations in this work will maintain the sources' punctuation, capitalization, and original spelling (without noting misspellings by sic). Whenever journals, diaries, and other archival materials are cited, a page number will be provided when possible, and if not, then the date of the entry.

of this sort of meeting as quarterly conferences or charge conferences, they should not allow any associations with the latter to color their first assumptions about quarterly meetings. Quarterly meetings two hundred years ago were much different from their modern progeny, containing not only a business session but also nearly every form of Methodist worship. Not surprisingly, the meetings typically lasted two days, if not longer. Attendees were not only those who came for the business, but also the many who came for worship, fellowship, or just the commotion itself. It was not uncommon for attendants—Methodists and non-Methodists alike—to number into the hundreds or thousands. For all these reasons, quarterly meetings were an especially crucial liturgical setting for early Methodists, and serve today as a particularly appropriate lens to gain focus on their worship.[21]

I wish to thank the many people who have supported me and made this work possible. The support of Yale University's Institute of Sacred Music and its director, Margot Fassler, has been invaluable. Many thanks also to those who have read sections of this book and have offered comments that have improved it: Mark Torgerson, Martin Jean, Cindy Zirlott, Bryan Spinks, and Beth Boardman. The comments of John Wigger, Karen Westerfield Tucker, Russell Richey, and my study group in the North American Academy of Liturgy have also been very useful. The excellent work of John Wigger and Russell Richey, in particular, has been influential in helping me see another way to approach early Methodist liturgical history.

My appreciation must also go to James White for his continued support and encouragement of this project. I extend gratitude to Don Meador, my former district superintendent, for showing me the continuing relevance of this research for modern Methodists. I also want to thank the fine staffs at the many archives and churches who have helped me, including those at Drew, Duke, the University of North Carolina, Garrett, DePauw, Lovely Lane, Old St. George's, Barratt's Chapel, and the United Methodist Church in Stratford, Connecticut. Finally, I thank my assistant, Josh McKee, for his excellent help at several critical junctures.

I also wish to thank the General Commission on Archives and

---

21. A specific benefit of looking at quarterly meetings as settings for worship rather than at particular liturgical texts is that they enable us to see how important liturgical rhythms and practices were firmly in place for Methodists before their organization as The Methodist Episcopal Church, and how John Wesley's sending over of the *Sunday Service*, his revision of the *Book of Common Prayer*, must be understood in this context.

History of The United Methodist Church for awarding this book the 1999 quadrennial Jesse Lee Prize in Methodist History.

This book could not have been completed without the support of my family. Foremost kudos must be given to the lights of my life: Carmen, Charissa, Rebekah, and Lois. The love and energy you all have shared with me provide the deep inspiration for this book. Thanks also to my much-loved siblings: Joe Martin, Judy Almaguer, and Pat Martin. Your support has made many dark times bearable.

CHAPTER 1

Quarterly Meetings as Settings for Worship in American Methodism

"These were our great festivals."
—*an early itinerant reminiscing about quarterly meetings*[1]

During the eighteenth century Methodism, whether as a reform movement within the Church of England or as a church in its own right, lived in a form of self-imposed diaspora. The polity, or form of organization, that its founder John Wesley had developed made it so. The majority of Methodists—in England and in America—lived in circuits, the standard unit of organization. At its most basic meaning, a circuit described the path of travel over which a traveling preacher went to preach his sermons each month, including typically two dozen or more preaching sites. As a lived experience, a circuit was an act of ecclesiastical dispersion. The idea of a Methodist preacher or minister in constant residence with the people was foreign to the eighteenth century. Conspicuously absent was the notion of local Methodism as parishes and itinerant preachers as pastors. Since the typical American circuit was a four-week circuit, traveled by two itinerant preachers spaced two weeks apart, the majority of American Methodists grew accustomed to hearing preaching from one of their itinerants every other week, on any day of the week, depending upon the plan of preaching appointments for that circuit.

By having its chief representatives serve as itinerant preachers, who

---

1. David Lewis, *Recollections of a Superannuate: or, Sketches of Life, Labor, and Experience in the Methodist Itinerancy,* ed. S. M. Merrill (Cincinnati: Methodist Book Concern, 1857), 61.

17

traveled constantly, the polity formed the Methodist people in the idea that they belonged to something that was dispersed across space. In other words, the idea of the Connection (or Connexion, to use a more original spelling) was embodied by the circuit riders. The every-other-week visitation and subsequent absence by an itinerant preacher served as a visible reminder that any one group of Methodists belonged to the whole (at least all those societies—to use the original Methodist term—under the care of that itinerant). As originally organized, although each part belonged to the whole, Methodism was Christianity in dispersion, a form of self-imposed diaspora. The dispersion existed in space and in time. Indeed the dispersion through space tended to create many of the liturgical rhythms of time for early Methodists.

But as Methodism developed in the eighteenth century it created a way for this dispersion to be erased on a regular basis. It created a way for the Connection, as it existed in the circuit, to be made visible within time and space. This way was the quarterly meeting. As the name suggested, four times a year the Methodists in the circuit gathered with their itinerants. Here at the quarterly meeting the individual Methodist could see the others with whom she or he belonged on the circuit. At the quarterly meeting Methodists could see the full range of offices that led the Connection. And, as it developed, at the quarterly meetings Methodists experienced the wide range of worship services that made up their liturgical repertoire. Indeed, there was such an ecclesiastical fullness in quarterly meetings that perhaps it is best to reserve the word "church" for these meetings rather than for the smaller parts of the circuit, the societies and classes.[2]

The genesis of quarterly meetings did not include such lofty aspirations. In its original design a quarterly meeting was simply to be a business meeting for a circuit. After the 1748 Annual Conference had expressed the hope that all the societies could be more "firmly and closely united together," one of the British itinerant preachers, John Bennet, borrowed an idea—and name—from the Quakers.[3] In fall 1748 Bennet scheduled quarterly meetings for parts of his own circuit

---

2. Compare the similar assessment in Russell Richey, *Early American Methodism* (Bloomington: Indiana University Press, 1991), 14, 20, 28-29. In his more recent book, *The Methodist Conference in America: A History* (Nashville: Kingswood, 1996), Richey likewise notes (p. 31) that conferences, which would include quarterly meetings, organized time and space within early Methodism.

3. See "John Bennet's copy of the Minutes of the Conferences of 1744, 1745, 1747 and 1748; with Wesley's Copy of Those for 1746," *Publications of The Wesley Historical Society* 1 (1896): 59.

and an adjoining circuit.[4] Bennet was ecstatic about the usefulness of these first meetings and scheduled more for the following winter and spring.[5] Wesley himself must have been impressed too, since the 1749 Annual Conference mandated these meetings and named Bennet as the person who would instruct the other preachers in how to hold them.[6]

Quarterly meetings grew steadily in prominence in mid-eighteenth-century British Methodism. However, it is not clear how widespread the meetings were in the initial years after the 1749 conference mandate. Bennet's journal for the period is sporadic and mentions only a few more meetings. Moreover, Bennet's role as promoter of quarterly meetings was most likely compromised by his growing estrangement with Wesley, a conflict that led to his leaving the Methodists in 1752. Despite Bennet's departure, quarterly meetings seem to have become prominent in Methodism by the 1760s. From midcentury onward there were increasing references to them in the Annual Conference's *Minutes* as they became more important in circuit administration. By the 1760s Wesley's own journal contains frequent clear references to them. By the early 1770s—around the time Methodism was introduced into America—quarterly meetings were prominent enough that they could be used to compare Methodists to other religious groups.

Throughout this time period, British Methodist quarterly meetings seem to have grown in scope. The meeting's original design to handle the temporal affairs of the circuit continually expanded as these meetings became the natural sites for the "assistants" (the chief itinerant on each circuit) to handle their oversight responsibilities. Thus, for example, quarterly meetings became the occasion for men to be approved as local preachers and exhorters.[7]

Just as significantly, the meetings grew in scope with respect to attendance and worship services.[8] Beginning in 1769, Wesley's journal

---

4. John Bennet journal (27 July 1748), 82-83. See also Frederick Hunter and Frank Baker, "The Origin of the Methodist Quarterly Meeting," *London Quarterly and Holborn Review* (January 1949): 28-37; and William W. Stamp, "Methodism in Former Days. III. On the Origin of Quarterly Meetings," *The Wesleyan-Methodist Magazine* (1843): 376-82.

5. For Bennet's excitement, see his letter to Wesley (22 October 1748) in Wesley, *Works* 26:335-36.

6. Minutes of the Methodist Conferences, from the First, Held in London, by the Late Rev. John Wesley, A.M., in the Year 1744 (London: John Mason, 1862): 1:708-9.

7. See, for example, the story of Richard Rodda in *The Lives of Early Methodist Preachers*, 4th ed., ed. Thomas Jackson (London: Wesleyan Conference Office, 1871), 2:308.

8. For more detailed documentation, see Lester Ruth, " 'A Little Heaven Below': Quarterly Meetings as Seasons of Grace in Early American Methodism" (Ph.D. diss., University of Notre Dame, 1996), 22-25.

includes accounts of quarterly meetings attended by large numbers. At times the crowds numbered in the hundreds or thousands. With respect to worship, quarterly meetings soon became liturgical settings. Preaching services were the most frequently reported type of service. But some accounts include mention of distinctive Methodist services like love feasts and watch nights.[9] Although the evidence is sporadic, there is enough to surmise that, at least occasionally, quarterly meetings had grown into events of some magnitude administratively, numerically, and liturgically. Judged by the earliest accounts, this was the type of meeting brought to America with the first itinerant preachers sent by Wesley in the 1770s.

Quarterly Meetings as American "Great Festivals"

The developmental trajectory of quarterly meetings becoming ritual events of some magnitude that had begun in England was accentuated in America. Accounts of quarterly meetings during the first fifty years of American Methodism typically stress the amount of worship that was done there. For example, in January 1819, George Coles, a Methodist preacher recently arrived from England, attended his first American quarterly meeting in southwestern Connecticut, noting all the worship he experienced there. What is significant about Coles's account is not how liturgically full his first American meeting was but how his description would have been just as accurate in 1779 as it was in 1819.

His description of Saturday began with a note about being introduced to the constituent groups of the fellowship:

> I rode to the Quarterly meeting at Weston where I was introduced to Mr. Ebenezer Washburn the Presiding Elder, and to Jas. M. Smith, Cyrus Silliman, Hawley Sanford Oliver Sykes & Samuel Bushnell, Preachers as also to several others of the Friends, Class Leaders,

---

9. The love feast was a Wesleyan adaptation of an early Church practice, filtered through and influenced by contact with the Moravians. The love feast combined a sharing of bread and water with testimony from the members, along with prayer and singing. See Frank Baker, *Methodism and the Love-Feast* (London: Epworth, 1957). A watch night service was Wesley's adaptation of how he understood early Christian vigils. Originating in the early 1740s, the services consisted of preaching, praying, singing, and praising God, by Wesley's own description. See "A Plain Account of the People Called Methodists" (1749), §3.1-2, *Works* 9:264. Compare also John Bishop, *Methodist Worship in Relation to Free Church Worship* (New York: Scholars Studies Press, 1975), 92-94 and Ted A. Campbell, *John Wesley and Christian Antiquity* (Nashville: Kingswood, 1991), 32-33 and 98.

Stewards, Local Preachers &c The Preachers treated me with respectful kindness, asked me to Preach & exhort &c[10]

Coles continues his account, noting the weaving of worship and business, and how provision was made for those Methodists who had traveled from home to attend the meeting:

The order of the Quarterly Meeting was as follows—On Saturday morning about 11 oclock meeting for worship began Mr. Washburn Preached and another Preacher gave an exhortation—after which the friends from a distance were billited among the friends on the spot 8 or 10 to a house as was convenient—When the congregation was thus dismissed the meeting for business ensued & when business was over some of the Preachers & friends repaired to Chapel again and held a meeting for Prayer and exhortation, which concluded about 8 oclock.

Sunday likewise was a full day, having multiple worship services that occupied nearly the entire day:

on Sunday Morning at 9 oclock the Love feast began—Public Preaching at 11 oclock, which was followed by exhortation, the Sacrament of the Lords Supper, Singing & Prayer—One new member was publicly received into society and one expelled, and the Bands of Marriage published for one "happy pair." The Sermons delivered by Mr. Washburn were good and powerful and during the exhortation given by Mr. Sykes on Sunday afternoon many cried out seemingly in the bitterness of their souls—The singing was solemn & moderately good.

Despite his basic familiarity with the meeting's content, Coles was, nonetheless, shocked by some of the behavior of his new American friends:

the noise on Saturday evening & at Love feast on Sunday morning was almost too much for me. I hope it was not offensive to Deity but it really seemed indecorus & unnatural—["So it seemed then," Coles adds in a later note in the manuscript.] . . . [There were] Married women without cap or bonnet in the house who think it no breech of decency to spit

---

10. George Coles journal, in Papers. United Methodist Church Archives-GCAH, Madison, NJ, 22 January 1819. See also George Coles, *My First Seven Years in America* (New York: Carlton & Porter, 1852), 49-52. "Friends" was a standard term used at the time to refer to other Methodists. Local preachers were licensed to preach but, in contrast to itinerant preachers, did not travel extensively and did not earn their living by preaching. Stewards handled the financial dealings of the circuit. Class leaders led the weekly meetings required of all Methodist members for accountability and support. Trustees were responsible for buildings.

on the floor in company. Preachers and others also who after receiving the Holy Eucharist . . . regaled themselves by spitting pretty freely within the altar.

Notwithstanding the spitting, much of what Coles observed had long before become standard features of the American version of quarterly meetings: two-day weekend format, business session, multiple preaching services, prayer meeting, administration of the love feast and the Lord's Supper, administration of pastoral rites, the renewal of fellowship among Methodists—ministers and nonministers alike—normally disbursed across long distances, and even exuberant shouting. Indeed this sort of quarterly meeting, one lasting several days and containing a variety of services and rites, could be said to be intrinsic to American Methodism, having emerged within the first decade of Methodist activity here and spread wherever Methodists went.

In no other setting in early American Methodism was the full array of Methodist liturgical activity regularly brought into such proximity as in a quarterly meeting. Originally designed as a business meeting to conduct certain affairs of the circuit, these meetings developed— particularly in America—into great worship "festivals." As such they are unique windows into the nature of early American Methodist worship in both practice and piety. Quarterly meetings typically contained the full range of services that early Methodists practiced. During worship at their meetings, Methodists often exhibited the loud exuberance and evangelical vehemence that was their trademark in this period, and here they experienced a fellowship that was so rich that they saw it as an eschatological foretaste. In their minds a quarterly meeting was not merely a business session or even a "great festival," it could also be a "little heaven on earth."[11] Here, in the midst of a quarterly meeting's communal activities, Methodists understood the grace of God to be operative.

Consequently, if anything is missing in the fullness of George Coles's account, it is a mention of revival, the most precious of Methodist aspirations and an element often found in accounts written by American-born preachers. Although not all quarterly meetings were occasions by which God's grace seemed to break out in power-

---

11. William Watters, *A Short Account of the Christian Experience, and Ministereal Labours, of William Watters* (Alexandria, VA: S. Snowden, 1806), 75-76. Many others in early Methodism expressed this sentiment.

ful effects upon the people, they often were. When this happened, the Methodists duly noted this "work of God" as a prominent part of their sacred history.

For example, this dimension of revival (couched in the theological terms of God's dealing with participants) was the central feature in the description of a June 1790 quarterly meeting:

> On Friday the eleventh I set out for Burke quarterly meeting in Georgia, where, on Saturday the twelfth, we had a very quickening season. The whole assembly of hearers were disolved in tears, while I enforced these words, "The eyes of the Lord are upon the righteous, and his ears are open unto their cry."[12]

The "quickening" only intensified on the following day:

> On Sunday the 13th, we had a large number of our friends to attend the love feast in the morning. But all seemed dull to me till just about the conclusion. I felt a desire to speak to the people, and in a few minutes a flame broke out in a most rapid manner; the doors were opened and the people thronged in till the large church could receive no more, but there was room enough in the hearts of the people. They truly looked like men drunken with new wine; poor hardened sinners were cut to the heart, and some that came cursing and swearing went away praising and glorifying God. This work began about eleven o'clock, and we waited more than an hour, and strove to quiet them so that we might preach to the people, but it was all in vain. I therefore went into the wood, and preached to about one thousand hearers, some of whom we left on the ground or floor about four o'clock; and I was informed by brother Hull (one of our Preachers who continued with them after my departure) that some of them were obliged to be carried home by their neighbours. . . . The same divine power attended our quarterly meeting, at Campbell-Town.

So important was the outbreak of the work of God in this account that this preacher failed to mention the one thing that, technically, defined the quarterly meeting—the business session.

Both the Connecticut and Georgia quarterly meeting accounts are good examples of typical descriptions of early American quarterly meetings in that the business session has receded into the background. Instead, the focus usually falls upon quarterly meetings as

---

12. B[everly] Allen, "Some Account of the Work of God in America," *Arminian Magazine* 15 (1792): 407-8.

"great festivals" or "quickening seasons," full of a variety of worship services, and, it is hoped, demonstrations of God's grace. It was this sense of liturgical fullness that Bishop Thomas Coke, writing to a British audience around 1785, emphasized in his description of American quarterly meetings:

> Their Quarterly-meetings on this continent are much attended to. The Brethren for twenty miles round, and sometimes for thirty or forty, meet together. The meetings always last two days. All the Travelling Preachers in the circuit are present, and they with perhaps a local Preacher or two, give the people a sermon one after another, besides the Love-feast, and (now) the sacrament.[13]

Indeed, Bishop Coke's description serves as a good summary of American developments in quarterly meetings in the late–eighteenth century, including such important aspects as the adoption of a two-day format, the attraction of large crowds with expectation of revival, and the presence of multiple worship leaders. In these ways quarterly meetings were visible demonstrations of the essence of the evangelical, exuberant, expanding Christianity that was American Methodism. The elements of Coke's summary will be used to organize the description of the developments in quarterly meetings.

"Always Two Days"—The Timing for Quarterly Meetings

The earliest quarterly meetings held in America, to a large degree, followed the format of contemporary meetings held in England. The first itinerants in America, all missionaries from England, duplicated the quarterly meetings with which they were familiar. The earliest quarterly meetings in America involved a business meeting surrounded by a preaching service, a love feast, and, perhaps, a watch night service. The first American meetings seem to have been held mainly on a single day, normally a Tuesday; on occasion, a preaching service was held on Monday. This format was standard for American meetings for several years.[14]

---

13. Thomas Coke, *Extracts of the journals of the Rev. Dr. Coke's five visits to America* (London: G. Paramore, 1793), 34-35.

14. Francis Asbury provides the first accounts of quarterly meetings held in America: a December 1772 meeting and one held the previous fall (in *JLFA* 1:59-60). The other main sources for descriptions of quarterly meetings prior to creation of The Methodist Episcopal Church in 1784 are Thomas Rankin, "The Diary of Reverend Thomas Rankin" (Ts. Garrett-Evangelical Theological Seminary Library, Evanston, IL), William Duke, "The Journal of William Duke

But by the spring of 1776 a new format for American quarterly meetings began to emerge. It involved two basic changes: the expansion of quarterly meetings from one-day to regular two-day events, and the move to hold the meetings on Saturdays and Sundays.[15] Both aspects represent adaptations to the earliest American practice, as Methodists sought to come to grips with the role quarterly meetings were playing in their societies and in their work with the broader populace. Changes in the manner of holding quarterly meetings occurred as crowds traveled far distances to attend, particularly during times of revival. With greater numbers swelling these meetings, they become increasingly important occasions for worship and evangelism.

A watershed for the first development—expansion from a one-day format—seems to have come during a revival that broke out in southern Virginia in 1776. An account of this revival by Devereux Jarratt, a Church of England priest sympathetic to the Methodists, provides clear evidence of a quarterly meeting that extended over several days.[16] As Jarratt describes it, the relationship between the revival and this expansion was not coincidental. The revival emerged in January 1776 in three places and soon spread throughout the entire circuit (which contained his parish). However, it was at the quarterly meeting in early May 1776 when "the windows of heaven were opened, and the rain of Divine Influence poured down" in earnest.[17] Jarratt's description of this revival notes the intensity of the experience for those in attendance and the breadth of area affected. The "work of God," as eighteenth-century evangelicals would call it, soon affected people from six counties adjacent to Jarratt's own. Although

1774–1776." (Ts. United Methodist Historical Society, Lovely Lane Museum, Baltimore, MD), John Littlejohn, "Journal of John Littlejohn" (Ts. Transcribed by Annie L. Winstead. Louisville Conference Historical Society, Louisville, KY. [Available on microfilm from Kentucky Wesleyan College, Owensboro, KY.), Nelson Reed, "Diary of Rev. Nelson Reed" (Ts. United Methodist Historical Society, Lovely Lane Museum, Baltimore, MD), Thomas Haskins, "The Journal of Thomas Haskins (1760–1816)" (Ts. Transcribed by Louise Stahl. Indiana State University, Terre Haute, IN), and *American Methodist Pioneer: The Life and Journals of The Rev. Freeborn Garrettson*, ed. Robert Drew Simpson (Rutland, VT: Academy Books, 1984).

15. The earliest histories note the same developments. See Jesse Lee, *A Short History of the Methodists, in the United States of America; Beginning in 1766, and Continued till 1809* (Baltimore: Magill & Clime, 1810; reprint, Rutland, VT: Academy Books, 1974), 42.

16. Devereux Jarratt, *A Brief Narrative of the Revival of Religion in Virginia in a Letter to a Friend*, 3rd. ed. (London: J. Paramore, 1786). Jarratt's parish was Bath, located in Dinwiddie County, Virginia, which is halfway between Richmond and the North Carolina state line. Within a short time after Methodism's first introduction in this general region in the early 1770s, the area was a hotbed for Methodist activity.

17. Jarratt, *Brief Narrative*, 9-10. See also W. Smith to "Dear Br.," undated letter (in Edward Dromgoole papers).

he does not specifically say so, the implication is that persons from these counties attended this particular quarterly meeting.

It appears that the intensity of the work, the excitement of the spontaneous revival, and the breadth of area represented by those in attendance were all contributing factors to lengthening this quarterly meeting from one day to several days. Jarratt makes it quite clear that there was a "second day of the quarterly meeting," Wednesday, May 1, on which the love feast was held.

The distancing of the love feast relative to the business session is a good indicator that quarterly meetings were expanding from one to several days. Originally both love feast and business session were held on the same day. In the majority of cases in America in the early 1770s this day was Tuesday. In contrast, this May 1776 Virginia quarterly meeting involved a multiple-day meeting as a development with increasing prominence. Sparked by this precedent, quarterly meetings in southern Virginia increasingly continued over several days. By 1779 most quarterly meetings in Virginia and in neighboring North Carolina were two-day events, the format increasingly standardized in this region.

This expansion necessarily involved some other internal changes. For example, in accounts of quarterly meetings of the 1770s, there is a growing sense that the circuit's official business was to be conducted in the intervals between services. These accounts reflect a growing opinion that quarterly meetings were settings for worship. Often they fail to mention the business session at all. In addition, the length of services at quarterly meetings grew as an accommodation to cultural preferences. Prominent itinerant Thomas Rankin once noted that Virginians desired long meetings.[18] The most interesting embodiment of that desire is what Thomas Rankin usually calls the "watchafternoon." The term, adapted from "watch night," was Rankin's attempt to describe the length and intensity of the service after a morning love feast.[19] In the strict sense the term "watchafternoon" is nonsensical since in traditional Methodist usage a "watch" was an adaptation of a vigil and thus necessitated a night setting. But the term was the best Rankin could find to describe adequately such a long, intense afternoon preaching service. The intensity of the people's religious expe-

---

18. Rankin diary, 175.

19. See Rankin diary, 181-83, 186, 189, 207-8, 218, and 229. Note that a watch night could conclude the original one-day Tuesday pattern for American quarterly meetings. See Duke journal, 4, 7, and esp. 17 where he noted that the day finished with a watch night "as usual."

riences itself reinforced this lengthening. At the May 1776 Virginia quarterly meeting, for example, a watch night did not end after its usual three or four hours but continued until two hours after sunrise because of the deep distress of the mourners.[20]

These same factors—growing attendance, greater distances traveled, and the connection to revival—apparently contributed to a similar meeting expansion from one day to several days on the peninsula formed by Delaware, and the eastern shores of Maryland and Virginia (the so-called Delmarva peninsula). Beginning at the very end of the 1770s and continuing into the next decade, attendance at quarterly meetings on the peninsula dramatically increased. For example, whereas quarterly meetings in Delaware drew several hundred people in the first part of 1779, by the end of the year estimates of attendance topped one thousand, and by the latter part of 1780 were approaching three and four thousand.[21] Large crowds became such an expected part of Delmarva quarterly meetings that by 1784 Freeborn Garrettson noted the regularity of seeing one to four thousand people.[22] Those attending would travel from across the peninsula. For instance, Asbury noted that the entire state of Delaware was represented at the August 1779 quarterly meeting near Dover, as well as at least three counties in Maryland, and also Philadelphia.[23] Methodist preachers saw these numbers as partial evidence of an emerging revival on the peninsula. The swelling of the crowd to seven hundred in February 1779 made Asbury articulate a hope for "a gracious revival of religion."[24] The even larger crowds of the early 1780s meant the same for Freeborn Garrettson: "the whole Peninsula would flame with the glory of God."[25]

Not surprisingly, as crowds grew, accounts of Delmarva quarterly meetings begin to reveal an expansion from one to multiple days. The first hints, as elsewhere, are suggestions that the meetings began on Monday with preaching to a very sizable crowd. By 1779 onward the meetings are clearly further expanded: preaching occurred over several days and the day of the love feast became separated from the day of the business session.

---

20. Jarratt, *Brief Narrative*, 14.
21. See *JLFA* 1:295, 308, 319, 345, 387; and Simpson, *Freeborn Garrettson*, 177, 178, and 182.
22. Simpson, *Freeborn Garrettson*, 122.
23. *JLFA* 1:308.
24. Ibid., 1:295.
25. Simpson, *Freeborn Garrettson*, 122.

The second dimension of the Americanization of quarterly meetings—placement on Saturday and Sunday—is closely related to the first: expansion from a one-day to a two-day format. Although the expansion from one to two days occurred prior to moving the meetings to weekends, the two aspects are related in that they originated in the same regions (Virginia and the Delmarva peninsula) for the same reasons (to facilitate crowds and to foster revival). And, like the internal expansion, moving quarterly meetings to weekends occurred first in Virginia but was soon followed by Delmarva.

Placement of the quarterly meeting on a weekend appears to have begun in Virginia in 1777.[26] Over the next couple of years—and particularly in 1779—the practice proliferated with accounts of weekend quarterly meetings in several different circuits. One Virginia itinerant preacher noted that between 26 October and 14 November 1779 he attended five quarterly meetings in Virginia and North Carolina, three of which were on Saturday-Sunday and two of which were on Tuesday-Wednesday.[27] By spring 1780 the preponderance of quarterly meetings in the region apparently followed the Saturday-Sunday format.

The adoption of this weekend format was similar in Delmarva, if a little later than in Virginia. At least two quarterly meetings had begun on a weekend day on the peninsula before 1780, as noted by Freeborn Garrettson.[28] A more permanent shift occurred in early 1780. The first entire weekend quarterly meeting appears to have been a Saturday through Monday meeting on 8-10 April 1780 in Delaware.[29] From summer 1780 the Saturday-Sunday format became dominant for Delmarva quarterly meetings.

Quarterly meetings in regions of Methodism outside of Virginia and the Delmarva peninsula do not appear to have expanded to a true two-day, weekend format until later, as this new format filtered into these areas. For example, quarterly meetings in New Jersey and the western shore of Maryland usually followed the one-day, Tuesday format into the early 1780s. Exceptions most frequently involved occasions in which preaching services extended into the night.

But preference for the two-day, weekend format soon spread across American Methodism. This preference found official expression at the

---

26. Littlejohn journal, 42-43.

27. Reed diary, 84-87; see also 62 and 72-73.

28. Simpson, *Freeborn Garrettson,* 78 and 156.

29. *JLFA* 1:344. See also Simpson, *Freeborn Garrettson,* 172, where Garrettson says the meeting began on Sunday; a suggestion of weekend-long meetings in summer 1779 can be found in *Freeborn Garrettson,* 156.

Annual Conference of northern preachers sitting in Baltimore under the leadership of Francis Asbury in late April 1780, when they passed this resolution: "Quest[ion]. 18. Shall we recommend our quarterly meetings to be held on Saturdays and Sundays when convenient? Ans[wer]. Agreed."[30]

This 1780 minute was initially more prescriptive than descriptive. The first clear account of a Saturday-Sunday quarterly meeting in the remainder of Maryland is not until 1783. The same is true for New Jersey and eastern Pennsylvania.[31] But the two-day, weekend format's convenience eventually won out. Within a few years after creation of the Methodist Episcopal Church in 1784, the adoption of two-day meetings was nearly universal. For example, of the thirteen quarterly meetings that Ezekiel Cooper noted from 1785 through 1787, only six were on the two-day, weekend format. By contrast, of the forty-eight meetings Cooper recorded from 1788 through 1799, only three were *not*.[32] Similarly, only seven of the eighteen quarterly meetings recorded in a steward's book for a New Jersey circuit from 1783 through 1787 clearly appear to utilize the Saturday-Sunday format, while only two of the next seventeen meetings in this circuit were clearly not on weekends.[33] From Maine to Georgia, from the East Coast to the wilds of Illinois and Missouri, wherever Methodism spread, quarterly meetings were most often two-day, weekend affairs.

Occasional variations did occur. One variation was a two-day format that started on Sunday and ended on Monday. Another was a three-day quarterly meeting that started on Saturday and ended on Monday. Of course, the older Tuesday-Wednesday schedule was retained in some areas as well. If a quarterly meeting was held in the town in which the presiding elder resided, it could be turned into a one-day affair. If the distance between circuits was short, one circuit's quarterly meeting could immediately follow that of another. City stations[34] also appear to revert frequently to one-day, weekday formats. Finally, the liturgical calendar had some influence on the scheduling of quarterly meetings. On at least one occasion the quarterly meeting

---

30. *Minutes*/1780, 12. An annual conference was the gathering of itinerant preachers for business concerning the whole movement.

31. For Maryland, see Haskins journal, 22. For Pennsylvania, see *JLFA* 1:443.

32. Ezekiel Cooper journal in Papers. Garrett-Evangelical Theological Seminary Library, Evanston, IL.

33. New Mills Circuit (NJ) Steward's book, 2-40.

34. A station was the assignment of responsibility for the societies of a small geographic area to an itinerant preacher or preachers, in essence collapsing a circuit to that area, even limiting it to the boundaries of one city or to one society.

was scheduled so that the second day fell on Good Friday, on which Devereux Jarratt was invited to preach and administer the sacrament.[35] Similarly, a few quarterly meetings were scheduled to coincide with Christmas. The December 1798 meeting for the Greensville circuit in Virginia was scheduled so that its second day fell on Tuesday, 25 December.[36] What was probably the first Methodist administration of the Lord's Supper in western Ohio occurred on that same day at a quarterly meeting near present-day Milford.[37] Quarterly meetings could also be scheduled so that they included Easter Sunday.

As the two-day, weekend format was becoming more widespread, it was also being revised into what might be considered a three-day format; namely, the Friday immediately preceding the quarterly meeting was designated to be kept by Methodists as a day of fasting. The 1780 Annual Conference had originally stipulated that the Friday after the quarterly meeting should be kept as a fast day. Probable irregularity in keeping the fast prompted the added stipulation four years later that a reminder of the fast was to be written on all class papers. The 1785 *Discipline*, the first produced after the Christmas Conference that created the Methodist Episcopal Church, picked up both stipulations and fused them into one, replacing the requirement in the (inherited British) "Large Minutes," which called for fasts on the last Friday in September and on the Fridays after New Year's Day, 25 March, and "Midsummer-day."[38] By 1792 the provision was changed so that the fast was held on the Friday preceding the quarterly meeting.[39] The instruction to write a reminder on class papers was kept and, at least in some regions, followed.[40] Some Methodists did regularly keep this fast although, as one itinerant noted, it was "too generally neglected."[41]

With the widespread adoption of the two-day, weekend format, the internal order of ritual elements underwent a correlated standardization. Typically, the meeting began around midday on Saturday after arrival in the morning. (Traveling might have begun several days ear-

---

35. *JLFA* 1:440.

36. Greensville Circuit (VA) Steward's book.

37. Milford Circuit (OH), Report of Committee of 2nd Conference.

38. "Large Minutes," Q. 56, *Works* (Jackson) 8:328.

39. *Discipline*/1792, 26.

40. See the New Haven (OH) Class Meeting Records for 1806, 1808, and 1811.

41. See Nathaniel Mills, Journal. Ms. United Methodist Historical Society, Lovely Lane Museum, Baltimore, MD, 7 February 1812, 5 April 1811, and 19 July 1811. See also Coles journal, 2 April 1819; David Dailey, Diary. Ms. St. George's United Methodist Church, Philadelphia, PA, 28 January 1814; and *JLFA* 1:613.

lier, depending upon the length of the trip.) A preaching service usually began the meeting, followed by the business session in the afternoon. On occasion, a preaching service could be held simultaneously with the business session. An evening preaching service often concluded the day. A common New England variation had prayer meetings on Saturday evening, either in several homes or in a centralized location. After retirement to the various places of sleep, family prayer services were often held.

Sunday was an equally full day. Most frequently the day began with a love feast, often followed by the Lord's Supper. The remainder of the day was spent in preaching services. The first most commonly began at 11 A.M., but a later starting time around noon was also used. Preaching frequently carried into the midafternoon and evening. Other rites—baptisms, weddings, funerals, and ordinations—were conducted at any time of the weekend. Departure, at least for the preachers, was usually on Monday.

Many exceptions to the order can be found due to the fluidity and extemporaneity with which American Methodists approached their worship. Each element of the order was a semiautonomous ritual unit that could be moved at discretion, although the order previously described was the most common. On very rare occasions, for example, the business session was held on Sunday morning or at night after the preachers had retired. The Lord's Supper was probably the unit that moved most frequently. To begin with, there was the basic question of whether to administer it or not. Sometimes it was omitted. When it was administered, it could fall into a variety of time slots throughout the weekend. One common location was after the Sunday morning preaching. It was also placed after the Sunday afternoon preaching or after a preaching service on Saturday. The Lord's Supper could even exchange places with the love feast on Sunday so that the sacrament was administered first and was followed by the love feast. All these variations show that, while early Methodist worship tended to follow certain patterns, great flexibility was allowed in actual Methodist practice. The common order was more a tendency than a mandate.

"Much Attended To"—The Crowds at Quarterly Meetings

One of the most striking aspects of many American quarterly meetings was their size. The crowds were consistently large enough that the normal attendance for a quarterly meeting became the unofficial standard for measuring any crowd and a shorthand way of saying that a large congregation was in attendance at other events. If an itinerant wanted to say that a worshiping congregation was uncharacteristically large, it was enough for him to note that he had rarely seen such large crowds except at a quarterly meeting.[42]

Even some of the earliest accounts speak of "large congregations" at the preaching services. By the mid-1770s, Virginia and Maryland accounts indicate that large numbers of people traveled some distance to attend. And in the summer of 1776, with the eruption of a revival in southern Virginia, Rankin noted that he preached at a quarterly meeting to "the most numerous congregation" that he had seen in America.[43] By 1780 three to four thousand were attending quarterly meetings on the Delmarva peninsula. Over time the estimates increased, sometimes reaching seemingly unbelievable heights. One itinerant reported between six and seven thousand at a 1791 Maryland quarterly meeting. Another estimated ten thousand at a quarterly meeting in southern Virginia in 1787. Even in more remote regions the numbers were sizable: a 1787 quarterly meeting in the Redstone circuit in western Pennsylvania drew an estimated one thousand participants in the dead of winter.[44]

Significantly, the possibility of large crowds at an extended meeting did not depend upon a city being in close proximity. Coke was amazed that four thousand attended one Annual Conference in southern Virginia's Mecklenburg County even though there was no nearby town.[45] The participants' willingness to travel created the ability to gather such large crowds. As noted earlier, the distances crossed were frequently significant. The Philadelphians in attendance in August 1779 at the meeting in Dover, Delaware, traveled over fifty miles by land. Such endeavors were not unique, even if the more commonly reported maximum distance traveled was around twenty to thirty miles. Frequently, accounts of significant travel were taken as evidence that a revival had broken out. Early Methodists relished these accounts of great individual achievement in traveling to quarterly

---

42. See Cooper journal, 14 September 1789; and *JLFA* 1:412.

43. Rankin diary, 181.

44. These estimates come from the following sources, respectively: Cooper journal, 13 August 1791; [Philip Cox], "An Extract of a Letter from Philip Cox, Elder of the Methodist-Episcopal Church in America (then Preacher) to Bishop Coke, dated, Sussex-county, Virginia, July 1787," *Arminian Magazine* 13 (1790): 92-93; and "The Journal of Robert Ayres." Ts. United Methodist Church Archives-GCAH, Madison, NJ, 23.

45. Coke, *Extracts*, 70.

meetings, as in the stories of an individual who journeyed two hundred miles in four days or of two teenage sisters who walked thirty-five miles alone to attend.[46]

The desire for large crowds also encouraged the preference for the Saturday-Sunday format. Sunday was the best day to draw a crowd. Itinerants' rough estimates of attendance typically noted that the numbers on Sunday were twice as large as on Saturday. Reasons for this increase include the Methodists' own emphasis on Sunday as the Sabbath and the fact that, since it was usually the one day when they were free from work, others, including slaves, were more likely to attend on Sunday. Accommodating the unique situation of slaves was surely a part of the appeal for the Saturday-Sunday format, especially in its origins in places like the Delmarva peninsula where the membership was largely Black. Consider itinerant Benjamin Lakin's complaint about a Kentucky quarterly meeting being moved from the weekend. Although excluding Sunday had obtained the desired end of preventing "disorderly persons" from attending, Lakin noted that it meant Blacks were prevented too.[47] In addition to greater attendance of slaves, others noted that Sunday attracted more wealthy people, who seemingly were too disinterested to attend on other days, and more poor people, "especially those of our own society," who could not spare the time or procure horses otherwise.[48]

This willingness to travel significant distances in order to create a special event was an important part of early American culture, especially in regions where the quarterly meeting's extended format first emerged: southern Virginia and the Delmarva peninsula. As Russell Richey has noted, quarterly meetings in these regions were a particular Methodist expression of a broader cultural tendency to create community by assembling for a special occasion.[49] In this middle

46. Cf. [Laban Clark], *Laban Clark: Autobiography about his early life from 1778 to 1804: Circuit Rider for the Methodist Episcopal Church,* ed. E. Farley Sharp (Rutland, VT: Academy Books, 1984), 4; and George Peck, *Early Methodism within the bounds of the old Genesee Conference from 1788 to 1828: or, The first forty years of Wesleyan evangelism in northern Pennsylvania, central and western New York, and Canada. Containing sketches of interesting localities, exciting scenes, and prominent actors* (New York: Carlton & Porter, 1860), 78-80.

47. Benjamin Lakin, Journal. Ms. on microfilm. Washington University Library, St. Louis, MO. Some of Lakin's journal can be found in William Warren Sweet, *The Methodists* (Chicago: University of Chicago Press, 1946), 24 August 1815.

48. Lee, *Short History,* 42.

49. Russell Richey, "The Chesapeake Coloration of American Methodism," in *Methodism in its Cultural Milieu,* ed. Tim Macquiban (Oxford: Applied Theology Press, 1994), 117-18. Richey's conclusions are an application of the thesis in Rhys Isaac, *The Transformation of Virginia 1740–1790* (Chapel Hill: University of North Carolina Press, 1982), 88-114.

Atlantic region community was defined more by event than space. As such, not only did Methodist quarterly meetings attract large crowds in this general area, meetings of other religious groups—Quaker, Baptist, Presbyterian, and United Brethren—were large as well.[50]

"Much Attended To"—Methodist Categories for People and Services

The large crowds at quarterly meetings raise an auxiliary issue, which is important for understanding the nature of early Methodist worship and evangelism: the distinction between services and rituals that were open for all to attend, and those that were accessible only to members of a Methodist society. Such a distinction was formal in that the American *Disciplines*, following the British *Large Minutes*, recognized both "public" worship and meetings and restricted societal meetings and rituals.

The formal disciplinary distinction was reinforced by the colloquial vocabulary of early Methodists. The colloquial meaning of "public," for example, was fully consonant with the disciplinary meaning, designating those sorts of services in which any and all might participate. The term was most commonly used for the preaching service, often resulting in phrases like "public preaching" or "public exercises." As Robert Ayres once stated, describing the second day of a 1787 quarterly meeting: "Our Society meeting being over [referring to the early morning love feast and Lord's Supper] we began public preaching at about 12."[51] The corresponding term for those assembled at public worship is "congregation," which referred to an assembly consisting of Methodist members and nonmembers alike. In the same way that "public" could be opposed to "societal" to designate a generally accessible service, "congregation" was opposed to "society" to designate those in attendance at such a service.

And attend they did. To use an early Methodist idiom, nonsociety

---

50. For a description of a widely attended Quaker yearly meeting see James Meacham, Journal. Ms. Special Collections Library, Duke University Library, Durham, NC, 22 May 1791. For a Baptist "great meeting" see Mills journal, 16 July 1815. For numerous examples of "sacramental meetings"/quarterly meetings among the United Brethren, a German pietistic denomination, see Samuel S. Hough, ed., *Christian Newcomer: His Life, Journal and Achievements* (Dayton: Board of Administration, Church of the United Brethren in Christ, 1941). For Presbyterian sacramental seasons in America see Leigh E. Schmidt, *Holy Fairs: Scottish Communions and American Revivals in the Early Modern Period* (Princeton, NJ: Princeton University Press, 1989), 50-68.

51. Ayres journal, 23.

members "flocked like doves to their windows" in their eagerness to attend Methodist preaching services.[52] Indeed nonmembers regularly outnumbered members at public exercises. In 1791 Bishop Thomas Coke put the ratio for "our regular Sunday's congregations" as five non-Methodists to every Methodist.[53] By his own admission, Coke states that his estimate is a conservative one—he made it "with safety"—and did not include children, which would raise the ratio even more. Other estimates, both by scholars today and by Methodists then, place the number of adherents to members at around 6:1.[54]

In contrast to public services, Methodists also conducted rituals and meetings that they designated "societal," implying that access was restricted to members or those who had obtained special permission to attend. Not surprisingly, in the colloquial expressions of early Methodists these rituals and meetings were called "private," to provide symmetry with the term "public." These private meetings included gatherings of the society as a whole and of its smaller units, the classes and bands. The restricted meeting often occurred immediately prior to or after the public preaching service. A usual pattern was for the itinerant to conduct the public exercises, dismiss the congregation, and then meet the class or society.

In addition to the restricted nature of these meetings, certain rituals normally conducted exclusively for society members were considered private. The foremost example was the love feast, the ritual of distinct Methodist identity bar none. The Lord's Supper was most often private but occasionally was open to certain nonmembers. Finally, the business session, whose membership was even more tightly governed by the *Discipline*, was also considered a restricted meeting.

This Methodist differentiation between types of worship services

---

52. Rankin diary, 121; and Joseph Pilmore, *The Journal of Joseph Pilmore*, ed. Frederick E. Maser and Howard T. Maag (Philadelphia: Message Publishing Co. for the Historical Society of the Philadelphia Annual Conference of The United Methodist Church, 1969), 119.

53. Thomas Coke, "Letter to Samuel Seabury, Philadelphia, 14 May 1791," in *A Letter to a Methodist*, 4th ed. (Baltimore: George Lycett, 1869), 44.

54. See John Wigger, *Taking Heaven by Storm: Methodism and the Rise of Popular Christianity in America* (New York: Oxford University Press, 1998), 4; and *JLFA* 3:314. In 1805 Bishop Francis Asbury placed the ratio of nonmembers to members at 10:1, estimating that Methodists had around one hundred thousand members with another million "who regularly attend our ministry" (see *JLFA* 3:310 and 3:162). Perhaps these ratios are too high for later periods when it became more "respectable" to join the Methodists. In 1824 Freeborn Garrettson noted that Methodist membership stood at around half a million (the *Minutes* actually report around 329,000) while the "quiet hearers" who "sit under our ministry" numbered more than a million; see Simpson, *Freeborn Garrettson*, 351.

correlated to differentiations between types of worshiping individuals. The terms that Methodists used can be arranged along a continuum, showing a Wesleyan order of salvation at work in the background. All are experiential categories, likewise revealing the Methodist emphasis on "experimental religion," as they would call it, or "experienced religion," as we might call it. Some of the most common Methodist terms, indicating progression in states of grace or faith, were, in order: "unawakened," "awakened"/"seeker," "mourner," and "believer"/"professor." Someone who had lapsed from a state of grace or faith was a "backslider."

The terms indicate a common agreement in the evangelical nature of early Methodist soteriology, which was so universal that, even though they were understood with various nuances, a common use and basic meaning must be seen in them. "Unawakened" refers to people who had yet to respond positively to the operations of God's grace upon them. For the Methodist preacher, this is the presumed state for anyone who first comes to hear preaching, although exception would be made, of course, for visitors who had a living relationship with God through another church. An unawakened person is, as the bishops' commentary on the 1798 *Discipline* stated, someone "whose whole life is sin, and who are at the best only 'like unto whited sepulchres, which indeed appear beautiful outward, but are within full of dead men's bones, and of all uncleanness'."[55] The first step of progression in grace is being "awakened," or giving an initial response to prevenient grace, particularly as the gospel was heard through preaching. As the Methodists used the term it implied some degree of quickening, a sensibility to one's sinfulness and to God's saving provision. This growing sensibility was called "conviction." Methodist conversion narratives typically recall the initial degrees of feeling guilt and the search to find peace through God's forgiveness. Thus the term "awakened" was used synonymously with the term "seeker." Among the awakened there was a smaller subgroup called the "mourners." These were people under the most acute sense of sinfulness and conviction as well as a need for grace. While both the awakened and mourners were under conviction, the latter were portrayed as in the throes of despair and ripe for experiencing justifying

---

55. *The Doctrines and Discipline of the Methodist Episcopal Church in America, with Explanatory Notes by Thomas Coke and Francis Asbury,* 10th ed. (Philadelphia: Hall, 1798; reprint, Rutland, VT: Academy Books, 1979), 121. Earlier in this commentary (p. 73), the authors emphasize the danger of allowing the "unawakened" to society meetings and love feasts.

grace. Similar in many ways to the awakened and mourners, backsliders were considered to have once experienced saving grace but then fallen away. Like the distinction between the awakened and mourners, backsliders might be under either a small or great sense of conviction for their faithlessness.[56]

In contrast to these terms which, for the most part, indicate those who had never experienced saving grace (backsliders being the exception), Methodists had two terms to indicate those who had such an experience: "professor" and "believer." Of the two, professor was probably the more frequently used. "Professors" of religion were the ones who could profess religion, giving testimony to having experienced a sense of God's pardon of the "guilt of sin" (justification) or the cleansing effect of God's love on the "remains of sin" (sanctification).[57] Such an emphasis on testimony had larger liturgical implications since testimonials were an important part of several Methodist rituals. The term "believer" was also used for professing Christians in the sense that they had exercised saving faith.

The mixed nature of worshiping congregations among the early Methodists can be seen in the way the terms were often juxtaposed to show different reactions among the congregation. The most frequent—and nearly universal—expression was to say that a particularly moving sermon or exhortation had caused the mourners to cry and weep for mercy but had caused the professors to become happy and shout for joy. Such a categorizing of people and responses was often portrayed poetically, with rich biblical allusions: one itinerant noted at a 1788 meeting that there were "Sinners struck with the hammer of Conviction Mourners a laying at the pool and Christians a Echoing the Glorious praise of the Lamb."[58]

The early Methodists expected this diversity of reactions in their worship, aware that the very same message of salvation and grace—whether in sermon, testimonial, or hymn—might arouse anything from the deepest cries of despair to shouts of joy, depending upon the spiritual state of the individual. Such expectations were an intrinsic part of early Methodism. They were planted already in Francis Asbury's

---

56. See the similar order of salvation inherent in Philip Gatch's description of different types of grace: "convincing," "convicting," "converting," "sanctifying," and "perservering" (in a sermon on John 10:9, part of a sermon outline book among his papers [Papers. Ohio Wesleyan University Library, Delaware, OH]).

57. The phrases are Philip Gatch's from his sermon on John 10:9 (ibid.).

58. Meacham journal, 19 December 1788. The reference to the pool is probably an allusion to the story of Jesus healing the invalid in John 5.

at a 1772 Maryland quarterly meeting (the first American ser- this setting of which we have an account). Asbury divided the typical Methodist "flock" into categories that would remain standard for decades to come: a flock contained those under deep conviction, true believers, those sorely tempted, those groaning for full redemption, and backsliders.[59] Little changed as Methodism crossed into newly settled regions. A description of the work in 1788 Kentucky noted that "some sinners were awakened, some seekers joined to society, and some penitents converted to God."[60] Given the rest of this account, it could have continued that some believers were entirely sanctified.

The Methodists' use of these categories is potentially confusing for the modern observer because the threshold for membership in a society was not where one would first expect: at the transition from being a mourner to a believer or professor. Instead, the threshold was at the point where a person went from being unawakened to awakened. Or as the General Rules for the United Societies stated it, membership was open to anyone who could meet the "only condition," namely, "a desire to flee from the wrath to come, to be saved from their sins."[61] Those with this desire were expected to bear the concomitant "fruit," which the General Rules specifically detailed, but Methodists in this early period understood this as requiring only a desire to be saved and not an experience of salvation itself as the threshold for membership.

This minimal threshold for membership created an important dynamic for societal rituals: even if the disciplinary provisions for limiting access to societal members were strictly kept, the societal rituals were still attended by both those considered saved and those not yet saved. Indeed, access to and use of the societal rituals were seen as mandatory participation in the "means of grace," an idea behind which stands the Wesleyan notion of salvation as synergistic response to God's grace. The common consequence of the mixed nature of a societal ritual was that individual responses to grace might vary greatly. At the same love feast some Methodists might be more deeply convicted, becoming mourners in the most intense agonies of seeking a sense of peace in God's forgiveness, while others experience the joy

---

59. JLFA 1:59.

60. [James Haw], "An extract of a letter from James Haw, elder of the Methodist Episcopal church in America, to Bishop Asbury: written from Cumberland near Kentucke, about the beginning of the year 1789," *Arminian Magazine* 13 (1790): 203-4.

61. Compare Ayres journal, 7 (1786): "Met a large society after preaching, who were chiefly seekers, and some babes in Christ."

of receiving assurance of this forgiveness (justification), or even the next stage of sanctification. Reports from the period commonly summarized the results of God's work in worship in these very terms: so many were convicted, so many justified, so many sanctified. In the Methodist understanding, the normal ways that God had appointed for persons to experience salvation (the "means of grace") were the same whereas the results of the grace experienced might differ, depending on the spiritual state of the individual worshiper. Such diversity of experience was true whether the service was public (open to everyone) or private (restricted to Methodist members). The diversity in private rituals can be confusing if the correct threshold for membership is ignored.

"All the Travelling Preachers with a Local Preacher or Two"—The Nature of Liturgical Presidency at Quarterly Meetings

In early March 1814 Henry Boehm, the presiding elder for the Schuylkill District of the Philadelphia Conference, attended a quarterly meeting for the Northampton circuit in his district.[62] Over the weekend Boehm preached five times and administered the Lord's Supper. As Boehm noted in his journal, what was unusual about this quarterly meeting was not the number of services but that there were no other ministers—whether itinerant preachers, local preachers, or exhorters—to assist him. This was an unusual case. Because their presence was expected (or required) at the business session, numerous itinerants, local preachers, and exhorters were normally in attendance at quarterly meeting.[63] The typical circuit had several local preachers and exhorters for each of its itinerants. Additionally, preachers and exhorters often crossed circuit boundaries in order to attend meetings in other circuits. The result was a wealth of ministers

---

62. Henry Boehm journal, 5-6 March 1814. Much of Boehm's material can be found in J. B. Wakeley, *The Patriarch of One Hundred Years; Reminiscences, Historical and Biographical of Rev. Henry Boehm* (New York: Nelson & Phillips, 1875; reprint, Abram W. Sangrey, 1982). A presiding elder had general oversight for a grouping of circuits known as a district and, after 1792, specific authority for conducting the business session at a quarterly meeting. For more information on the development of this office see Fred W. Price, "The Role of the Presiding Elder in the Growth of The Methodist Episcopal Church, 1784–1832" (Ph.D. diss., Drew University, 1987).

63. Local preachers were licensed to preach but did not regularly travel a circuit or earn their living by preaching. Exhorters too were licensed for public speaking but were not to preach from a biblical text. The nature of exhortation will be considered in a subsequent chapter. The

in attendance, all usually eager to exercise their gifts. This abundance shaped quarterly meetings' liturgical dimensions, both in the number of services that could be reasonably held and in the manner in which leadership was shared within any one service.

With an abundance of ministers at quarterly meetings, more services could be held without exhausting ministers' energies. It was the unusual absence of this support that Boehm, echoing the sentiments of other preachers in similar circumstances, was lamenting. Preaching itself was not a burden, but such sheer amounts in a short time period surely taxed the already overly extended physical resources of an itinerant preacher. But multiple ministers made multiple, long services much easier. As Francis Asbury once noted, because numerous preachers and exhorters were present, it would have been "no burden to have tarried in religious exercises all the night," even after a very full day that included preaching, a love feast, and a four-hour watch night.[64]

The usual abundance of preachers and exhorters made possible not only numerous services but also simultaneous services. Indeed worship at quarterly meetings was often a flurry of activity. If preachers from a neighboring circuit were present, for example, they could conduct a service while the business meeting was in session. Similarly, simultaneous preaching services could be held, as in the case of a Delmarva quarterly meeting in which the congregation was divided between the Methodist meetinghouse and the Episcopal church.[65] Simultaneous preaching services were often held when the crowd's size made it impossible to reasonably gather in one place. Holding a love feast and a preaching service at the same time was also possible, particularly if the size of the crowd gathering outside of the building made it seem prudent. At an 1808 meeting, for example, Seth Crowell

---

ratio of local preachers and exhorters to itinerant preachers for a circuit was large, though precise calculation is difficult. A conservative estimate of the ratio of local preachers to itinerant preachers in a circuit appears to be about 3:1. See Lee, *Short History*, 255, 362; Lorenzo Dow, *Extracts from Original Letters, to the Methodist Bishops, Mostly from their Preachers and Members, in North America: Giving an Account of the Work of God, Since the Year 1800. Prefaced with a Short History of the Spread and Increase of the Methodists; with a Sketch of the camp meetings* (Liverpool, 1806), iv; and *JLFA* 3:283, 311, 314, 322, 402, and 522. The typical circuit also had several exhorters as evidenced by the various quarterly meeting records. Of course, actual attendance at quarterly meetings fluctuated. At the August 1809 quarterly meeting for the Hockhocking Circuit in Ohio (probably held as a camp meeting) the two itinerants were joined with seven local preachers and fourteen exhorters; at the meeting the following February, the two itinerants had the assistance of only one local preacher and two exhorters. See Hockhocking Circuit (OH) "Book of Records." Ms. Ohio Wesleyan University Library, Delaware, OH.

64. *JLFA* 1:202.
65. Boehm journal, 2 July 1815.

preached out in the street from a wagon while the love feast was conducted inside.[66]

The numerous preachers and exhorters in attendance also created a distinctly American version of a Methodist preaching service: one with multiple sermons and exhortations in succession. As Bishop Coke noted for a British audience in the 1780s in describing a "custom peculiar to the American Preachers," when there were multiple preachers present "the Preachers that have not preached, give each of them a warm exhortation."[67] In fact, the common practice allowed not only a sermon followed by multiple exhortations but multiple sermons followed by exhortations. American preachers and exhorters were accustomed to speaking to their congregations in wave after wave.

Another factor involved in the variety of services possible in a quarterly meeting was the fact that the one to whom the polity gave authority to hold the business session also had unique ritual authority. This was true already within the polity of British Methodism under which American Methodists initially operated. This polity gave authority to hold quarterly meetings to the assistant for the circuit, who also had authority to conduct love feasts and watch nights. Not surprisingly, both of these services were regular parts of quarterly meetings in America as in Great Britain.

When American Methodism organized as the Methodist Episcopal Church in 1784, their revised polity continued to make itinerants with distinctive ritual authority responsible for holding the quarterly meeting. In 1787, the assistants' quarterly meeting responsibilities were shifted to deacons, along with the assistants' responsibility to hold love feasts and watch nights. But placement of this responsibility with the deacons was only temporary. The first several *Disciplines* after the 1784 Christmas Conference show this sort of fluidity in several respects as the Methodists worked out some ambiguities arising from grafting new ecclesiastical categories onto their former societal polity. The 1792 *Discipline* moved the responsibility for holding quarterly meetings to presiding elders, who, of course, had full sacramental authority.

In actuality the connection between quarterly meetings and (presiding) elders had existed since 1784, although it was not officially recognized in the *Disciplines* before 1792. The regular attendance of

---

66. Seth Crowell, *The Journal of Seth Crowell; containing an Account of His Travels as a Methodist Preacher for Twelve Years* (New York: J. C. Totten, 1813), 82.

67. Coke, *Extracts*, 112-13. Compare Haskins's journal, 31.

elders at quarterly meetings was certainly what enabled Coke to note in the mid-1780s that American quarterly meetings had the "Love-feast, and (now) the sacrament" since administration of the sacrament of the Lord's Supper required an elder.[68] In fact, the office of presiding elder could be said to have been created for the very purpose of presiding at quarterly meetings. For Thomas Ware, one of the earliest itinerants and a participant in the Christmas Conference, that certainly was the case. Commenting late in his life, Ware states:

> After our organization [as a church], we proceeded to elect a sufficient number of elders to visit the quarterly meetings, and administer the ordinances; and this it was that gave rise to the office of presiding elders among us.[69]

Presiding at quarterly meetings would not have been a strange task to the first class of Methodist elders since almost all of them had previously served as assistants in circuits. Of the thirteen elders ordained at the Christmas Conference, all had been assistants before and twelve were currently serving as assistants, having been appointed to that capacity the previous spring.

Simply put, under normal circumstances a quarterly meeting brought together those people, itinerant and local, who held the full range of liturgical authority and ministries within Methodism. This occurrence contributed to the richness of the liturgical activities at American quarterly meetings.

Conclusion

In 1804 a subtle, but significant, change occurred in the *Discipline:* a new phrase, "quarterly meeting conference," appeared. In some instances it was a simple lengthening of the nomenclature as one name was substituted for the other. However, in several instances, the change indicated a novel attempt to distinguish the quarterly meeting as a whole from the business session now designated as the "quarterly meeting conference." For example, the passage that had charged presiding elders to be present at quarterly meetings and "to call together

---

68. Coke, *Extracts*, 35.

69. Thomas Ware, "The Christmas Conference of 1784," *Methodist Quarterly Review* 14 (1832): 98. See also Thomas Ware, *Sketches of the Life and Travels of Rev. Thomas Ware, who has been an Itinerant Methodist Preacher for More than Fifty Years* (New York: Lane & Sandford, 1842), 106-7 and 115. Another aspect of Ware's statement is naming quarterly meetings as the locus for sacramental administration. This issue will be considered more fully in a later chapter.

at each quarterly meeting" all the various ministers now read "to call together at each quarterly meeting a quarterly meeting conference" of the various ministers.[70]

All the individual terms were familiar ones. The term "conference" was understood well enough: it was the term that Methodists used for a business meeting, particularly the itinerants' Annual Conference. And the phrase "quarterly meeting conference" itself was no surprise, having begun to seep into popular usage well before the official change in the *Discipline*.[71]

What made the 1804 change striking was that it made official what had been unofficial, but obvious: the business aspect of quarterly meetings was only a part—perhaps even a small part—of the whole. Subtlety gave way to clarity as the polity finally recognized what had long ago become the norm in practice. What the polity had once recognized as the whole (the business session *technically* was the quarterly meeting) had now become a part—the quarterly meeting conference. The original term, "quarterly meeting," now officially referred to the entirety of the events: arrival, preaching services, family prayer, prayer meetings, love feast, sacrament, pastoral rites, fellowship, and departure, along with the conference.

Again, in 1804, the polity's official language finally caught up with reality. That which had started as one British itinerant's idea for a helpful business meeting had become an American "great festival." The business, though important, was often moved to the periphery as quarterly meetings became the first true extended meetings for American Methodist worship and revival.

---

70. *Discipline*/1804, 19.
71. See Meacham journal, 13 October 1792.

CHAPTER 2

Public Worship at Quarterly Meetings: Preaching Services

"It is the power of God: the Lord is in this place!"
—visiting Quaker encouraging people not to run from a Methodist preaching service[1]

"Spend and be spent in this work," the early *Disciplines* said to the Methodist itinerants. "This work" was *the* work: saving souls. Initially eschewing all forms of settled parish ministry in favor of itinerant preachers, early Methodist polity emphasized the itinerants' role as evangelists. The business of these preachers, as John Wesley had first instructed, was not "to preach so many Times, and to take care of this or that Society" but it was "to save as many Souls as you can."[2] Not surprisingly, a common way in which some expressed the essence of their ministry was to say, echoing other foundational Methodist documents, that they were calling sinners "to flee from the wrath to come."

Nothing was more pervasive in early Methodism than the impulse to evangelize. An evangelical spirit imbued all aspects of the faith, including the way Methodists worshiped, particularly in public services. Open to both Methodists and non-Methodists, public services were opportunities for Methodists to evangelize people along the entire soteriological spectrum from those unawakened to those seeking

---

1. John Ffirth, *Experience and Gospel Labors of the Rev. Benjamin Abbott; to which is annexed a Narrative of his Life and Death* (New York: Carlton & Phillips, 1853), 187.
2. These passages were inherited from the eighteenth-century British polity document, the "Large Minutes" (Q. 26), and are thus traceable to John Wesley himself. See *Works* (Jackson) 8:310.

sanctification. Here Methodists offered God's grace, warned of the consequences for failing to receive that grace, and experienced grace, whether it was in first awakenings of sensibility to God or in entire sanctification's joyful rest.

Quarterly meetings were full of these public services. In order of prominence, quarterly meetings included preaching services, prayer services ("prayer meetings" and family prayer), watch night services, and pastoral rites (weddings, funerals, and baptisms). All of these were considered public in the sense that polity did not restrict attendance to Methodists only. With preaching services in the forefront, public worship at quarterly meetings offered God's grace to the full range of human conditions recognized by Methodists.

Preaching Service Basics

The predominant Methodist public service was the preaching service. At least two but more commonly four to five such services took place at any quarterly meeting. If there were only two, one would be held on Saturday and the other on Sunday. In most meetings, there were four or five services; two would fall on Saturday and two or three on Sunday.

The precise timing of these services on the two days evolved like many elements in early Methodist worship: in the midst of variety, certain patterns tended to emerge. The first service on either day would usually start around 11 A.M. On Saturday this time allowed for participants to complete their travel; on Sunday it provided time to conduct the private or "societal" rituals, such as a love feast or the Lord's Supper. If there were two more services in the day, they would typically occur at midafternoon and early evening. If there was only one more service after the 11 A.M. service it was held at either time, although on Saturday a late afternoon or early evening slot was desirable to allow time for the quarterly meeting conference and on Sunday a midafternoon setting allowed time for the people to travel home.

Methodists generally showed great variety in their selection of sites for preaching services. Only the most minimal requirements had to be achieved: a place for a preacher to stand and be heard and a place for people to gather. Outside of quarterly meetings, many—perhaps, in some places, most—preaching services were not held in meeting-houses built for worship. Methodists were initially more concerned with the utility than the ritual sacrality of a space, although the increasing number of Methodist-built meetinghouses indicates some preference for distinctive space. Accordingly, people were used to attending Methodist preaching services in stores, taverns, even out in the woods. The itinerants' plans of circuit preaching appointments show this variety. Few preaching services on a typical circuit were held in meetinghouses; most were in homes, or possibly schools or courthouses.[3] Only in older, more established regions did the number of meetinghouses proliferate.

Therefore the selection of a site for a quarterly meeting, and its preaching services, was not necessarily dictated by the availability of a Methodist meetinghouse. Instead the quarterly meeting conference, which apparently chose sites under the direction of the presiding elder, rotated the meeting sites. Particular choices seem to have been guided only by a desire to make the meetings accessible to people in various parts of a circuit, and by the need for a space that could accommodate the expected crowd. Meetings were often rotated among several regular sites in no particular order. If needed, an "extra" quarterly meeting could be scheduled, presumably in a location more convenient to part of a circuit when the circuit was extremely large.

This meant that the preaching services at a quarterly meeting used any large building or space available to them, singularly or in combination. If no one space was large enough, the congregation could be divided for several simultaneous preaching services. Preaching services were held in Methodist meetinghouses, other churches, schools, courthouses, and homes, if necessary. Even an abandoned distillery or a tobacco warehouse could be pressed into service.[4] Barns were a particularly favorite setting.

Preaching services were frequently held outside, especially if the crowd was large. The move outdoors could be either planned or unplanned. In either case, little preparation was needed. A wagon was brought up in which the preachers sat. Perhaps a chair was placed in it upon which the speaker stood. A less desirable, but some-

---

3. See, for example, the two plans (one for the Vincennes, Indiana, circuit; the other for the Marietta, Ohio, circuit) from the early 1820s in John Stewart, *Highways and Hedges; or, Fifty Years of Western Methodism* (Cincinnati: Hitchcock and Walden; New York: Carlton and Lanahan, 1870), 105, 139. See also Raymond Martin Bell, *Methodist Circuit Plans 1777–1825* (Washington, PA: R. M. Bell, 1984).

4. Cf. George Peck, *The Life and Times of Rev. George Peck, D.D.* (New York: Nelson & Phillips, 1874), 82; and *JLFA* 1:597.

times necessary, alternative was a stump or rock. At some services the preacher stood at the window of the meetinghouse and preached simultaneously to people inside and out. However, congregations preferred the woods for the sake of the shade. If the preaching was planned for outside—a common occurrence from the 1770s onward—an arbor could be built for the congregation.[5] To assist the preachers, a stand or stage could be built, as in the case of a 1790 quarterly meeting.[6] More simply, an available site with good shade and promising acoustics was selected.

Whether inside or out, Methodist preaching services most typically included seating arrangements segregated by both gender and race. Separation of women and men had been a long-standing feature of British Methodism and was continued in American practice. If anything, American leaders recommitted themselves to this "primitive, prudent, and decent" practice to the point of recommending separate doors in new construction.[7] Although liturgical legislation reveals occasional failure to follow certain practices, the practice of separated seating by gender was very common through the early nineteenth century.[8]

Within a meetinghouse the easiest way to separate men and women was to designate different sides for each, although a variety of different approaches was tried at larger-than-normal quarterly meeting congregations. One way was to keep the women in the meetinghouse and move the men outside for a separate preaching service. If the preaching service was in a barn, the floor could be designated for women with men relegated to the loft. If the entire congregation was in the woods, separate areas for women and men were maintained.[9]

5. *JLFA* 1:308. Asbury describes an August 1779 meeting in Delaware. Devereux Jarratt, the Anglican priest in southern Virginia, claimed to have preached in arbors in the early 1770s before he made contact with the Methodists. See Devereux Jarratt, *The Life of the Reverend Devereux Jarratt* (Baltimore: Warner & Hanna, 1806), 96.

6. William Jessop, Journal (1788). Ms. United Methodist Church Archives-GCAH, Madison, NJ, 4 July 1790.

7. *Minutes; Taken at a Council of the Bishop and delegated Elders of the Methodist Episcopal Church: Held at Baltimore, in the State of Maryland, December 1, 1790* (Baltimore: Goddard and Angell, 1790), 7.

8. Compare Frederick A. Norwood, "When They All Sat Together in Dayton," *Methodist History* 25.1 (October 1986): 34-40.

9. See, respectively, David Dailey, Diary. Ms. St. George's United Methodist Church, Philadelphia, PA, 13 February 1820; David Lewis, *Recollections of a Superannuate: or, Sketches of Life, Labor, and Experience in the Methodist Itinerancy,* ed. S. M. Merrill (Cincinnati: Methodist Book Concern, 1857), 69; John Littlejohn, "Journal of John Littlejohn." Ts. Transcribed by Annie L. Winstead. Louisville Conference Historical Society, Louisville, KY. [Available on microfilm

In addition to gender separation Methodist preaching services also commonly involved segregated seating by race. As with gender separation, various means were used. If the entire congregation could be held in a meetinghouse, Blacks were restricted to one area, perhaps the gallery or balcony. If the congregation was too large, Whites would be gathered inside and Blacks outside, with the windows left open so that all could hear. Preaching services located outdoors also involved segregated seating, even to the use of partitions at times.[10]

Two other sorts of segregation in seating probably occurred at public services, although evidence is sketchier: gathered seating for the preachers apart from the people, and separation of the Methodists from the non-Methodists. The former is the more easily recognized in available accounts. For example, on a couple of occasions itinerant Ezekiel Cooper spoke about sitting "among the people." In one instance he was late in arriving and in the other he had not planned to speak. But in both cases Cooper eventually moved to the pulpit area where the other preachers were gathered.[11]

Concentration of Methodists within the congregation is even less well documented, but it is implied in some descriptions of early public services. Consider one 1809 public service (a watch night service held outside a quarterly meeting) where Daniel De Vinné and five young friends stumbled in. All found seats close to the door except for De Vinné, who was forced to pass "up the aisle, to within one seat of the altar, and [be] seated in the midst of praying Methodists." De Vinné was embarrassed, probably to the great amusement of his friends.[12]

In terms of internal order, a preaching service had two parts. The first part rarely varied as to its components and their order. It contained successively: hymns, extemporaneous prayer, reading of the biblical text, sermon(s), and exhortation(s).[13] A preaching service

from Kentucky Wesleyan College, Owensboro, KY.], 148; John Campbell Deem Autobiography. Ms. Ohio Wesleyan University Library, 42-43; and W. P. Strickland, *The Life of Jacob Gruber* (New York: Carlton & Porter, 1860), 87-88.

10. See Ann Taves, *Fits, Trances, and Visions: Experiencing Religion and Explaining Experience from Wesley to James* (Princeton, NJ: Princeton University Press, 1999), 106.

11. Ezekiel Cooper journal in Papers. Garrett-Evangelical Theological Seminary Library, Evanston, IL, 5 March 1796 and 8 September 1798.

12. Daniel De Vinné, *Recollections of Fifty Years in the Ministry* (New York: Tibbals & Co., 1869), 9-11. Compare Miram Fletcher, *The Methodist; Or, Incidents and Characters from Life in the Baltimore Conference* (New York: Derby & Jackson, 1859), 1:129, 142.

13. Looking at the writings of contemporary British Methodists, Adrian Burden outlines a similar order for them. See *The Preaching Service—The Glory of the Methodists: A Study of the Piety, Ethos, and Development of the Methodist Preaching Service*, Alcuin/GROW Liturgical Study 17 (Bramcote: Grove Books Limited, 1991), 22.

typically commenced with someone stepping into the chancel or onto the stage and lining out the first hymn, normally two lines at a time, for the congregation to sing. Occasionally the inexperience of the leader made this a humorous sight as when one itinerant, so scared in his first attempt to line out a hymn, closed his eyes after every two lines and soon was reading only the first two lines of every stanza. According to this preacher, the congregation sang his abbreviated form of the hymn "O for a Thousand Tongues to Sing" fairly well.[14] At a hymn's conclusion, someone, most commonly the appointed preacher, would kneel in the pulpit and pray extemporaneously. Afterward, the preacher would rise, go to the preaching spot, and read the scripture text for the sermon. A long text might consist of four to five verses from one biblical book. Evidence is extremely sparse that anyone followed the instructions in the 1792 *Discipline* to read two complete biblical chapters in a morning preaching service and one complete chapter in the afternoon service. Preaching and exhorting, which will be described in more detail later in this chapter, followed immediately.

A preaching service's second part consisted of whatever might occur after the preaching and exhortation. What *did* occur varied widely (and sometimes wildly). The simplest completion for a preaching service was a concluding extemporaneous prayer followed by a hymn. The more complex—and, in Methodist thought, more desirable—ending for a preaching service was the "work of God," to use an early term. In this case, God was understood to become so powerfully present that the people became engaged in seeking grace in its various dimensions. As mourners began to cry for a sense of peace through the forgiveness of their sins and some "professors" struggled in prayer to experience sanctification, believers would begin to shout the praises of God, exhort those close to them, or begin praying for others. Meanwhile, ministers—itinerant preachers, local preachers, exhorters, and class leaders—would spread through the worship space to find those most earnestly engaged with God's grace, all the while themselves praying, exhorting, and shouting. The time

---

14. George Brown, *Recollections of Itinerant Life: Including Early Reminiscences* (Cincinnati: Carroll & Co., 1866), 64. Which hymnal might have been used in any particular service is an open question. Although those published by The Methodist Episcopal Church itself would have been used frequently, some individuals would most probably have used any number of "unauthorized" hymnals. These seem very prevalent in early Methodism, existing in both unpublished and published form. There were at least seventeen such hymnals published by Methodists between 1805 and 1843, according to Charles A. Johnson, *The Frontier Camp Meeting* (Dallas: Southern Methodist University Press, 1955), 193.

was one of intense engagement with the grace of God as in this 1788 meeting:

> the power of the lord came down so powerfully that the crys of the people stopd public preaching the preachers & exhorters went then among the people praying with & exorting them as Paul the Jaylor to believe on the Lord Jesus Christ. . . . it is suposd 100 found peace in the Lord in them two days & nights.[15]

This "work of God," which will also be described in more detail later, could continue for hours or days.

Three other activities were commonly undertaken during a preaching service. One possibility was insertion of a public collection. Whereas most money collected to support the ministers and pay for expenses was raised in the classes and brought to quarterly meetings for disbursement, occasionally a general collection was taken from whoever might be in attendance at a preaching service.[16] Not only did non-Methodists contribute, but they sometimes assisted in the gathering itself as in the case of a militia officer, in full dress uniform, collecting money from his soldiers at a 1795 Long Island quarterly meeting.[17]

A public collection, although made sporadically, could be a significant source of revenue for a circuit. Commonly a single public collection represented 10 to 20 percent of the money available for a circuit during a quarter.[18] If the classes had been especially lax the percentage increased: one public collection made up over half of quarterly funds for the Edenton, North Carolina, station in 1824.[19] Frequently, the monies were used to offset deficiencies in paying support to the presiding elder, families of the itinerant preachers, or even the itinerants themselves. A public collection could also be used to retire building debts or even to pay for an itinerant's new horse.

---

15. Daniel Grant letter to John Owen. Letters. David Campbell Papers, Special Collections Library, Duke University Library, Durham, NC, 10 July 1788.

16. In some instances "public collection" means a general collection made of the society members during administration of the Lord's Supper. But it most commonly referred to a collection made from members and nonmembers alike at a public service. The ambiguity in terms happened because, as will be discussed in chapter 4, some sacramental administrations occurred in a public setting, although communing itself was restricted. In this case, perhaps the normal sacramental collection was taken from everyone and was thus a "public collection."

17. Cooper journal, 17 May 1795.

18. See, for example, the various entries in the "Steward's Book for the New Mills Circuit (NJ)" and the Stratford (CT) quarterly meeting conference records. The Stratford records hold two interesting suggestions: in some circuits public collections were quite frequent and summertime collections were larger both absolutely and proportionally.

19. Edenton (NC) quarterly meeting conference records, 28 February 1824.

Another common occurrence was not as useful or welcome as a public collection: disruptions by those in attendance. Such disruptions seem fairly frequent, at least compared to late-twentieth-century experience. They show the popular nature of Methodist preaching services, both in the sense that the services were open to everyone and that they attracted a wide variety of people with varying social sensibilities. One common disruption, which still occurs today, was the noise of rambunctious children. Efforts to quiet them often met with minimal success. As one presiding elder found out when he attempted to quiet a three-year-old boy with a stern "Little boy, you must not talk!" from the pulpit, to which the child responded defiantly, "I will talk!" to the great embarrassment of his mother.[20] (This little boy was left at home with relatives during the next quarterly meeting.)

Adulthood did not necessarily guarantee better behavior. Preaching services were disrupted in various ways. Non-Methodist observers and hecklers would fight; show up with eggs to pelt the congregation; exhibit their drunkenness; clown by joking, laughing, and imitating Methodist practices; or even chop wood immediately outside the door in order to disrupt a service. Some disruptions were quite sinister, as in the case of a Virginia quarterly meeting during which a gang arrived to stone the meetinghouse and whip some of the blacks in attendance.[21]

Some disruptions were intended as protests to Methodism's ministry or theology. Those with some complaint against Methodism would often bring that complaint into a preaching service. Preachers had to be ready to counter a wide variety of attacks, from someone asking for the return of their pledge to a building fund or entering a debate about doctrine in the middle of a sermon to someone expressing their displeasure with the harsh tone of Methodist preaching as did "two dressy girls" who walked out of a service with "an impudent air."[22] At times the Methodist preacher could be an unwitting aid to denominational hubris. James Finley, for example, wanting to include a visiting clergyman from another church in the service, invited

20. Chauncey Hobart, *Recollections of My Life. Fifty Years of Itinerancy in the Northwest* (Red Wing, MN: Red Wing Printing Co., 1885), 11.

21. "Diary of Rev. Nelson Reed" (Ts. United Methodist Historical Society, Lovely Lane Museum, Baltimore, MD), 109.

22. Cooper journal, 28 August 1791; [John Smith], "The Journal of John Smith, Methodist Circuit Rider, of his Work on the Greenbrier Circuit, (West) Virginia and Virginia," *The Journal of the Greenbrier Historical Society* 1.4 (October 1966): 26; and Coke, *Extracts of the journals of the Rev. Dr. Coke's five visits to America* (London: G. Paramore, 1793), 40-41.

him to say the final prayer. The visitor stood up and prayed for the Methodists, the "poor, ignorant, misled people" who were "doing more harm than infidelity itself and hindering the progress of the pure Gospel."[23] Another sort of direct attack on Methodist ministry was the frequent attempts of some to forcibly remove relatives or friends who had come under conviction and were being prayed for by Methodists. Sometimes they threatened with a weapon to gain compliance.

Methodists were not defenseless. Preachers often had a stock of sharp, quick-witted responses to common disturbances, developed through sheer repetition. Moreover, some Methodist men acquired an informal status as liturgical "bouncers." A good example is Ezekiel Dimmitt, who lived in a center of Methodist activity along the branches of the Little Miami River in southwest Ohio. He gained a reputation for muscular strength and an "iron grasp," his willingness to use these to suppress disturbances, and his ability not to let his role "detract from his spiritual enjoyment" of worship.[24]

A final common staple of preaching services was the "invitation," an offer by one of the preachers or exhorters for mourners to gather in a designated place for the prayers of the faithful. Most likely originating in the late-1790s, the practice increased in prominence, importance, and ritualized nature. Several accounts of the origin of this practice exist.[25] Although accounts include differing details, they share many common features. The first is that the invitation for mourners to move to a specified location for prayer was first done in the 1790s, probably in the latter half of that decade. The second is that initially the invitation was a natural, spontaneous act to facilitate a ministry that was already commonplace: prayer with mourners for their justification. Having preachers, exhorters, and the Methodist people themselves spread through a liturgical space to pray with mourners under deep conviction was a very frequent scene. The

---

23. James B. Finley, *Autobiography of Rev. James B. Finley; or, Pioneer Life in the West,* ed. W. P. Strickland (Cincinnati: Methodist Book Concern, 1853), 299-300.

24. Undated sketch of Ezekiel Dimmitt in Philip Gatch papers (Papers. Ohio Wesleyan University Library, Delaware, OH).

25. J. B. Wakeley, The *Patriarch of One Hundred Years; Being Reminiscences, Historical and Biographical of Rev. Henry Boehm* (New York: Nelson & Phillips, 1875; reprint, Abram W. Sangrey, 1982), 134-36; [James Jenkins], *Experience, Labours, and Sufferings of Rev. James Jenkins, of the South Carolina Conference* (n.p.: Printed for the author, 1842), 79-80; Jeremiah Norman, Journal. Ms. Stephen Beauregard Weeks Papers. Southern Historical Collection, University of North Carolina, Chapel Hill, NC, 11 March 1798; Minton Thrift, *Memoir of the Rev. Jesse Lee. With Extracts from his Journals* (New York: Bangs and Mason, 1823), 243; and Samuel W. Williams, *Pictures of Early Methodism in Ohio* (Cincinnati: Jennings & Graham, 1909), 68-69.

original phenomenon was the same as the innovation: the faithful praying with mourners. The new element was the direction of movement through the liturgical space: instead of the prayers dispersing through the space, those wanting prayer were collected in one place.

As a portend of other innovations during this period, the invitation was increasingly ritualized so that its features became standard. One standardized feature was development of distinct spaces, with specific names, for gathering mourners. Mourners were invited to either come to the altar or to a mourner's bench. In both cases, the names expanded previous terms. Methodists called the space around the communion table and the railing the "altar."[26] The name generally became associated with whatever space in which the mourners gathered, particularly the space immediately in front of a stand in an outdoor preaching service.[27] Similarly, the pew or bench at which mourners might be gathered acquired a technical name, the "mourner's bench," and designation of such a spot became commonplace.[28]

Another ritualized feature was the means by which the believers prayed for the mourners. The consistent elements of this feature were the mourners' desire for the prayer of the church, expressed as desiring the prayer "of the faithful" or "of the people of God," and the "professors" willingness to pray.[29] However, the manner of praying for the mourners sometimes acquired more ritualized form, such as the "praying circle" in which the kneeling mourners were surrounded by Methodists all praying simultaneously.[30] This practice inspired at least one hymn describing such a scene:

26. Cf. Joseph Snelling, *Life of Rev. Joseph Snelling, Being a Sketch of His Christian Experience and Labors in the Ministry* (Boston: John M'Leish, 1847), 114-15; and De Vinné, *Recollections*, 9-11. Hence the invitation could also be called an "altar call."

27. E.g., David Dailey, *Experience and Ministerial Labors of Rev. Thomas Smith, Late an Itinerant Preacher of the Gospel in the Methodist Episcopal Church* (New York: Lane & Tippett, 1848), 87-88; and Joshua N. Glenn, "A Memorandum or Journal of the first part of my life up to the twenty third year of my age." Ms. on microfilm. Library of Congress, Washington, D.C., 17. Of course, much of this applies to the organization of the ground for a camp meeting, after their emergence about the same time.

28. Compare Henry Boehm, Journal. Ms. Henry Boehm Papers, United Methodist Church Archives-GCAH, Madison, NJ. [Microfilm copy at Iliff Theological Seminary, Denver, CO.], 5 July 1801; and W. P. Strickland, ed., *Autobiography of Dan Young, A New England Preacher of the Olden Time* (New York: Carlton & Porter, 1860), 54-55; to Strickland, *The Life of Jacob Gruber*, 51.

29. See Glenn journal, 17 and 79; and John Ellis Edwards, *Life of Rev. John Wesley Childs: For Twenty-Three Years an Itinerant Methodist Minister* (Richmond and Louisville: John Early, 1852), 37. Note the very communal nature of the prayer desired. The accounts often emphasize a desire for a prayer of the people, not just an individual.

30. Taves, *Fits, Trances, and Visions*, 100-101. See also Nathan Bangs, Journal. Ms. Nathan Bangs papers. United Methodist Church Archives-GCAH, Madison, NJ, 5 October 1805; and Snelling, *Life of Rev. Joseph Snelling*, 73-74. Compare Dailey, *Experience and Ministerial Labors of Rev. Thomas Smith*, 148-50.

Come, and let us form the circle,
With the mourners let us pray,
They are griev'd and broken-hearted,
And they know not what to say.

Have you faith to pray for mourners?
Come and form the social ring;
They with deep distress are groaning,
While they hear their neighbours sing.[31]

At times these circles also used some form of circular dance or march while the participants prayed and shouted.

Proclamation in Preaching Services

There was great emphasis in early Methodist theology on the importance of the present time. "Now" was the favorite adverb of time. This "now," as represented in Methodist worship, contained both a sense of great opportunity and of great urgency. Because faith was portrayed as the premier precondition for experiencing saving grace, a speaker at a Methodist public meeting could emphasize both the present opportunity for experiencing grace ("all people can respond, if they have faith!") and the present urgency to do so ("all people must respond; have faith!").[32]

The desire to expound effectively both the opportunity and necessity of salvation was the typical goal of the early Methodist sermon. As portrayed by Edward Dromgoole, one of the earliest American preachers, a sermon should be persuasive, leaving the mind filled with conviction and the heart with resolution.[33] Dromgoole emphasized that humans had several capacities, all of which must be addressed

---

31. Enoch Mudge, *The American Camp-Meeting Hymn Book. Containing a Variety of Original Hymns, Suitable to be Used at Camp-Meetings; and at Other Times in Private and Social Devotion* (Boston: Burdakin, 1818), 119.

32. Compare the ending of John Wesley's sermon 43, "The Scripture Way of Salvation," §3.18, *Works* 2:169: "If you seek it by faith, you may expect it as you are; and if as you are, then expect it now. It is of importance to observe, that there is an inseparable connexion between these three points,—expect it by faith, expect it as you are, and expect it now!" Although Wesley was here presenting an invitation to sanctification, his thought is just as applicable to the antecedent experience of salvation, justification.

33. Edward Dromgoole, "The Art of Preaching" (in his papers [Papers. Southern Historical Collection, University of North Carolina Library, Chapel Hill, NC. (Available on microfilm from the University of North Carolina.)]). Dromgoole was admitted into the itinerancy in 1775. He quit active traveling several years later but remained an active local preacher and influential presence in southern Virginia well into the nineteenth century.

for the sermon to be effective. A sermon should begin by instructing the understanding. Then the preacher should arouse imagination and appeal to the conscience. The ending should excite the affections.

Whether or not most preachers agreed with Dromgoole's precise technique, they would agree with his goal: a sermon must be persuasive in disclosing the opportunity and the necessity of salvation. Good preaching was pointed and moving. Theological sophistication was a secondary goal, if it was one at all. Instead, the Methodist preacher tried to speak forcibly and plainly. As Bishop Asbury urged, the Methodist preacher was to "feel for the power, feel for the power, brother."[34] Listeners of those who found "liberty" to preach powerfully would have felt this power; such listeners could say: "We *felt* as well as heard the word of truth."[35] A crucial part of the preacher's ability to speak in this manner appears to have been the level at which the listeners felt akin to the preachers. It was not hard for average listeners to recognize themselves in the Methodist preacher. The typical preacher had little if any formal theological education. His training was most commonly by a form of apprenticeship, being mentored by a more experienced preacher and learning to preach by preaching.[36] With there being no educational requirement, oftentimes very little time passed between one's conversion and first attempts at preaching. Thus early Methodist preaching was in the vernacular. As one scholar has pointed out, often the only thing that distinguished the Methodist preacher and his listener was the side of the pulpit on which each was located.[37]

The typical Methodist sermon was a topical exposition of a very short biblical passage (two to four verses). The text could be as short as one word. "Mercy" was the text for one particularly moving quarterly meeting sermon, for example.[38] These early Methodist preachers

---

34. Quoted in John H. Wigger, *Taking Heaven by Storm: Methodism and the Rise of Popular Christianity in America* (New York: Oxford University Press, 1998), 77. I am indebted to Wigger generally for his insights on Methodist preaching and exhortation. See Wakeley, *Patriarch*, 441. An assessment of Asbury's own preaching can be found in Todd E. Johnson, "The Sermons of Francis Asbury: Reconstruction and Analysis," *Methodist History* 33.3 (April 1995): 149-61. Many of Johnson's comments about Asbury seem true generally for Methodist preachers.

35. Elbert Osborn, *Passages in the Life and Ministry of Elbert Osborn, an Itinerant Minister of the Methodist Episcopal Church, illustrating the Providence and Grace of God* (New York: Published for the author, 1847–1850), 37. (Emphasis in original.) "Liberty" was the universal term used by preachers to describe what they felt when preaching effectively. See Russell Richey, "The Chesapeake Coloration of American Methodism," in *Methodism in its Cultural Milieu*, ed. Tim Macquiban (Oxford: Applied Theology Press, 1994), 120.

36. Wigger, *Taking Heaven by Storm*, 71-79.

37. Ibid., 49.

38. Finley, *Autobiography*, 290.

might choose their text well in advance of preaching or at the very moment they stood up to preach. Delivery was almost always extemporaneous. The result was that a Methodist sermon was most often an exposition of the doctrine of salvation. Indeed, the *Discipline* urged preaching the full scope of the order of salvation in every sermon.[39] Because Methodists considered grace immediately available whenever they preached, sermons usually ended with an "application."

Existing outlines of sermons from this period (see the sampling in appendix A) show a consistency in many of these elements.[40] If these surviving outlines are any indication, a Methodist preacher typically divided his sermon into three sections. First he identified his text and provided an introduction of some sort. As the itinerant John Price instructed himself in his sermon outline book from 1814–1816, it was important to "introduce the subject by some reflections from the chapter" or "introduce by explaining the context."[41] Some such introduction was followed by the body of the sermon, often a topical exposition that could reach six or seven main points. In the final section of the sermon the preacher sought to "apply" the sermon to his hearers. Philip Gatch, for instance, uses a variety of phrases in his outlines to remind himself to direct his rhetoric in this way: "then apply," "then enforce the word of my text, and conclude," "lastly apply and so conclude," and "now apply."[42] The Word must never rest simply in some distant abstraction.

Perhaps even more than in sermons, this emphasis on the immediacy of grace was evident in Methodist exhortation, particularly within public preaching services. A common feature of such services, an exhortation was the occasion when the offer of grace in the sermon was applied very specifically to that congregation. Through the exhortation a congregation was informed that now was the moment to respond in faith and that they were the specific ones God was calling

---

39. See the bishops' commentary in the 1798 *Discipline*, 86-87.

40. Large collections of sermon outlines can be found in the Philip Gatch, James Meacham, John Price, and George A. Reed manuscript collections. For a printed collection of sermons in the period immediately after the one under consideration see Shipley Wells Willson and Ebenezer Ireson, ed., *The Methodist Preacher: or Monthly Sermons from Living Ministers*, vols. 1 and 2 for 1830 and 1831, 2nd. ed. (Boston: C. D. Strong, 1832). The northeastern United States is disproportionately represented in this collection and some degree of educational respectability was intended (note the listing of degrees and an extended quotation from Virgil's *Aeneid* in Latin).

41. John Price sermon book. During these years Price was preaching in Maryland and Pennsylvania. Compare the sermon outline labeled "Exaltation of Christ" in the papers of George Reed.

42. Gatch sermon outline book. Gatch was a prominent preacher, first as a Virginia itinerant and later as a local preacher in Virginia and Ohio. He began preaching in the 1770s.

upon to do so. This focus sometimes gave exhortations precedence over preaching. As Bishop Coke noted, "More good has been done in most instances by the exhortations than by the sermon: more souls have been awakened and converted to God."[43] More good was done "in most instances" because an exhortation was the time when people were informed that God's grace was specifically for them and that there would be serious, specific consequences if they ignored the offer.

This function of exhortations demonstrates the point at which they were related to—and distinct from—preaching. The purpose of exhortation seems to have been to make absolutely sure that the word of God never remained in the abstract but was applied forcefully to those gathered in a particular worship service. Indeed, on the infrequent occasions when sermons accomplished this in an effective manner on their own, exhortations could be omitted. Thus an itinerant once observed, "It seemed no trouble for the preachers to preach, and every Sermon seemed to take such effect that it was judged unnecessary to be followed by exhortation."[44] The underlying suggestion that sermons often were not so effective shows that exhortations were the fulfillment of sermons in applying and making specific the issues of salvation and judgment raised in the sermons.

Methodist exhorters used a range of rhetorical strategies to accomplish this task. As one early itinerant noted:

> To declaim, to advise, to warn, to persuade, to entreat with tears, all are comprised in the ample range of exhortation. And, in doing this awfully sublime work, the depths of human learning may be opened, the wide field of revelation explored, its doctrines brought up, its promises spread out, together with the rousing of Sinai's thunder, and the blood and groans of Calvary . . . in the winding up of the sermon, exhortation comes in as an auxiliary; then the holy effort resembles an army in the act of storming the castle.[45]

Methodist exhorters would pick and choose from this range of rhetorical strategies to subvert any resistance listeners had toward the gospel. In some instances this consisted of speaking the listeners' own minds, raising their objections, then using whatever means necessary

43. Coke, *Extracts*, 112-13. See also *JLFA* 3:327.

44. Benjamin Lakin, Journal. Ms. on microfilm. Washington University Library, St. Louis, MO [Some of Lakin's journal can be found in William Warren Sweet, *The Methodists* (Chicago: University of Chicago Press, 1946)], 8 September 1815.

45. Charles Giles, *Pioneer: A Narrative of the Nativity, Experience, Travels, and Ministerial Labours of Rev. Charles Giles* (New York: G. Lane & P. P. Sandford, 1844), 85.

to erase the objections. An exhortation could start, for example, by posing the question of why people would "not come and seek the Lord Jesus Christ" and then answer its own question (because of fear and pride), at the same time attempting to move the listeners to overcome those obstacles.[46] This approach could be quite effective. Francis Asbury once marveled at how one exhorter's method of "proposing cases of conscience, and answering them, and speaking about Christ, heaven, and hell . . . carries all before it."[47]

An exhorter's tendency to exegete the listeners' thoughts and motivations highlights the chief difference, in theory at least, between exhorting and preaching: the relationship of the speaker's words to those of the biblical texts. Strictly speaking, preachers were to "take" a text while preaching and exhorters were not so prescribed. In other words, sermons offered exposition of a biblical text while exhortations applied the gospel to the listeners' immediate situation. The terminology of "taking a text" and the distinction between preaching and exhorting were long-standing features in Methodist polity on both sides of the Atlantic. And it is clear that many American Methodists kept this distinction in mind.

But in actuality the difference between a sermon and an exhortation was not nearly so sharp. Rather than neatly distinguished modes of discourse, preaching and exhorting were more points of differing emphasis along a continuum. Many sermons were little more than topical expositions to which some biblical text was joined. Moreover, the sermon portion called the "application" held a similar function to an exhortation. Meanwhile, exhortations could hardly avoid biblical exposition. As one itinerant put it, an exhorter "might *steal* a text," introducing a subject by quoting a biblical passage, but not telling where it could be found.[48] In addition, although only formally licensed preachers could preach, all preachers and the informal class of exhorters could give exhortations. In other words, sermons might sound like exhortations because the same people performed both types of speech-acts.

Two unpublished exhortations found in the papers of George A. Reed (reproduced in appendix B) exhibit the close relationship between

---

46. Jenkins, *Experience*, 125-31. This exhortation seems to be one of the few published.

47. *JLFA* 1:308-9.

48. Alfred Brunson, *A Western Pioneer: or, Incidents of the Life and Times of Rev. Alfred Brunson, A.M., D.D., Embracing a Period of over Seventy Years* (New York: Carlton & Lanahan, 1872) 1:89. The full quotation is also in Wigger, *Taking Heaven by Storm*, 29.

exhorting and "stealing a text."[49] The first exhortation begins with a quotation from Isaiah 55:6a, namely, Seek the Lord while he may be found. This brief quotation is not fully explored, but serves to launch the exhorter's attempts to create greater interest in religious serious-ness. Perhaps the most interesting aspect of the exhortation is the manner in which it weaves together material from a variety of sources. This exhorter uses standard Methodist terminology (refer-ence to the "means of grace," albeit expanded to include camp meet-ings and prayer meetings), other biblical allusions (reference to the Israelite king, David, and Hebrews 12:14, a favorite Methodist proof-text), and popular religious expression (religious duty consists of tacit acknowledgment of the Scriptures and living a moral life) to move the listeners to action. The second exhortation is mostly a stringing together of randomly selected biblical texts. The first two-thirds of the exhortation is a fusion of at least twelve biblical texts, selected around themes of impending judgment and the necessity of salvation in Christ. The cumulative effect establishes that the exhorter's urgent warning is in actuality a warning from God.

Exhortations were most often delivered after the sermon, as the ser-mon's normal culmination. But in the flexible, fluid world of early Methodist worship even this simple relationship allowed for a wide variety in actual practice. It was not uncommon for a sermon to be followed by multiple exhortations, all delivered by different people. At a 1783 quarterly meeting, for example, Francis Asbury's sermon was followed by four exhortations, the latter two occurring after a brief intermission.[50] The exhortations themselves, particularly if there were several, could take longer than the sermon itself. A variation when multiple sermons were preached was the use of exhortations to provide transitions between the sermons.

After it became common to invite mourners to move forward in the worship space, exhorters often issued this invitation for a preaching service. An 1802 service, in which Bishops Francis Asbury and Thomas Whatcoat had both spoken, climaxed with another preacher inviting at the close of his exhortation "all who [were] in distress to come forward and join in prayer."[51] Such closing exhortations with

---

49. Untitled exhortations in George A. Reed papers. Authorship is unclear. George A. Reed (1793–1843) was originally from Winchester, Virginia.

50. Thomas Haskins, "The Journal of Thomas Haskins (1760-1816)." Ts. Transcribed by Louise Stahl, Indiana State University, 31.

51. William Colbert, "A Journal of the Travels of William Colbert Methodist Preacher thro' parts of Maryland, Pennsylvania, New York, Delaware, and Virginia in 1790 to 1838." Ts. United Methodist Church Archives-GCAH, Madison, NJ, 4:80.

invitations to mourners became the norm for Methodist preaching services.

But this norm was not rigidly observed. It was often spontaneously decided whether it was appropriate to exhort or not. Even where the preachers and exhorters consulted ahead of time on the number of sermons and exhortations in a service, a decision could be postponed to the moment itself. The speaker could respond to divine leading as he thought appropriate. If necessary, several exhortations could be given by preachers and exhorters in various parts of the meetinghouse. Or if a preacher or exhorter thought the presence of God was so imminent that the "work of God" was on the verge of erupting, the sermon could be interrupted so that an exhortation could be given. At one preaching service, for example, a preacher named John Adams pulled on the coat of the preacher currently speaking in the pulpit "that he might stop for me to exhort; for I felt the resurrection power of Christ in my soul, and as soon as I began to exhort, the power went through the assembly."[52]

A sudden eruption of exhortation was common in Methodist worship whenever the "work of God" broke out. At these times exhortation joined shouted praise and extemporaneous prayer as spontaneous responses of "professors" who felt the imminent presence of God. Such spontaneous exhorting was particularly linked closely with shouting. As one Methodist described such an occasion, "I went through the house shouting and exhorting with all possible ecstacy and energy."[53] The distinction between shouting and exhorting on such occasions was the audience: shouted praise was directed toward God and exhortation to sinners. Such speech underscored in an amazingly clear way the dual vocation of experiencing grace, as Methodists understood it. Experiencing grace should lead to the worship of God on the one hand and evangelistic mission on the other.

Both established believers and the newly converted participated in this sort of exhortation. Typically a new convert, fresh from the experience of pardon and peace found in justification, would rise from his or her kneeling position and immediately begin to shout and exhort. This was the case with one woman converted at an 1801 Kentucky quarterly meeting. Initially convicted at a preaching service earlier

52. [John Adams], *The Life of "Reformation" John Adams, an Elder of the Methodist Episcopal Church,* ed. Enoch George Adams (Boston: George C. Rand, 1853), 1:52.

53. [John M'Gee], "Commencement of the Great Revival of Religion in Kentucky and Tennessee, in 1799, In a Letter to the Rev. Thomas L. Douglass," *MQR* 4 (1821): 190.

that year, she reportedly had remained speechless for five weeks. Finally, at the quarterly meeting, she gathered with the mourners when a preacher prayed for them. As she began to pray aloud "her soul was set at liberty."[54] She arose, praising God and exhorting other people.

Like shouting and inspired praying, this sort of immediately inspired exhortation broke down barriers of gender, age, and race that might otherwise have kept some from active leadership in worship. While the classic form of exhortation (that normally appended to a sermon) was usually performed by a licensed preacher or exhorter, all sorts of people joined in the spontaneous version. Quite frequently, multiple exhortations—in the dozens or perhaps hundreds—would be given simultaneously as "professors" spoke to the sinners closest to them. In this case women, children, and Blacks participated as fully as the officially licensed preachers and exhorters.

Their ability to exhort effectively in this setting seems to have led some women to engage in the more classic form of exhorting. Apparently without license, individual women would at times deliver the exhortation after a sermon. At an 1804 quarterly meeting, for example, Sarah Edmondson "mounted a bench after the preachers were done speaking, and gave a powerful exhortation."[55]

The rhetorical power of exhortations to move listeners, whether delivered by women or men, was due to a variety of factors. One was the rapport an exhorter could build with a listener. On the one hand, exhorters were popular in the sense that they spoke in the common language and knew from their own experience the thoughts of their listeners' hearts. Conversely, listeners readily identified with the exhorters, taking seriously their admonitions and promises as concrete examples of effective grace. The conviction of Daniel De Vinné began precisely in this manner. Uneasy with his religious background, De Vinné one night heard an exhorter who "began to tell how some people felt in regard to religion. . . . The very thoughts and intents of my heart was laid open; and it really seemed as if everybody was looking at me."[56] Within a few months, De Vinné was a Methodist, and eventually a Methodist preacher.

---

54. Henry Smith, *Recollections and Reflections of an Old Itinerant* (New York: Lane & Tippett, 1848), 61. For a similar phenomenon in a class meeting see Finley, *Autobiography*, 181-82.

55. Colbert journal 5:27. See also Ebenezer Francis Newell, *Life and Observations of Rev. E. F. Newell, who has been more than Forty Years an Itinerant Minister in the Methodist Episcopal Church* (Worcester, MA: C. W. Ainsworth, 1847), 185.

56. De Vinné, *Recollections*, 9-11.

This example suggests that the easiest form of exhortation was to profess what God had done in one's own experience and then offer that as a promise to the listeners. Typical of their early ministry, one itinerant reports of how "hard-hearted sinners" wept while he testified, as he "told what great things the Lord had done for my soul, and what he was willing to do for each and every one of them."[57]

Sinners were not the only ones who wept during exhortations. Often exhorters, taking their dire theology seriously, would begin to cry as they exhorted. They were aware of the pathos this created in the congregation and would point it out if they felt it would move the listeners. As one exhorter called to a fellow preacher at the end of an exhortation, "O! Bro. Hibbard, weep with me, let us weep for poor sinners whom we cannot persuade."[58] Such emotion would have pleased John Wesley who rebuked preachers who became too comfortable in associating with unrepentant sinners and, instead, encouraged prophetic tears combined with "vehement and importunate exhortations."[59]

Many exhorters began by singing a hymn. This hymn might focus on offering the promise of saving grace or it might issue a stern warning to sinners who remain unmoved. An early hymn entitled "A Warning to Sinners" encouraged:

> Stop poor sinner stop and think
> Before you farther go
> Will you sport upon the brink
> Of everlasting woe
> Once again I charge you stop
> For unless you warning take
> E'er you are aware you'll drop
> Into the burning lake
>
> Say have you an arm like God
> That you his will oppose
> Fear you not his iron rod
> With which he'll break his foes
> Can you stand in that great day
> When his Judgment he'll proclaim

57. Finley, *Autobiography*, 186. See also William M. Wightman, *Life of William Capers, D.D., One of the Bishops of the Methodist Episcopal church, South; Including an Autobiography* (Nashville: Southern Methodist Publishing House, 1858), 80; and Carolyn De Swarte Gifford, ed., *The Nineteenth-Century American Methodist Itinerant Preacher's Wife* (New York: Garland Publishing, Inc., 1987), 48.

58. Billy Hibbard, *Memoirs of the Life and Travels of B. Hibbard, Minister of the Gospel, Containing an Account of his Experience of Religion; and of his Call to and Labours in the Ministry, for Nearly Thirty Years* (New York: Totten, 1825), 250-51.

59. See "Large Minutes," Q. 13, *Works* (Jackson) 8:304.

When the earth shall melt away
Like wax before the flame.

Though your hearts be made of steel
Your foreheads lined with brass
God at length will make you feel
He will not let you pass
Sinners then in vain will call
though they now despise his grace
Rocks and mountains on us fall
to hide us from his face

But as yet there is a hope
you may his mercy know
Though his arm be lifted up
He still forbears the blow
'Twas for sinners Jesus died
Sinners he invites to come
None that come shall be denied
He says there yet is room.[60]

However distasteful it might be to some modern observers, the creation of fear of God was obviously an important factor in motivating the multitudes to respond to the Methodist message. Belief—and fear—that there was truly "a wrath to come" for the unrepentant sinner amounted to an article of faith among Methodists. And large segments of the populace readily accepted such a portrayal of God's justice.

Methodist exhorters did not hesitate to use the popular acceptance of this portrayal of God to create vivid, specific fear in their listeners. One exhortation chastised the congregation for being fearful of a thunderstorm that passed during the service but remaining unconcerned about the storm that would come on the day of judgment.[61] On another occasion, the speaker related the story of a sick young woman who had resisted her parents' best efforts to get her to experience religion. The story climaxed with the woman's dying words, in which she regretted that her parents' last memory of her would be of her descent to hell. For Joshua Glenn, a young man in the congrega-

---

60. "A Warning to Sinners," undated, unsigned hymn in a ms. hymnal labeled "Spiritual Songs," Edward Dromgoole papers.

61. Cooper journal, 8 July 1798. Ezekiel Cooper, the speaker, was one of the most theologically sophisticated, articulate preachers of his day. This sort of theology was not on the margins of early Methodist thought.

tion who had been resisting his own parents' efforts, the fear of both hell and leaving his parents in such sorrow was too much. His period of intense mourning began at that moment.[62]

Hell, judgment, and punishment were important theological categories in early Methodism. Contemplation of these three generated both an honest fear and an ability to describe them in detail. The sense of potential disaster for the unrepentant was expressed in one hymn in late-eighteenth-century Methodist hymnals that compared their fate to those who enjoyed God's right hand:

> While they enjoy his heavenly love,
> Must I in torments dwell?
> And howl, (while they sing hymns above),
> And blow the flames of hell?[63]

An intellectual understanding of hell was supplemented for some by visions and dreams that made specific—and awful—the biblical references to hell. In one of these dreams a Methodist saw a vision of hell as a vast pit with a lake burning with fire. Vast multitudes of souls were dragged down, step-by-step, into this torment. Flames of fire emanated from the mouths and nostrils of the damned. As he awoke from the dream the visionary heard his instructions: "Go, and declare what you have seen."[64]

The Methodist understanding of hell was based on a broader theological basis than simply biblical literalism. Their understanding of judgment was a natural corollary to the Methodist doctrine of holiness as requisite for heaven. If holiness is the necessary condition and qualification for being able to enjoy heaven,[65] then conversely sinfulness renders someone fit only for hell. In both cases one's eternal destiny is portrayed as a continuation of the trajectory of one's earthly condition. With respect to hell, the uneasy dispositions caused by

---

62. Glenn journal, 10.

63. Stanza 4 of *Hymns* #78 ("Describing Hell"), Wesley, *Works* 7:177. The hymn also appeared in American edited collections. See, for example, hymn 16 in *A Pocket Hymn-book, designed as a Constant Companion for the Pious. Collected from Various Authors*, 5th ed. (New York: W. Ross, 1786), 18.

64. Graham Russell Hodges, ed., *Black Itinerants of the Gospel: The Narratives of John Jea and George White* (Madison, WI: Madison House Publishers, 1993), 54-56. Compare the dream in Ffirth, *Benjamin Abbott*, 7-9. For more on dreams and visions in early Methodism, see Wigger, *Taking Heaven by Storm*, 106-24.

65. See Richard Allen, *The Life Experience and Gospel Labors of the Rt. Rev. Richard Allen* (New York: Abingdon, 1960), 88-89. This notion could be found in Wesley's earlier sermons; see Sermon 45, "The New Birth," §3.2-3, *Works* 2:195-96. But see Wesley's later qualification in Sermon 89, "The More Excellent Way," §8, *Works* 3:226.

sinfulness in this world would only be accentuated in the next. A person's body would be tormented by fire while his or her soul was tormented by the wrath of God and the continuing unease of dealing with sins like "pride, malice, and envy . . . grief, desire, fear, rage, and despair."[66] On top of these torments the damned will mourn in response to the worst punishment of all: the loss of joyful communion with God, without which no one could be at rest.

For some, the agonizing scenes that occurred in Methodist preaching services were an explicit anticipation of hell. Preaching places became filled with mourners under deep conviction for their sin, agonizing for a sense of peace that came only with the experience of the forgiveness of justification. "Heartrending cries" and "throbbing lamentations" crescendoed. As one itinerant described it, their cries "strikingly put one in mind of the hopeless shrieks or screams of the damned beneath."[67]

The zealous Methodist exhorter often found it necessary to do no more than call unrepentant sinners' attention to the distress of the mourners around them. Against this background hearers were likely to welcome the offer of a gracious Savior:

> Sinner come and trust the Saviour
> He invites you to his arms
> He from Heven came to save you
> Come and vew his Hevenly charms
> He can save you he can save you
> Fly for Safety from all harms
>
> Tho your sins are red like Scarlett
> He can make them white as snow
> Come put on the shineing garment
> Which the Savour will bestow
> He can save you he can save you
> And will bless you here below
>
> If you feel you are unworthy
> He hath given you the space
> To behold your lost condition

---

66. Jonathan Crowther, *A True and Complete Portraiture of Methodism* (New York: J. C. Totten, 1813), 195. Compare John Wesley's similar understanding in Sermon 73, "Of Hell," §2.3, *Works* 3:37.

67. Ezekiel Cooper, "A brief account of the work of God in Baltimore: written by E. C. in an Epistle to Bishop Asbury" Ts. (also in George A. Phoebus, comp., *Beams of Light on Early Methodism in America* [New York: Phillips & Hunt; Cincinnati: Cranston & Stowe, 1887], 88).

Freely now be savd by grace
He can save you he can save you
Come behold his smileing face.[68]

The "Work of God" in Preaching Services

Early Methodists worshiped no distant Deity. God often answered their deepest, prayer-filled aspirations by sweeping into the midst of a worshiping congregation. So intense was the experience that normally congregants did not even attempt an explanation in theological prose but used a rich fusion of biblical allusions and poetic images to describe this transforming, powerful, acutely imminent presence of God. One itinerant described such an occasion as a time when "the Aweful presence of God was sweetly with us."[69] Another spoke of how "the Lord broake out wonderfully."[70] For lack of a better shorthand term, I will follow early Methodist precedent in designating this phenomenon the "work of God."

Methodist theology stressed subjective experiences of grace or "experimental religion." This stress made visitations of God at Methodist worship extremely desirable, even necessary. These visits were the times when people experienced salvation. God's presence was experienced as grace that saved by overwhelming worshipers with divine and personal love. Although this phenomenon was not restricted to preaching services (or, for that matter, preaching services at quarterly meetings), these services proved a reliable source for apprehending the dynamics of the "work of God."

The visitation of God's presence in preaching services was evidenced by various reactions by the worshipers, depending upon their state of faith. Bishop Coke succinctly described the varying responses when the "work of God" broke out at a preaching service held in conjunction with an Annual Conference in Baltimore around 1790:

> Out of a congregation of two thousand people, I suppose two or three hundred were engaged at the same time in praising God, praying for the conviction and conversion of sinners, or exhorting those around them with the utmost vehemence: And hundreds more were engaged

---

68. Hymn 24, "Invitation," in Ebenezer Hills, Hymnal. Ms. Ezekiel Cooper Papers. Garrett-Evangelical Theological Seminary Library, Evanston, IL.

69. William K. Boyd, ed., "A Journal and Travel of James Meacham," *Annual Publication of Historical Papers of the Historical Society of Trinity College* 9 (1912): 71.

70. [Richard Sneath], "Diary," in *The History of Bethel Methodist Episcopal Church Gloucester County New Jersey 1945*, comp. Mrs. Walter Aborn Simpson (n.p., 1945), 96.

in wrestling prayer either for their own conversion or sanctification. The great noise of the people soon brought a multitude to see what was going on.[71]

Several groups can be identified in Coke's description: mourners engaged in prayer for conversion (justification), some "professors" of religion engaged for sanctification, and other "professors" immersed in praise, prayer, or exhortation, or any number of these. I will consider the experience of each in developing a fuller understanding of what happened when the "work of God" erupted.

For the mourner, the "work of God" was a time of deep, agonizing distress. Having taken the Methodist message to heart, a mourner became aware of a hybrid of burdensome convictions: separation from God, personal helplessness before a God of justice, the guilt of sin, remorse over sinful acts, fear of eternal judgment and punishment, and sensitivity to life's transience, to name a few.

The intensity of this spiritual experience should not be underestimated. As portrayed by early Methodists (and every biography from the period has a similar conversion narrative), it was a time of stark personal despair. The agony was overwhelming:

> A Sinner rebel here I stand
> Exposd to Hell on every hand
> Under thy Scalding wrath to lye
> And wether threw Eternity
>
> Naught but the brittle thread of Life
> That saves my soul from endless Grief
> Over the awfull gulph I tread
> Soon shall be numberd with the dead
>
> A frowning God I now can see
> An awfull sentance waits for me
> Depart ye cursed how shall I
> Beneath his awfull vengance lye
>
> To God I dare not lift mine eyes
> That God whose Goodness I dispise
> That God that sent his son to die
> For Rebel Sinners such as I.[72]

---

71. Coke, *Extracts*, 109.
72. Hymn 12, "Awakning," in Ebenezer Hills ms. hymnal.

Because of the intensity of the mourning, the time was filled with a desperate search to find peace and rest. The preachers and exhorters declared that peace could be found in God's pardon and acceptance experienced in justifying grace, but the mourners who had not yet experienced pardon remained under the shadow of God's righteous conviction.

Even the possible source of relief, a view of Christ, could intensify the grief. The story of William Watters, who became a Methodist in the early 1770s and advanced to be an itinerant preacher, is typical in this regard. Under deep conviction from attending Methodist preaching services and prayer meetings, Watters reached a point where he was so overwhelmed by his mourning that he was "unfit for any worldly business." Like many others, he secluded himself for private prayer. While praying, the "eyes of his mind" saw "Christ on the cross bleeding, and bearing the sins of the whole world in his own body, and dying to make a full atonement." The vision only intensified his despair; he was convinced that he had trampled Christ's "most precious blood under my unhallowed feet" and had been despising the "spirit of grace." Watters, unable to bear this burden alone, began to meet again with the Methodists to secure their prayers.[73]

Watters's account is typical because of the emphasis it places on prayer. Since one aspect of typical mourning was a feeling of personal inability to find peace, the time of mourning was one of intense, repeated prayer, both privately and with others praying for the mourner. The peace they desired could come only from God; prayer was the appropriate posture of the soul while the mourner waited for God to answer.

The timing of God's answer seemed to vary as individual periods of mourning varied. One itinerant, reporting a 1789 revival in Baltimore, noted that while some were converted within a day or two after being convicted, or even on the same day, most had been awakened but not justified for some time.[74]

Mourners expressed their grief in a variety of ways. Typically they were so filled with honest despair that they could not contain the feelings. Tears and sighing were common. So were "heartrending cries" and "throbbing lamentations." During the 1789 Baltimore revival, for

73. William Watters, *A Short Account of the Christian Experience, and Ministereal Labours, of William Watters* (Alexandria: S. Snowden, 1806), 5-11.
74. Cooper, "A brief account" (Phoebus, *Beams of Light,* 89).

example, the Methodist services were full of mourners crying out "Save Lord! save or we perish!" with "gushing tears" and "writhing agitations." Hearing the shouts and praises of others only accentuated their mourning: "Has the Lord no mercy for me? What shall I do? Save! Save! Save! Lord save from the wrath to come! Save or I sink into hell!"[75]

At times the mourners' demonstrations were more directly attributed to the power of God. As God had convicted these people of their sins, God also physically brought them to the ground. One preacher, speaking in Petersburg, Virginia, in 1788, noted that even before he had completed his sermon "the power of God" was manifested in dropping a woman from her seat where she appeared as if dead for a time.[76] This falling, sometimes accompanied by stupors of various lengths, was a common phenomenon at early quarterly meetings. Most experienced Methodists took it as a sign that God was present. As Richard Whatcoat, one of the first two elders ordained by John Wesley, marveled at a 1796 meeting: "How awful yet How pleasing to See one fall as Dead under the Power of God."[77]

The deep convictions experienced during the "work of God" were sometimes connected with visions. In a typical example, one mourner attempted to flee from the "work of God" by going home. Struck down by the power of God when arriving home, he entered a "convulsed and speechless state." After a time he awoke to some degree of consciousness and exclaimed, "O, hell! hell! hell!" The Methodists gathered around and prayed. After another period of stillness, he awoke and exclaimed first, "O, heaven! heaven! heaven!" and then, springing to his feet, "Glory! Glory! Glory!" To the Methodists eagerly gathered around he related a vision of hell and then of Christ's personal intercession in heaven for him.[78]

As this account shows, the intensity of despair that characterized the period of mourning was matched, and even exceeded, by the ecstasy of joy that accompanied justification. After spending several days in prayer with the Methodists, William Watters experienced an exuberant sense of liberation:

---

75. Ibid., 88.

76. Thrift, *Memoir of Jesse Lee*, 94-95.

77. Richard Whatcoat, Journal. Ts. Garrett-Evangelical Theological Seminary Library, Evanston, IL, 31 January 1796.

78. Finley, *Autobiography*, 306-7.

My burden was gone—my sorrow fled—my soul and all that was within me rejoiced in hopes of the glory of God: while I beheld such fulness
and willingness in the Lord Jesus to save lost sinners, and my soul so
rested on him, that I could now for the first time call Jesus Christ,
"Lord," by the Holy Ghost given unto me.[79]

The joy was intensely personal because the experience of grace was
so personal. In characteristically Wesleyan fashion, the accounts of
the newly justified reveal a deep feeling of personal recognition of
God's grace. God's grace is *for me*, she or he could now say, or to put
it in the idiom of Christ's passion, "now I know Christ died for me."[80]

The intensity of both the mourning and justification's ecstasy was
due in large part to the Methodist emphasis on "experimental" religion. In the popular Methodist understanding, "if a man's sins were
forgiven, he would know it."[81] This emphasis on affective knowledge
of a state of grace gave an easily discernible demarcation between
mourner and professor. If one did not know his or her sins were forgiven, then they were not forgiven. Mourners knew what they were
seeking: a knowledge of forgiveness. They knew when they were justified: they would feel God's pardon in their hearts. Those who had
this feeling could profess the experience to others and they did so
with great joy:

> O! how I have longed for the coming of God
> I sought him by praying and searching his word
> In watching and fasting my soul was oppress'd
> Nor would I give over till Jesus had blessed.
>
> The tokens of mercy at length did appear
> According to promise he answered my prayer
> And glory is opening in floods on my soul
> Salvation from Zion is beginning to role
>
> I'll sing and I'll shout and shout and I'll sing
> O! God make the nations with praises to ring
> With loud acclamations of Jesuses love
> And carry us all to the City above.[82]

---

79. Watters, *Short Account*, 15.

80. Strickland, *Life of Jacob Gruber*, 63. The Methodist expressing this sentiment had come from
a background of popular Calvinistic theology and had been convinced that only the elect were
eligible for grace.

81. Thrift, *Memoir of Jesse Lee*, 7.

82. Untitled hymn dated 21 August 1803 in Henry Bradford ms. hymnbook. Compare Richard
Allen, *A Collection of Hymns and Spiritual Songs* (Philadelphia: T. L. Plowman, 1801; reprint,
Nashville: A.M.E.C. Sunday School Union, 1987), 58.

The experience of justification was marked by visible demonstrations, just as the mourning had been. As the spiritual distress had overflowed to the point of expression, so now did the joy of pardon's peace. Indeed, the distinct demonstrations of the two states vividly marked the spiritual transition that Methodists saw occurring. Whereas mourning was commonly marked by crouched or prostrate bodily postures, tears, and crying, justification was marked by a contrasting set of behaviors. The newly justified would typically rise from the ground where they had been lying or kneeling in prayer and begin to shout. In Methodist terminology, the newly justified "got happy." These demonstrations marked the conversion of John Adam Granade during the "work of God" in a 1799 Tennessee meeting. As the "power of God as a rushing mighty wind" came across the congregation Granade began to whisper "Adoration to God and the Lamb!" The more he repeated this phrase the stronger his voice became until he began to shout "Glory to God! Glory and adoration to God and the Lamb forever!" Granade spent the remainder of the day praising God. After communing the next day he began again, spending the day in exhortation to other mourners and shouting praise to God.[83] Clapping, jumping, testifying to one's experience, and participation in praying for other mourners were other common activities after justification.

In addition to mourners in search of justification, times when the "work of God" erupted frequently included "professors" seeking sanctification. Expectation of this more elevated state of grace was a fundamental part of early Methodist soteriology. In their understanding, as "professors" grew in spiritual maturity they would eventually reach a point where they would "feel the remains of sin and the roots of bitterness springing up in them" and seek the activity of God within themselves, which would bring them "into the liberty of loving the Lord our God with all the heart, soul, mind, and strength and our neighbor as our self."[84] This awareness triggered an experience not unlike conversion: a period of searching prayer climaxed by a recognizable experience of the blessing sought. The demands of experimental religion remained constant; early Methodists presumed that if someone had been cleansed from sinfulness, then she or he would affectively know

---

83. R. N. Price, *Holston Methodism: From its Origin to the Present Time* (Nashville: Publishing House of the Methodist Episcopal Church, South, 1904): 2:7-8.

84. David L. Steele, ed., "The Autobiography of the Reverend John Young, 1747–1837," *Methodist History* 13.1 (October 1974): 37-38.

it and could testify to it. This belief tended to emphasize sanctification as a discernibly clear event at an identifiable point in time.

While accounts of people experiencing sanctification during the "work of God" are not nearly as numerous as accounts of justification, they reveal a common rhythm. Just as mourners could cry for justification, "professors" wept "in distress for sanctification."[85] Terms used for mourning were often applied to the desire for sanctification: "professors" were "much exercised for holiness of heart" at one quarterly meeting.[86] The experience of delivery was also similar: one woman's prayer for sanctification reached a high pitch at which point she began to cry, "O! thou dost hear! thou art nigh! O thy glory! O!!" After a period when she knelt silently, slumped over a chair, she arose, speaking praise and testifying of the "blessing."[87] Given the similarity to the experience of justification, early accounts often speak of the "work of God" as one work of grace, experienced in various dimensions. These reports often noted figures for how many were convicted, how many justified, and how many sanctified at a meeting.[88]

Quarterly meetings and other extended settings for worship provided a useful time for Methodists to recommit themselves to this distinctive doctrinal system and urge members to experience sanctification. This occurred in several ways. First, a quarterly meeting brought the average Methodist in contact with a wider range of Methodists than she or he normally saw in the local class and society. The frequent eruptions of the "work of God" in this setting produced testimonies—sometimes many of them—that brought others under conviction for this "second blessing." Second, a typical quarterly meeting brought together larger numbers of Methodists than the preachers normally addressed. A conscientious presiding elder would see this occurrence as an opportune time to encourage Methodist distinctives like sanctification. As the presiding elder of the Baltimore District informed his bishop in 1802, he made it a point to preach "perfect love and holiness" every Saturday at his quarterly meetings.[89]

The reference to Saturday suggests a phenomenon hinted at in other accounts: there were greater concentrations of Methodists in the con-

---

85. William Jessop journal, 4 January 1788.

86. Seth Crowell, *The Journal of Seth Crowell; containing an Account of His Travels as a Methodist Preacher for Twelve Years* (New York: J. C. Totten, 1813), 24.

87. Hibbard, *Memoirs*, 237.

88. See, for example, the accounts of quarterly meetings in Colbert journal 4:93-94; and Jessop journal, 14 February 1790.

89. *Extracts of Letters, Containing some Account of the Work of God since the Year 1800* (New York: J. C. Totten, 1805), 47.

gregations earlier in extended meetings, before the larger crowds of Sunday. This helps explain the greater concentrations of sanctification experiences early in extended meetings. Accounts that speak of striking experiences of sanctification sometimes note that they occurred on Saturday, while not mentioning concomitant justifications. Other such accounts specify a worship setting other than a preaching service, like an evening prayer meeting or watch night service, where presumably the concentration of Methodists to non-Methodists would be higher.[90]

By no means were other "professors" silent or still when the "work of God" broke out. While mourners were under deep conviction and some "professors" wrestled in prayer for sanctification, other Methodists were busily engaged in very exuberant worship. Their exuberance took several forms, expressed both bodily and vocally. As one early hymn said approvingly, "They'd stamp and clap & tumble, & roar & cry & scream."[91] Methodists were so demonstrative that they were often mimicked. One young Ohio Lutheran, for example, jumped and shouted in a mocking manner to aggravate his acquaintance, John Campbell Deem, then under the first sense of awakening. Deem retaliated by hitting him.[92]

As noted above, Methodists' vocal participation in the "work of God" tended to take one of three forms: shouted praise, exhortation, or prayer for those under conviction, or any combination of these. Relying on inspired extemporaneity in all three forms, Methodist participation was truly a communal work of the whole church. Racial, gender, and age barriers broke down in ways—exuberant ways—that would have appeared unseemly in more established churches. Any who were so inspired, regardless of their social status, were welcome to speak up, to get up, to get happy. For women to pray zealously for their neighbors during a "work of God," for example, was in Methodist sensibility a natural demonstration of the gracious power of God in their midst. But others held different opinions. To some, Methodists were "short lived blazes of Enthusiasm and intemperate zeal," whose influence was "principally felt among the Negroes & poorer & lower classes of the People" and whose worship was filled "with all that confusion, violence, and distortion of the body, voice &

---

90. N. Bangs journal, 27 Wednesday (perhaps October 1805; Bangs's dating seems confused); Colbert journal 4:134. Compare the number of sanctifications to conversions for several 1806 camp meetings in Boehm journal, 13-17 June 1806 and 8-12 August 1806.

91. Hymn entitled "Come All my Tender Brethren, &c" in Bradford ms. hymnbook.

92. Deem autobiography, 29.

gestures that characterizes such a boiling hot religion"; indeed, the Methodists were "not far behind the Shakers."[93]

The exuberant manner of early Methodist worship, which some have labeled the "shout tradition," was not without internal controversy. Although the dominant tradition within the first several decades of American Methodism, it was never without its critics, some of whom were other Methodists.[94]

The emergence of the shout tradition has both regional and racial markers. In the first two decades of Methodism in America, southern Methodists (Maryland and Delaware southward) were generally more exuberant than northern, and Black Methodists more exuberant than White. However, it would be inaccurate to say that White Methodists merely adapted the more vibrant African spirituality of their Black counterparts: certain strains of European Methodism had their own distinctive exuberance and White Methodists—southern and northern—appear to have quite willingly and freely engaged in the exuberance on their own.[95] Nonetheless, the American shouting tradition appears to have had some distinctive element in the level of its exuberance. Whatever its regional and racial origins, before long it achieved dominance in early Methodism.[96]

The distinctiveness of this tradition is shown by the reaction whenever British preachers first contacted it in America. Joseph Pilmore, one of the first two itinerants sent by Wesley, was flabbergasted when he first traveled to Maryland.[97] Thomas Rankin, Wesley's general assistant

93. Thomas Wallcut, Letter to James Freeman, Thomas Wallcut papers. American Antiquarian Society, Worcester, MA, 31 October 1789.

94. For an analysis of the development of this tradition see the two works by Ann Taves: *Fits, Trances, and Visions,* 76-117; and "Knowing Through the Body: Dissociative Religious Experience in the African- and British-American Methodist Traditions," *The Journal of Religion* 73 (1993): 200-222. I am indebted to these works in my discussion. The latter article provides a short summary of the extent of dissociative religious phenomena among British Methodists under the ministry of John Wesley.

95. Winthrop S. Hudson, "Shouting Methodists," *Encounter* 29 (1968): 82-83. For an interpretation of the influence of African spirituality on eighteenth-century American religious exuberance, see Mechal Sobel, *The World They Made Together: Black and White Values in Eighteenth-Century Virginia* (Princeton, NJ: Princeton University Press, 1987), 180-203. Sobel argues that demonstrations of ecstatic exuberance were part of the Black contribution to the interracial religious synthesis in eighteenth-century Virginia. More recent works have issued cautionary notes about overemphasizing a direct causal relationship between race and ecstatic expressions; e.g., Christine Leigh Heyrman, *Southern Cross: The Beginnings of the Bible Belt* (New York: Knopf, 1997), 49, 277 n. 26.

96. For an assessment of the cultural context for Methodist exuberance see Wigger, *Taking Heaven by Storm,* 110-24. See also Nathan O. Hatch, *The Democratization of American Christianity* (New Haven: Yale University Press, 1989), for a description of Methodism's place within American society.

97. Joseph Pilmore, *The Journal of Joseph Pilmore.* ed. Frederick E. Maser and Howard T. Maag

here, never appeared to be fully comfortable with it. Thomas Coke, one of the first bishops, took some time to acquire a taste for it. The decisive factor he saw in its favor was that the shouting came with numerous convictions and conversions. Eventually he saw it as being like the noise that the visionary in the book of Revelation had heard.[98] When George Coles first heard a Methodist shout in 1819 after a recent immigration from England, he thought it was very "indecorus & unnatural." Within a short time, however, he had changed his mind. Returning to his journal, he inserted "So it seemed then."[99]

Some never changed their minds about the exuberance. Within American Methodism a certain minority remained uncomfortable with what they saw as unscriptural disorder in worship. In 1809, for example, the minority was distinct enough in the Annapolis, Maryland, society that the itinerant there could speak of two parties: the shouters and the "anti-shouters."[100] By the second decade of the nineteenth century, the minority elsewhere had grown enough to begin public argument, as in the small book *Methodist Error*, probably written by a Methodist in Philadelphia.[101] Despite some strongly worded attacks, the shout tradition remained prominent through the first part of the nineteenth century, especially in those locales where American Methodism retained its original soteriological emphases, strong African influence, devaluation of formal education, and initial social position.

Early Methodism had several commonly accepted images to explain the nature of the "work of God" and to note that it had occurred. The most prominent was to say that there had been a "shout of a king in the camp." The phrase was a universal colloquialism among early Methodists. Joseph Pilmore used a version of the phrase already in 1769.[102] It was taken up in the 1770s by Thomas

(Philadelphia: Message Publishing Co. for the Historical Society of the Philadelphia Annual Conference of the United Methodist Church, 1969), 138.

98. Thomas Coke letter to Ezekiel Cooper, 7 July 1789 (in Ezekiel Cooper papers).

99. Coles journal, 22 January 1819. Compare the assessment of Henry Bradshaw Fearon, a visiting English businessman, concerning his observation of a service at Philadelphia's Ebenezer Church in 1817. According to Fearon in *Sketches of America; A Narrative of a Journey of Five Thousand Miles through the Eastern and Western States of America* (London, 1818; reprint, New York: August M. Kelley, 1970), 166, American Methodists generally had more "fanatical violence" in their services than their British counterparts.

100. H. Smith, *Recollections*, 257.

101. *Methodist Error* (1814; reprint, Trenton: D. & E. Fenton, 1819). Ann Taves has identified the author as John Fanning Watson, a member of the St. George's Society in Philadelphia (*Fits, Trances and Visions*, 76).

102. Pilmore, *Journal*, 91 and 111: "shout of a King in Zion."

Rankin, the first general assistant.[103] It remained in constant use through the entire period under consideration in this study. Joshua Glenn, who began to preach around 1820, used the phrase in the same way as the first American Methodists.[104] Indeed, the phrase was perhaps *the* way in early Methodism to say that God had attended a worship service with divine power and that the people had responded favorably. Its status as a standard shorthand way of saying exactly that is reflected in this 1805 letter: "we had some glorious display of the power of God the last Sabbath at Quarterly meeting I have reason to believe some were sanctified we had a glorious shout of a King in the Camp."[105]

While descriptive of literal shouted praise in Methodist worship, this phrase has clear biblical rootage in 1 Samuel 4:5-7. That passage is part of the narrative of Israelite war with the Philistines. When the ark of the covenant entered the camp of the Israelites, they raised such a great shout that the story says the ground shook. The Philistine response, upon learning that the ark had arrived, was to acknowledge that "a god has come into the camp."[106]

Several points of association drew Methodists to this story in validating their practice of shouting. The story overflows with images of God's imminent presence, the people of God responding vocally to God's presence, the assurance that comes from that presence, and the contrasting fear from the opposition, all with a strong background of active warfare. With their tendency to see themselves as a new Israel, their spiritual condition as a sojourn to the promised land, and their ministry as spiritual warfare, the Methodists viewed this story as a version of their situation. The "shout of a King in the camp" was a concise way of explaining their sense of God's presence and validating their practice of shouting by aligning them with a precedent in salvation history. Since shouting was a crucial but controverted part of early Methodism's self-identity, the importance of its sanction through the identification of biblical rooting for the practice cannot be underestimated.[107]

While not nearly as pervasive as the "shout of a king in the camp," a second biblical image commonly used to explain the work of God

---

103. Rankin diary, 119.
104. Glenn journal, 85.
105. Samuel Coate letter to Ezekiel Cooper, 5 March 1805 (in Ezekiel Cooper papers).
106. Note this description of a time of shouting in New York City in the Cooper journal, 23 May 1795: "We had a small shout of joy & gladness at the entrance of the Ark into the Camp."
107. For a collection of hymns that demonstrate shouting's importance, see appendix C.

was to say that another Pentecost had occurred in a worship service. Methodists liked this image for several reasons. Not only did it come from the Christian Scriptures and thus emphasize distinctly Christian themes like the coming of the Holy Spirit, it contained several elements that reminded Methodists of the way they perceived God to be in their midst. The story of the first Pentecost (Acts 2) emphasized God's presence in saving power with a strong sense—literally—of movement. A mighty wind blows through God's people; flames of fire appear and spread.

These elements were attractive to early Methodist spirituality because Methodists liked to emphasize *feeling* God's presence, and not simply emotively but as a physical sensation. As one described his experience of God at a quarterly meeting, "it apeart to me as if the powr could sensible be feld as far as the sound [of shouted praise] reacht." This same itinerant once noted that the work of God was "better felt than explained."[108] This sort of piety was naturally attracted to a biblical story like the Pentecost narrative, which contained vivid images to express the power of God's presence in sensible ways. To early Methodists, the coming of God in power in the midst of their gatherings involved a corporate experience of movement. What they felt when the "work of God" erupted seemed like a Pentecost. Thus on one occasion, during a 1787 revival in Virginia when the "work of God" erupted even before preaching began, the itinerant used a Pentecost analogy as he struggled to describe the intensity of God's presence:

> Saturday the quarter-meeting for Sussex-circuit began at Brother Jones's chapel; but before the preachers got there, the work broke out; so that when we came to the chapel, above sixty were down on the floor, groaning in loud cries to God for mercy.... [On Sunday] We preached to them in the open air, and in the chapel, and in the barn by Brother Jones's house, at the same time. Such a sight my eyes never saw before, and never read of, either in Mr. Wesley's journals, or any other writings concerning the Lord's pouring out the Spirit, except the account in scripture of the day of Pentecost. Never, I believe, was the like seen since the apostolic age: hundreds were at once down on the ground in bitter cries to GOD for mercy. Here were many of the first quality in the country, wallowing in the dust with their silks and broad-cloths, powdered heads, rings, and ruffles, and some of them so convulsed that they could neither speak nor stir: many stood by, per-

---

108. Boehm journal, 20 July 1800 and 9 June 1800.

secuting, till the power of the Lord laid hold of them, and then they fell themselves, and cried as loud as those they just before persecuted.[109]

These biblical images were part of a larger vocabulary used to assess worship services. The vocabulary, consisting of words and phrases universally understood and used across the scope of early Methodism, constituted a repertoire of semitechnical phrases. The general thrust of the whole repertoire was to emphasize an affective assessment of God's presence and of the ways in which humans experience grace.

The most standard term in this vocabulary was "melting." Like many words that Christians have appropriated throughout history, the term "melt" appears to have originated in the general culture but was transformed and expanded by distinctive religious usage. In its original setting the term roughly meant the same as the modern "move," as in "that moved me to tears." In the mouths of Methodists the term became a catchword to describe people deeply affected by the presence of God. Where the "operations of the Holy Spirit were very powerful," Asbury said, "there was a general melting."[110] When the "great power of the Lord was with us," another noted, it was "a time of melting."[111] In emphasizing the affective sensing of God's power, another gloried after a 1795 quarterly meeting that "the melting Power of God was felt."[112] In fixing the object of the melting, Methodists spoke with a united voice: God's loving power melts the heart.

The universal use of the melting terminology was only the beginning of a wonderfully rich range of related terms and biblical allusions. From speaking of melting it was only a short step to speak of God's presence as a fire spreading from heart to heart (with an obvious Pentecost connection) or even exploding within a congregation. At one quarterly meeting's preaching service the preacher noted that

---

109. [Philip Cox], "Extract of a Letter from Mr. Phillip Cox, dated Brunswick-County, Virginia." *AM* 11 (1788), 92-93. Note the participation of Virginia gentry, identified by their clothing. For early Methodists, such nonsimplicity in clothing was worldly and sinful. For an assessment of early Methodists' socioeconomic placement see Wigger, *Taking Heaven by Storm.*

110. *JLFA* 1:295. Use of the term is so widespread that it would be fair to say that every primary source from this period uses the term somewhere in a similar fashion. Compare Richey, *Early American Methodism,* 3, who equates the term with Methodist experience of intense community. I am not at odds with this different emphasis as I will show in chapter 5 where intense fellowship will be connected with God's saving activity. Note also that a "melting" heart could be considered a characteristic of Jesus. See hymn 70 in *Pocket Hymn-book* (1786), 71: "Thy tender heart is still the same / And melts at human woe."

111. Boyd, "Journal and Travel of James Meacham," 70.

112. Whatcoat journal, 22 March 1795.

God's presence was so dramatic that it was like fire applied to gunpowder, which created a tremendous explosion.[113] The breaking out of the "work of God" could be called "wildfire" too.[114] Early descriptions of God's presence during the "work of God" also speak of it being like electricity running from person to person, energizing the whole.[115] Water images for God's loving presence were equally frequent, particularly to emphasize spiritual refreshment. At one quarterly meeting a Methodist noted, "we had a very gracious shower to fertilize our souls."[116] At another service God showered down "a sweet flow of Divine Love" upon some while "pointed arrows shot some souls" under conviction.[117] Worshipers could be "tender" or "hard." A service could be a "cold dead time" or full of "life & love."[118] Early Methodists mixed and matched these images as they struggled to find language adequate to express their experience and their affections. When all else failed, it was enough to describe a service full of God's presence as a "feeling time."[119]

The extent of this vocabulary clearly shows how important worship's affective aspects were to early Methodists. The breadth of terms is a sign of how much they dwelt on these aspects. Unfortunately, this affective vocabulary was not balanced by objective sensibility to God's presence in worship and sacraments. Liturgical categories using feeling and experience reigned supreme. When no warmth of heart or refreshment of spirit was experienced in more formal worship, Methodists tended to critique it harshly, without appreciating liturgy's more subtle formative aspects or any general sense of God's omnipresence. With specific reference to sacraments, the lack of objective theological categories could lead to a functional understanding of worship. Sacraments were often mistakenly seen as merely human activities achieving some one-dimensional function. It appears, for instance, that infant baptism was broadly seen as merely a rite to name a child.[120]

---

113. Cooper journal, 12 June 1796.

114. Strickland, *Life of Jacob Gruber*, 40.

115. Ibid., and [Sampson Maynard], *The Experience of Sampson Maynard, Local Preacher of the Methodist Episcopal Church* (New York: Printed for the author, by Wm. C. Taylor, 1828), 236. For an extended use of the electricity image to describe the phenomenon of bodily stupor under God's power see Giles, *Pioneer*, 74-75.

116. John Early, "Journal of Bishop John Early who lived Jan. 1, 1786–Nov. 5, 1873" (Ts. Southern Historical Collection, University of North Carolina, Chapel Hill, NC), 22 May 1813.

117. Sneath, "Diary," 66.

118. Colbert journal 2:93; Cooper journal, 21 February 1789.

119. Glenn journal, 79.

120. See, for example, the dispute over the proper name for a child presented by two different women in William Ormond journal, 3 July 1797.

All of this allowed, the typical Methodist terminology for assessing worship implied a wonderfully optimistic appraisal of God's presence. Truly they saw grace—understood as God's imminent presence to save in overwhelming personal love—as the essence of their worship. But their language also reveals that their understanding of worship's efficacy rested primarily on human response, whether worshipers felt something in their hearts. It would seem only a short step from such criteria for judging worship to a manipulative pragmatism, which sought to manufacture the desired human feelings. But this pragmatism was tempered—albeit not eliminated—in the early period by a constant refrain that redirected the theological focus back to God: the "work of God" was ultimately God's work. In the earliest Methodist understanding, the "work of God" was a work of grace.

Conclusion

Early Methodists had a clear goal for their quarterly meetings' preaching services. They prayed for God to be present; they longed for God to be present; they hungered and thirsted for God to be present. In their estimation God often was present, since they could feel the gracious presence in their hearts. They could see the effects of that presence in the variety of reactions in the worshipers: from the first awakenings to God to the joyful, clapping testimonies of those entirely sanctified. Although they honed their skills in preaching and exhorting in fervent hope that God would use their efforts, the "work of God" often erupted independent of any human effort. Often the moment when worshipers experienced God's saving power occurred when the liturgical speech addressed God rather than exhorted sinners. Methodists were willing to live with the unpredictability of grace. Because of a pervasive evangelical ethos, they were willing to see God pour out grace in whatever manner God might choose.

Early Methodist preaching was intended to encourage worshipers to make strides in the journey toward sanctification, and as we have seen God used this preaching to great effect. There were other elements of public worship that were equally important within the quarterly meetings, however, and it is to these that we turn our attention in chapter 3.

Public Worship at Quarterly Meetings: Prayer Services, Watch Nights, and Pastoral Rites

"We fell on our knees. I instantly felt the power of God, the people began to pray, and we soon had a time of power."
—scene at a Kentucky quarterly meeting watchnight, 1803[1]

Monday, 12 February 1787, was the second day of a New Jersey quarterly meeting. As itinerant Ezekiel Cooper described it, the day started in a fashion typical for a meeting's second day: with a 9 A.M. love feast at which "the Lord was with us indeed in a very powerful manner." At 11 "publick" worship began. The first service to be conducted was a funeral: "a corps was brought into the Preaching House the sight of which called aloud be ye also ready after Mr Sparks & Mr Whatcoat were done speaking the corps was intered." But that was not the culmination for that morning's worship. After the funeral—seemingly immediately afterward—a young bride and groom were married. Cooper was pleased. The proximity of the funeral to the wedding colored the latter, making it in Cooper's opinion "the most solemn weding I ever saw." One can imagine the look on the young couple's faces as they marched to the front of the meetinghouse as the casket was being carried away.

And yet that was still not the end for that day's public worship. After a short intermission a preaching service was held in which Cooper and one other man preached. The juxtaposition of services that day perhaps inspired the content of Cooper's sermon; in his

---

1. Benjamin Lakin, Journal. Ms. on microfilm. Washington University Library, St. Louis, MO. Some of Lakin's journal can be found in William Warren Sweet, *The Methodists* (Chicago: University of Chicago Press, 1946), 16 September 1803.

journal he makes a parenthetical remark that "some are dying others are marrying but soon we all shall be laid in the grave."[2]

To meld the themes in this manner, emphasizing life's transience even in the midst of great joy as a backdrop to an evangelistic appeal, would not have been out of character in an early quarterly meeting's public worship. As with preaching services, early Methodism's evangelical ethos saturated all its public services, influencing the way in which they were conducted.

Although not as prevalent as the more prominent preaching services, other early Methodist forms of worship open to the public were often part of the liturgical scheme at early quarterly meetings. These other public services included prayer services, watch night services, and administration of pastoral rites (baptisms, weddings, and funerals). All were considered opportunities to hear the word of God's grace and, one hoped, to experience the outpouring of God's power.

Prayer Meetings and Family Prayer

Services for prayer became regular features of many quarterly meetings as American Methodism entered the nineteenth century. Two forms of this service, "prayer meetings" and "family prayer," were included in quarterly meetings. The two forms were similar in that their goal was to provide extended time for repeated extemporaneous prayer. Preaching or exhortation in these services was spotty and not the central feature. The two forms differ with respect to their usual settings: family prayer was conducted in a domestic setting with a small circle of kin and associates, while prayer services were often held with larger numbers and in a more public venue. However, as with so many other aspects of early Methodist worship, sharp distinctions should be avoided. Fluidity existed between these two types of prayer services. This continuum was especially evident at quarterly meetings, where on many occasions the prayer meetings were appointed to take place in homes, and due to the numerous visitors in a home, attendance at a family prayer service might swell to several dozen.

With respect to formal prayer meetings, the most common time for

---

2. Ezekiel Cooper journal in Papers. Garrett-Evangelical Theological Seminary Library, Evanston, IL, 12 February 1787. See also George A. Phoebus, comp., *Beams of Light on Early Methodism in America* (New York: Phillips & Hunt; Cincinnati: Cranston & Stowe, 1887), 65.

scheduling these in northern states (especially New England and New York) was the Saturday on which quarterly meetings opened. Accounts of nineteenth-century meetings in this region usually include reference to a prayer meeting on Saturday night or, less frequently, Saturday afternoon.[3] The prayer meetings were held either in a central location or dispersed throughout the community, with several being held simultaneously in different homes.

When the latter occurred, a prayer meeting was hardly distinguishable from a family prayer service, given the number of visitors usually accommodated in a single house for quarterly meetings. Daily family prayer was a long-standing Methodist tradition, enjoined by the *Discipline,* although actual levels of obedience are hard to ascertain. Whatever its frequency at other times, the close proximity of Methodists to their preachers during quarterly meetings probably ensured that family prayer was held regularly. This became a period of endearing fellowship as it became the time of prayer for the Methodist "family." Thus Catherine Livingston Garrettson, one of twenty staying at a home during a quarterly meeting, once noted that "my dear Lord was of a truth among us while waiting before Him in family prayer."[4]

Prayer services followed a simple order: a sequence of several extemporaneous prayers by different people. The prayers were separated by hymns. Exhortations appear to have been a frequent addition and even a sermon followed on occasion, although the precise order is impossible to tell. The service leader would typically call on individuals to pray, though some regions entertained a manner of selection relying upon greater direct inspiration. This explains the

---

3. For Saturday night examples see James P. Horton, *A Narrative of the Early Life, Remarkable Conversion, and Spiritual Labours of James P. Horton, Who has been a Member of the Methodist Episcopal Church Upward of Forty Years* (n.p.: Printed for the author, 1839), 32; Elbert Osborn, *Passages in the Life and Ministry of Elbert Osborn, an Itinerant Minister of the Methodist Episcopal Church, illustrating the Providence and Grace of God* (New York: Published for the author, 1847–1850), 32; Billy Hibbard, *Memoirs of the Life and Travels of B. Hibbard, Minister of the Gospel, Containing an Account of his Experience of Religion; and of his Call to and Labours in the Ministry, for Nearly Thirty Years* (New York: Totten, 1825), 127-28; and William Colbert, "A Journal of the Travels of William Colbert Methodist Preacher thro' parts of Maryland, Pennsylvania, New York, Delaware, and Virginia in 1790 to 1838." Ts. United Methodist Church Archives-GCAH, Madison, NJ, 4:91. For Saturday afternoon see Abner Chase, *Recollections of the Past* (New York: Joseph Longkin, 1848), 29-31. By the 1810s, preachers in this region called Saturday night prayer meetings "customary." See James B. Finley, *Autobiography of Rev. James B. Finley; or, Pioneer Life in the West,* ed. W. P. Strickland (Cincinnati: Methodist Book Concern, 1853), 286-87; and David Lewis, *Recollections of a Superannuate: or, Sketches of Life, Labor, and Experience in the Methodist Itinerancy,* ed. S. M. Merrill (Cincinnati: Methodist Book Concern, 1857), 114.

4. Catherine Livingston Garrettson diary, 71-72. Compare the account of men in family prayer in Abner Chase, *Recollections of the Past* (New York: Joseph Longkin, 1848), 27.

shock of one presiding elder at the practice of his new district: instead of the leader calling upon specific individuals, any who felt inspired to do so would pray.[5]

Men were not the only ones called upon to pray, both women and children also were selected and some were recognized as being especially "gifted" in public praying. Some prayer meetings in mixed-gender congregations even centered on women's praying. At one memorable quarterly meeting several women had prayed in succession when a young woman, a non-Methodist "in high glee," walked to the center of the barn and said she would stop any woman who tried to pray. As one Methodist woman after another tried to pray, this intruder grabbed each pray-er by the hair and pulled her to the floor. Eventually several of the Methodist women began to pray simultaneously that God "would lay his hand upon her." The intruder became paralyzed and fell to the floor. Two of her companions, braving the praying Methodist women, pressed through the crowd and dragged their friend from the barn by her clothing.[6]

The praying of children could also be respected. In fact, children were sometimes called upon to pray publicly. William Keith, a New England Methodist, saw children's giftedness in praying as a sign of the "work of God" among them. He found the prayers of children in his neighborhood, some of them not older than ten, nothing less than astonishing. He heard one eight-year-old girl praying in a manner "beyond my abilities to express." Another thirteen-year-old girl prayed so movingly at a prayer meeting that Keith decided her "language seemed more like that of some celestial being than any human creature."[7]

Whoever was praying, Methodist public prayer was accompanied by several distinctive actions. The most prominent was kneeling. During this period, kneeling was *the* Methodist posture for prayer, without exception. Both the one praying and all those who acquiesced in the prayer knelt. The act and the posture were synonymous: Methodists praying meant Methodists kneeling. In fact, willingness to kneel functioned as a kind of bodily "Amen" to a prayer. Unwilling-

---

5. Finley, *Autobiography*, 286-87. Finley notes that the same principle applied in the preaching service as these "prophets"—both men and women—would interrupt a sermon to deliver their "impressions." Once, when Finley quieted a woman who had interrupted his sermon, the congregation was incensed.

6. Chase, *Recollections*, 23-31.

7. William Keith, *The Experience of William Keith. [Written by Himself.] Together with Some Observations Conclusive of Divine Influence on the Mind of Man* (Utica: Seward, 1806), 15.

ness to kneel, not an infrequent occurrence at Methodist public services since nonmembers frequently outnumbered members, indicated an individual's denial of a Methodist prayer. The individual's motivation could range from uncertainty about the Methodists to outright rejection of them. From a Methodist's perspective, refusal to kneel during prayer could be evidence of some grave spiritual flaw, described in terms such as being "dead to God."[8]

Methodist public prayers involved at least two other participatory actions. The first was the raising of hands during prayer. Although references to the practice are few, it occurred in both northern and southern states and among both Blacks and Whites.[9] When Methodists did raise their hands in prayer, in their own estimation, they were only imitating angelic practice. One young Delmarva girl, Hetty Clogg, after a vision of heaven in 1817, reported seeing angels holding up their hands in prayer and people raising their hands in song.[10] In addition, Methodists frequently voiced spontaneously an "amen" while another was praying. When done, this congregational response might invigorate the prayer to pray more fervently, even though outsiders frequently thought it rude.

Just as kneeling was *the* bodily posture for Methodists' prayers, a visible expression of the nature of their piety, extemporaneity was *the* verbal mode of Methodist praying, an expression of the affective nature of that piety. The importance of extemporaneous prayer in early Methodism cannot be overstated. Reliance on written prayers was often considered a mark of spiritual immaturity or a lack of "experimental religion." By contrast, the ability to pray extemporaneously was considered evidence that the "miracle" of conversion had been wrought in the prayer, who now had a wealth of items in the heart to be expressed before God. If advised to read prayers, a Methodist would insist that he or she would rather pray "out of the heart."[11] If someone felt he or she could not pray without a book then reading prayers was suggested, but only as an intermediate step until the person could pray extemporaneously.[12] This overwhelming

---

8. Jessop journal, 4 January 1788.

9. Rankin diary, 120-21; [John] Adams, *The Life of "Reformation" John Adams, an Elder of the Methodist Episcopal Church*, ed. Enoch George Adams, vol. 1 (Boston: George C. Rand, 1853), 1:172.

10. David Dailey, Diary. Ms. St. George's United Methodist Church, Philadelphia, PA, 27 April 1817.

11. Charles Giles, *Pioneer: A Narrative of the Nativity, Experience, Travels, and Ministerial Labours of Rev. Charles Giles* (New York: G. Lane & P. P. Sandford, 1844), 264.

12. John Littlejohn, "Journal of John Littlejohn." Ts. Transcribed by Annie L. Winstead. Louisville Conference Historical Society, Louisville, KY. [Available on microfilm from Kentucky Wesleyan College, Owensboro, KY], 32.

preference meant that prayer in prayer meetings and family prayer was almost sure to be extemporaneous. References to Methodists using books to pray in these settings are extremely rare.

Methodist preference for extemporaneous prayer was probably not simply a matter of spirituality. The position of early Methodism within society most likely contributed to the distaste for reading prayers, especially in areas where the Anglican Church had been strong. As Rhys Isaac pointed out in his study of eighteenth-century Virginia, the reading of services from the *Book of Common Prayer* in Anglican parishes was part of a web of social relationships that emphasized a gentry-centered social order.[13] In contrast, some Methodists, both Black and White, came most often from social groups that had high rates of marginal literacy.[14] Extemporaneous prayer may have been necessary as well as having been a highly valued option. In addition, in this cultural setting, extemporaneity was seen as an attack upon the values of the gentry, precisely the sort of statement that Methodists constantly made.

This is not to say that Methodists preferred extemporaneous prayer for merely negative reasons. Rather, extemporaneous prayer was preferred because it was the most sympathetic way to express the affective, intense nature of Methodist spirituality. The goal in extemporaneous prayer was poignancy, rather than proper grammar or tasteful construction. When reflecting on their praying, Methodists were likely to feel retrospective guilt if they thought they had become too concerned with well-sounding turns of phrases. Those considered gifted in praying were recognized as being able to grapple with the affective language of the heart and vocalize this in a moving way for and with whom they prayed. As one woman's giftedness was described thus: her prayers were "deep and affecting."[15]

Understanding these contexts—early Methodist spirituality and societal position—brings a different perspective to the frequently cited statement by Jesse Lee concerning Methodists' preference for extemporaneity. In his book, *A Short History of the Methodists*, Lee described the introduction in American Methodism of John Wesley's revision of the *Book of Common Prayer* commonly known as the *Sunday Service*:

---

13. Rhys Isaac, *The Transformation of Virginia 1740–1790* (Chapel Hill: University of North Carolina Press, 1982), 63-65, 260-64.

14. Compare John H. Wigger, *Taking Heaven by Storm: Methodism and the Rise of Popular Christianity in America* (New York: Oxford University Press, 1998), 72. Wigger notes that some preachers improved their literacy as a result of their conversion and ministry.

15. C. Garrettson diary, 97.

At this time the prayer book, as revised by Mr. Wesley, was introduced among us; and in the large towns, and in some country places, our preachers read prayers on the Lord's day: and in some cases the preachers read part of the morning service on Wednesdays and Fridays. But some of the preachers who had been long accustomed to pray extempore, were unwilling to adopt this new plan. Being fully satisfied that they could pray better, and with more devotion while their eyes were shut, than they could with their eyes open. After a few years the prayer book was laid aside, and has never been used since in public worship.[16]

Many modern commentators have looked harshly on this preference for extemporaneity, particularly as they see it as a rejection of the *Sunday Service*.[17] The bias of these commentators is shown in their failure to appreciate the various contexts within which early Methodists lived, worshiped, and preferred extemporaneous prayer. Additionally, they fail to question whether the *Sunday Service* was rejected due partly to qualities Wesley himself had instilled in early Methodism: its "experimental religion"-based piety and a polity rooted in itinerant ministry. Nor do they consider whether even the more "Anglican" of the early Methodists themselves might have been somewhat ambivalent about the strict necessity for reading prayers, as suggested in this 1786 statement by Bishop Coke in a letter to Freeborn Garrettson: "I would have you introduce y.e Prayer-book everywhere, so far as you possibly can without giving *great* offense: but I w.d not give *great* offense to precious Souls even for y.e best of forms."[18] Indeed, on the other side of this letter, Wesley himself noted that he "constantly" added extemporaneous prayer to morning and evening prayer.

Thus when commentators disparage American Methodism as some sort of caricatured perversion of a "true" Wesleyan approach to prayer and worship, they fail to understand the early Methodists.

---

16. Jesse Lee, *A Short History of the Methodists, in the United States of America; Beginning in 1766, and Continued till 1809.* (Baltimore: Magill & Clime, 1810; reprint, Rutland, VT: Academy Books, 1974), 107.

17. See, for example, Frank Senn, *Christian Liturgy: Catholic and Evangelical* (Minneapolis: Fortress, 1997), 550.

18. Thomas Coke letter to Freeborn Garrettson, n.d. Ms. John Wesley Papers, United Methodist Church Archives-GCAH, Madison, NJ. Coke's letter is on the reverse side of Wesley's letter to Garrettson, dated 25 February 1786. Note that in 1784 most—but not all—of the American itinerants had come from an Anglican background; see Thomas Ware, *Sketches of the Life and Travels of Rev. Thomas Ware, who has been an Itinerant Methodist Preacher for More than Fifty Years* (New York: Lane & Sandford, 1842), 106.

Given the piety they inherited and the social position they held, the Methodists naturally felt as if reading prayers, even from Wesley's own revised version of the *Book of Common Prayer,* could "destroy the energy of divine worship so much, that the life of religion is lost."[19]

Of course, it is fair to ask whether something important could be lost when American Methodists did not integrate the *Sunday Service* more fully into their liturgical life. Wesley himself would seem to suggest an answer: regular use of the prayer services from his service book would ensure that Methodists participated in a full, well-balanced diet of prayer. Wesley designed Methodist societal worship to complement—not as a substitute for—the prayer services from the *Book of Common Prayer.* In isolation, Methodist societal worship could be considered essentially defective since it would be in danger of lacking a balance of the "four grand parts" of prayer (deprecation, petition, intercession, and thanksgiving).[20] Whether the lived experience of Methodist prayer actually resulted in such defectiveness is another question. It is hard to imagine active Methodists not being exposed to all these types of prayer over time.

As noted before, the experience of being moved or melted in worship, as they would say, was very desirable to early Methodists. This experience was often the criteria by which they decided that God had attended their prayers. When a "remarkable spirit of prayer" was poured out on the preachers during one Annual Conference, one expressed his joy by saying, "O what a heaven of heavens I feel."[21] Poetry, not prose, was needed to describe these experiences of prayer:

> I have just come in from prayer, where God was so near one, that nature shrank, while the cloudless, blazing beams of Jehovah dark with excessive brightness sunk me to the ground, and as a Rainbow encircled me about, and what could I say while tears rolled like floods, my broken heart for joy made a noise.[22]

---

19. George Bourne, *The Life of the Rev. John Wesley, A.M., with Memoirs of the Wesley Family. To which are subjoined, Dr. Whitehead's Funeral Sermon: and a Comprehensive History of American Methodism* (Baltimore: George Dubbin and Murphy, 1807), 344. Some early itinerants did try to follow Wesley's directions in use of the *Sunday Service* for Sunday worship. Thomas Haskins was one. Beginning in late January 1785 he began to read prayers from it. He continued several weeks but finally quit, noting, "Altho' this [the service from the *Sunday Service*] is most excellent in itself, yet I scarcely think it will be of much use among us, as a people." See Haskins journal, 49 (entry for 23 January 1785).

20. See "Large Minutes," Q. 45, *Works* (Jackson) 8:322.

21. Thomas Coke, *Extracts of the journals of the Rev. Dr. Coke's five visits to America* (London: G. Paramore, 1793), 151.

22. Sarah Jones letter to Edward Dromgoole, n.d. (in Dromgoole papers).

The intense and immediate reaction of those who listened to the extemporaneous prayers of early Methodist preachers and exhorters indicates that praying often functioned as a form of indirect exhortation or sermon, as speech that moved worshipers to joyous communion and deep introspection. Indeed, Francis Asbury once noted that prayers moved people more than preaching at times.[23] For example, John Campbell Deem noted the tremendous effect a prayer had in awakening him, using terms that others had used for their reactions to exhortations and sermons. While a twelve-year-old boy prayed, Deem felt the boy was describing his own character and struggles as if from personal familiarity. When the boy concluded his prayer with "O God, if there is mercy for such a wretch, let him now feel it," Deem was brought under immediate conviction.[24]

Some pray-ers, surely aware of the effects of their prayers, emphasized the connection between praying and exhorting more directly. Some moved back and forth between the two, changing their intended audience—from God to people to God—as they went. Others just couched their exhortation in the form of a prayer. After morning family prayer in one well-to-do Delmarva Methodist family, a guest who was a United States senator was much agitated since he felt the pray-er had shaken a "brimstone-bag" over him. When asked why, the prayer was honest in his intention: "To save you from hell, sir."[25]

Because of Methodists' universal preference for extemporaneous prayers, few examples of early Methodists' prayers still exist. Two examples that do are prayers found in the George A. Reed manuscript papers (reproduced in appendix D).[26] Undated and unsigned, they

---

23. *JLFA* 1:194. Asbury himself was known for deep, affective prayers. See Johnson, "Sermons of Francis Asbury," 152.

24. John Campbell Deem, Autobiography. Ms. Ohio Wesleyan University Library, Delaware, OH, 32.

25. David Dailey, *Experience and Ministerial Labors of Rev. Thomas Smith, Late an Itinerant Preacher of the Gospel in the Methodist Episcopal Church* (New York: Lane & Tippett, 1848), 31. Such an exhortatory use of prayer shows a tendency to view people as the objects of worship, rather than the object being God. Such prayers are really directed at people instead of God. This approach is a troublesome adaptation of liturgical prayer's purpose. It is an amazingly short step from realizing that the overhearing of a prayer can be a moving experience to intentional planning of prayers to stimulate a certain response in the human hearer. Methodists seemed prone to make this step. Unfortunately, this transition can occur when pray-ers are moved by a deep evangelistic zeal. The general lack of objective sensibilities for worship—in this case the extreme affective liturgical piety among Methodists—only accentuates the tendency to use prayers in this manner.

26. Untitled Prayers, George A. Reed papers. For other examples of prayers or summaries of prayers see Meacham journal, 22 March 1789; Jessop journal, 11 August 1790; Richard Allen, *The Life Experience and Gospel Labors of the Rt. Rev. Richard Allen* (New York: Abingdon, 1960), 44-45; [James V. Watson], *Tales and Takings, Sketches and Incidents, from the Itinerant and Editorial Budget of Rev. James V. Watson* (New York: Carlton & Porter, 1857), 96; and the humorous account in

are examples of freely composed prayers in early Methodism. Based on internal clues, at least one of these prayers (the one designated "Prayer 1" in appendix D) was spoken in a liturgical setting.

If these prayers are reliable indicators, a typical early Methodist prayer would have been a synthesis of phrases and thoughts from several sources. Foremost among these were biblical quotes or allusions as well as standard phrases from Methodist piety. Scriptural quotes/allusions seem especially important for early Methodist praying; the ability to use them freely was seen as a sign of special ability in praying.[27] Similarly, the use of standard phrases from their shared piety probably created communal recognition and acceptance of the prayer although to the outsider they would have seemed nothing more than "a rant of miserable, low, familiar jargon."[28] The other defining quality of early Methodist prayer vocabulary was the use of archaic personal pronouns for God (thee, thou, thine) and archaic verb forms. These archaic forms, common in every example of Methodist free-composed prayer from the period, were probably related to the heavy use of scriptural allusions in these prayers.

Of the pious clichés Methodists used to describe the act of praying, none seems as frequent as talking about "visiting" or "waiting" before the "throne of grace."[29] The frequency of these clichés perhaps makes them the best terms to use to describe what Methodists understood to be happening at their various prayer services, including those at quarterly meetings. There is an obvious corporate element: prayer is God's people gathered together in hope before the presence of God. Before God, they meet and wait. The phrase "throne of grace" is a rich metaphor. It emphasizes their understanding of God's sovereignty and power as being fundamentally demonstrated in overwhelming, personal love. This understanding of the interdependence

George Peck, *Early Methodism within the bounds of the old Genesee Conference from 1788 to 1828: or, The first forty years of Wesleyan evangelism in northern Pennsylvania, central and western New York, and Canada. Containing sketches of interesting localities, exciting scenes, and prominent actors* (New York: Carlton & Porter, 1860), 152.

27. John F. Wright, *Sketches of the Life and Labors of James Quinn, who was Nearly Half a Century a Minister of the Gospel in the Methodist Episcopal Church* (Cincinnati: Methodist Book Concern, 1851), 146-47; and Daniel De Vinné, *Recollections of Fifty Years in the Ministry* (New York: Tibbals & Co., 1869), 49.

28. Frances Trollope, *Domestic Manners of the Americans*, 5th ed. (New York: Dodd, Mead & Co., 1927), 105.

29. Some variant of the phrase is in both of the prayers in the appendix. See also Giles, *Pioneer*, 71; W. P. Strickland, *The Life of Jacob Gruber* (New York: Carlton & Porter, 1860), 69-70; Meacham journal, 29 June 1791; Mary Avery Browder letter to Edward Dromgoole, 2 December 1777 (in Dromgoole papers); and Edward Dromgoole letter to Philip Gatch, 27 October 1813 (in Philip Gatch papers).

of God's love and God's power is central to their understanding of worship: there God encounters humanity with a wave of overpowering love.

Watch Nights

Watch night services appear to have been an integral component of the quarterly meetings held in America from the earliest days. Accounts by the general assistant, Thomas Rankin, reveal that the climax for most one-day quarterly meetings in the 1770s was a watch night service.[30] In 1775, William Duke notes that a watch night closed his meeting "as usual."[31]

The frequency of watch nights at quarterly meetings seems to have decreased over time, although they never completely died out. They did not develop a normative place within the two-day, weekend format of quarterly meetings that was rapidly taking hold. By the late-1770s, mention of watch nights is very sporadic. They had become only an optional element in the liturgical scheme of quarterly meetings. Yet in the decades that followed, they did continue to be held occasionally. Quarterly meetings that contained watch nights included a 1792 Maryland meeting, an 1802 Albany, New York, meeting, and an 1803 Kentucky meeting.[32]

Watch nights were related to preaching services in that both contained hymns, prayers, sermon(s), and exhortation(s). The close relationship between the two is seen in Rankin's grappling for a term to describe what he considered to be very long preaching services at Virginia quarterly meetings starting in 1776. For these daytime preaching services, which apparently lasted three to four hours, Rankin coined a new phrase: "watchafternoon."[33] Obviously derived from the term "watch night," it was the best Rankin could do to describe a preaching service that lasted as long as a watch night normally did. This term, "watchafternoon," shows a close connection between a watch night and a preaching service in terms of ritual

---

30. Rankin diary, 90-91, 109, 118, 120-22, 130-32, 141, and 152.

31. William Duke, "The Journal of William Duke 1774–1776." Ts. United Methodist Historical Society, Lovely Lane Museum, Baltimore, MD, 17.

32. See Colbert journal 1:52, 1:134 and Lakin journal 16 September 1803. See also C. R. Stockton, "The Origin and Development of Extra-liturgical Worship in Eighteenth Century Methodism" (D.Phil. diss., Oxford University, 1969), 58 n. 3.

33. Rankin diary, 181, 183, 186, 207-8, 218, 229. Rankin's use of the term appears to be unique among early itinerants.

content. Indeed, other accounts of watch nights indicate they contained the same elements found in a preaching service.

Even if their basic content was similar, there was a crucial difference between a watch night service and a typical preaching service: length. The watch night's greater length was due to repetition of the elements it shared with a preaching service. If the most basic ritual unit within a preaching service was hymn, prayer, sermon, and exhortation, then a watch night would repeat this structural unit several times until three or four hours had passed.[34] This length was not a peripheral issue, but was important for Methodist understanding of watch nights. By their length, particularly in a nighttime setting, Methodists were able to justify watch nights as an adaptation of the vigil form that appeared in the Anglican Church's own prayerbook, in accounts of the early church, and in biblical narrative, as the bishops argued in their commentary in the 1798 *Discipline*.[35] Their length helped Methodists to present the watch night as a Christian alternative to less holy, but more popular, nighttime exploits.

Watch nights also differed from preaching services in that they took place at night and therefore concentrated on themes appropriate for the night. Watch nights at quarterly meetings, as well as at other times, utilized a rich variety of appropriate biblical themes and images in preaching and singing (and presumably in exhorting and praying). A hymn in the collection published by Richard Allen that paraphrases a gospel parable, is one example:

> Ye virgin souls arise,
> With all the dead awake!
> Unto salvation wise,
> Oil in your vessels take:
> Upstarting at the midnight cry,
> Behold the heavenly bridegroom nigh.
>
> Then let us wait to hear
> The trumpet's welcome sound,
> To see our Lord appear,
> Watching let us be found;
> When Jesus doth the heavens bow,
> Be found—as Lord, thou find'st us now![36]

---

34. Compare the description of a watch night in Miram Fletcher, *The Methodist; Or, Incidents and Characters from Life in the Baltimore Conference* (New York: Derby & Jackson, 1859): 1:77-82.

35. *Discipline/1798*, 76-77.

36. Allen, *Collection of Hymns*, 87. This hymn first appeared as Hymn 64 in Wesley's *Hymns* (*Works* 7:160).

Inspired by the nighttime setting, watch nights emphasized motifs such as watching, praying, and readiness. Set against the backdrop of surrounding darkness—both literal and spiritual—watch night services contained calls to repentance and warnings of the transience of time, all placed within a framework of eschatological expectation of Christ's second coming. The themes of a watch night constituted a "kind of Advent piety" for early evangelicals, as others have suggested.[37] Thus the Methodists did sing:

> Thou Judge of quick and dead,
> Before whose bar severe,
> With holy joy, or guilty dread,
> We all shall soon appear;
> Our caution'd souls prepare,
> For that tremendous day,
> And fill us now with watchful care,
> And stir us up to pray
>
> To pray and wait the hour,
> That awful hour unknown,
> When, rob'd in majesty and pow'r,
> Thou shalt from heaven come down:
> Th' immortal son of Man,
> To judge the human race,
> With all thy Father's dazzling train,
> With all thy glorious grace.[38]

The selection of appropriate biblical texts for preaching was a key way in which these themes were made explicit. The texts for watch night sermons often functioned to heighten the congregation's awareness of the shortness of time, the need for readiness in judgment, and the conflict between the powers of darkness and of light. The text for an 1802 sermon, for example, was 1 Corinthians 3:13-15 (the Day will reveal the nature of each person's work).[39] The text for a 1792 sermon was Malachi 3:18 (see the difference between the righteous and the

---

37. Leigh E. Schmidt, "Time, Celebration, and the Christian Year in Eighteenth-Century Evangelicalism," in *Evangelicalism: Comparative Studies of Popular Protestantism in North America, the British Isles, and Beyond, 1700–1990,* ed. Mark A. Noll, David W. Bebbington, and George A. Rawlyk (New York: Oxford University Press, 1994), 101. Schmidt focuses his discussion on a very common setting for watch nights: New Year's Eve.

38. Hymn 12 in *Pocket Hymn-book* (1786), 14. This hymn was written by Charles Wesley and included in his *Hymns for the Watch-night* (1746).

39. Colbert journal 4:137.

wicked), which probably led the preacher to explore the need for the sanctified to separate themselves from "worldly" people.[40]

Indeed, watch nights seemed to early Methodists as natural settings for accenting their struggle with the powers of sin. This occurred at several levels. Some accounts speak of almost a palpable sense of powers opposed to God. In that case, preaching and exhortation seemed to have little effect whenever "the powers of darkness was most sencibly felt."[41] Watch nights thus also seemed to be appropriate times for "professors" to become aware of their own remaining sinfulness and thus seek sanctification; here they could "engage" God for this blessing though the "powers of darkness opposed."[42] At a more corporate level, watch nights also served to reinforce Methodism's countercultural stance. As Bishops Coke and Asbury asked rhetorically concerning watch nights in 1798, "shall the dissipates and profane revel and watch night after night, in the service of Satan, and shall we think it too much to watch and pray sometimes for a few hours together?"[43] An enthusiastic "no" resounded from the willingness of Methodists to worship in watch nights. Or, as they sang, the keeping watch for the coming of Christ was a mark of having experienced God's grace:

> Oft we have pass'd the guilty night
>   In revellings and frantic mirth,
> The creature was our sole delight,
>   Our happiness the things of earth;
> But O, suffice the season past,
> We choose the better part at last.
>
> We will not close our wakeful eyes,
>   We will not let our eye lids sleep,
> But humbly lift them to the skies,
>   And all a solemn vigil keep;
> So many nights on sin bestow'd,
> Can we not watch one hour for God?

---

40. Ibid. 1:52. Unfortunately Colbert does not say whether the preacher continued reading in Malachi 4, whose references to the coming Day of the Lord would seem to fit in a watch night. For examples of other watch night sermon texts, see Haskins journal, 3 (Hebrews 12:25: How shall we escape when warned from heaven?); and Littlejohn journal, 202 (Isaiah 21:11: "Watchman, what is left of the night?").

41. Lakin journal, 17 September 1803.

42. Colbert journal 4:137.

43. *Discipline/*1798, 76-77.

Dear object of our faith and love,
　We listen for thy welcome voice,
Our persons and our work approve,
　And bid us in thy strength rejoice,
Now let us hear the mighty cry
And shout to find the bridegroom nigh.[44]

Pastoral Rites

In addition to the more frequent preaching services and prayer meetings, quarterly meetings were sometimes occasions for administration of Methodism's pastoral rites: baptisms, weddings, and funerals.[45] Although not a regular part of every quarterly meeting, these rites were performed somewhat frequently. All three rites were public in their administration in that the *Discipline* did not restrict observation of them to Methodists. Everyone was eligible to watch them, even if in actual practice their administration—particularly weddings and, less frequently, baptisms—was often done in a smaller domestic setting.

The inclusion of pastoral rites into a quarterly meeting was a matter of convenience rather than liturgical necessity. There was nothing about either quarterly meetings or pastoral rites that made the latter's administration necessary in this setting. But since not all itinerants were ordained, while nearly every quarterly meeting had at least one ordained preacher present, it was often a convenient time to perform these rites for those needing them. As a notable case in point, at the famous November 1784 quarterly meeting in Delaware at which the newly ordained bishop, Thomas Coke, met the soon-to-be-ordained Francis Asbury, Coke noted that he baptized thirty to forty children and seven adults during the weekend.[46] Even before the arrival of

---

44. Stanzas 1, 2, and 4 of hymn 276 in *A Pocket Hymn-book, designed as a Constant Companion for the Pious. Collected from Various Authors*, 23rd ed. (Philadelphia: Henry Tuckniss, 1800), 267-68.

45. Although recognized technically as a sacrament, baptism was functionally grouped with weddings and funerals in early Methodist practice. Ministers demonstrated this association for baptism in a couple of ways: by distinguishing baptism from the Lord's Supper, by most regularly calling baptism an "ordinance" and the Lord's Supper "*the* sacrament"; and by linking baptism with other pastoral rites, by consistently grouping these together in the *Discipline*. Note that deacons were allowed to perform these pastoral rites; see *Discipline*/1785, 12; and *Discipline*/1787, 8. Beginning in 1788 bishops were allowed to ordain local preachers to deacon's orders without their first becoming itinerants, in contrast to the initial polity provisions in 1785–1787; see *Discipline*/1788, 6. In effect this enabled a more stationary ministry with respect to these pastoral offices. Ordinations were also conducted publicly but were less frequent in quarterly meetings since a bishop was required.

46. Coke, *Extracts*, 16. See also Ware, *Sketches*, 115. For a discussion of baptism in Methodism generally, see Charles R. Hohenstein, "The Revisions of the Rites of Baptism in the Methodist

such "legitimately" ordained preachers in 1784, quarterly meetings were convenient occasions for the administration of baptism as in the case of the 1780 quarterly meeting at which one of the preachers, ordained by the irregular 1779 Fluvanna presbytery, baptized.[47]

After the initial flurry in 1784, the relative necessity of conducting pastoral rites at quarterly meetings decreased over the years as the number of local deacons and elders increased in The Methodist Episcopal Church.[48] Thus, of the 111 weddings (from 1787–1813) and thirty-one baptisms (from 1788–1797) included in the records of the New Mills circuit in New Jersey, only three of each occurred during quarterly meetings. Weddings in particular seem to have been so infrequently performed at quarterly meetings that one preacher, who scheduled his own wedding after a quarterly meeting's preaching service, felt compelled to justify doing so to the crowd.[49] Baptism maintained a stronger connection to quarterly meetings, especially in missionary situations. The itinerant in St. Augustine, Florida, for example, noted that fifteen people (four children and eleven adults) were baptized at three different times during his first quarterly meeting in that city.[50] Waiting for an "extraordinary meeting" like a quarterly meeting (or camp meeting) to have one's child baptized remained popular enough in some areas that the 1831 South Carolina Annual Conference complained about this practice.[51]

If the relationship of baptisms and weddings to quarterly meetings was one of convenience, that of funerals was obviously one of coincidence. For example, the people who gathered for an 1814 quarterly meeting to be held by their presiding elder, Peter Moriarty, were surprised to discover that he had died suddenly and that the meeting's

Episcopal Church, 1784–1939" (Ph.D. diss., University of Notre Dame, 1990); and Gayle Carlton Felton, *This Gift of Water: The Practice and Theology of Baptism Among Methodists in America* (Nashville: Abingdon, 1992). For weddings and funerals see Karen Westerfield Tucker, " 'Till Death Us Do Part": The Rites of Marriage and Burial Prepared by John Wesley and Their Development in The Methodist Episcopal Church, 1784–1939" (Ph.D. diss., University of Notre Dame, 1992).

47. Reed diary, 94.

48. Disciplinary authorization to ordain local preachers as elders did not occur until 1812. However, a significant number of elders had located from active itinerancy well before then.

49. Ebenezer Francis Newell, *Life and Observations of Rev. E. F. Newell, who has been more than Forty Years an Itinerant Minister in the Methodist Episcopal Church* (Worcester, MA: C. W. Ainsworth, 1847), 139-40.

50. Glenn journal, 163-64.

51. Albert M. Shipp, *The History of Methodism in South Carolina* (Nashville: Southern Methodist Publishing House, 1884; reprint, Spartanburg, SC: The Reprint Company, 1972), 590. Compare *JLFA* 2:271.

first service was to be his funeral.[52] Generally, people who died at quarterly meetings were buried then.

The manner in which these pastoral rites were administered at quarterly meetings demonstrates the way early Methodists viewed their worship. They were less concerned about maintaining niceties of some fixed order for elements in worship and were more concerned about ritual acts contributing to Methodism's larger evangelical purposes. Methodists established the first element—disregard for ordo—by treating rites as autonomous units and emphasized the second—furthering their mission—by using administration of rites to preach, exhort, and pray evangelically.

For Methodists, convenience was a proper end. They administered the pastoral rites whenever it was necessary and convenient, with little concern for achieving some ideal ordo. While tendencies in arranging elements of worship emerged, there were no fixed rules. Although baptisms at quarterly meetings were frequently after the first preaching service on Sunday morning, for example, they were also administered at various occasions throughout the weekend or at the close of the day, in a home, when the preachers had gathered to retire. Multiple administrations were common when the baptizands chose different modes of baptism, which was often the case. William Colbert once baptized four by "sprinkling," then administered the Lord's Supper, and finally baptized Wyatt Chaimberlain by immersion in a creek.[53]

Regardless of the order in which they were administered, Methodist administrations of pastoral rites, like other Methodist worship, were opportunities to evangelize. This was particularly the case with funerals, since those occasions provided easy opportunity to talk about the transient nature of earthly life and the need to be aware of one's eternal destiny. One early hymn pointed this out vividly:

> Heark from the tomb a doleful sound
> My ears attend the cry
> Ye living men come view the ground
> Where you must shortly lie.
>
> Great God is this our certain doom
> And are we still secure

---

52. *Minutes*/1814, 1:241.
53. Colbert journal 4:129-30.

Still walking downward to the tomb
And yet prepare no more.[54]

So central were preaching and exhorting to funerals that Methodists very frequently used the phrase that someone had "preached a funeral."[55]

Of course, these were not the only themes possible at a Methodist funeral. It could also be an opportunity to rejoice in a fellow Methodist's promotion to heavenly fellowship. Indeed, all of the funeral hymns in one of the well-used early hymnals, the so-called *Pocket Hymn-book*, are triumphal in tone. The Methodists could sing to the departed:

> Happy soul, thy days are ended;
> All thy mourning days below;
> Go, by angel-guards attended,
> To the sight of Jesus, go.

Or they could sing comfort to each other as in this hymn for use at the loss of a Methodist woman:

> The soul of our sister is gone,
> To heighten the triumph above,
> Exalted to Jesus's throne,
> And clasp'd in the arms of his love.[56]

There were even special hymns of comfort for the deaths of infants.[57]

The impetus to evangelize was never far below the surface, however, and so Methodists seized opportunities to evangelize at all pastoral rites. Before their wedding at a quarterly meeting, Ebenezer

---

54. Bradford ms. hymnbook. Compare the anxiety of the funeral hymns in Stith Mead, *A General Selection of the Newest and Most Admired Hymns and Spiritual Songs, Now in Use. The second edition revised corrected and enlarged, and published by permission of the Virginia Conference held at Raleigh, (N.C.)* (Lynchburg: Jacob Haas, 1811), 168, 171.

55. For an example, see the Nathan Bangs journal, 9 August 1805. For examples of sermon texts see *JLFA* 1:334 (Ecclesiastes 9:10) and Thomas Mann journal, 16 November 1805 (Philippians 1:21). For examples of sermons see [Emory Prior], *A Funeral Sermon, Preached by the Rev. Mr. Prior, Minister of the Methodist Church at Baltimore, on the Death of Miss Christiana Lane, Who Departed this Life, Friday, October 5, 1792. Taken down in short hand* (Baltimore: Samuel & John Adams, 1792); and Joseph Crawford, *The Substance of a Sermon Delivered at the Funeral of Miss Nabby Frothingham, of Middletown, (Conn.) February 24, 1809. To a Numerous Crowd of Attentive Hearers, in the Methodist Meeting-house* (New York: John C. Totten, 1809). In both of these sermons, the preachers gave much attention to evangelizing their congregation by emphasizing the transience of life.

56. Hymns 180 and 185, respectively, in *Pocket Hymn-book* (1786), 170, 176.

57. Mead, *General Selection of Hymns*, 25, 178.

Newell and his fiancée, Fanny, fasted and prayed that God would give them a "public token of his favour" at their wedding ceremony. When "brokenhearted sinners" began to cry for mercy during the extemporaneous prayers before and after the reading of the rite, Ebenezer and Fanny were greatly pleased that God had answered their prayers. After the wedding, when her friends were congratulating her for getting a new name, Fanny took the remark as an opportunity to exhort her friends. She told them to be saved so that they too could receive a new name, "even the new name of Jesus!"[58]

Conclusion

Lorenzo Dow, the well-known, flamboyant Methodist preacher, was once preaching in a Methodist service and—as was his habit—standing near the altar rather than at the pulpit itself. Nearby there were two empty seats and, because the meetinghouse was fairly full, Dow sought someone to occupy the chairs. In one he placed a pious old woman who was using an ear trumpet to hear better. In the other he seated an old man who likewise had an ear trumpet. The old man was evidently "quite an opposite character" when compared to the pious woman, however. As he preached, Dow reportedly addressed first one, and then the other. Whenever he spoke of hell and judgment, he leaned close to the old man's ear trumpet. And whenever he spoke of heaven and happiness, he addressed himself to the pious Methodist woman.[59]

Whether or not this story is apocryphal, it does illustrate the dual nature of evangelism that existed in early Methodism's public worship services. Permeated with an evangelical ethos, Methodists sought to disclose in their public worship both the threats of hellish judgment and the promises of heavenly bliss. Believing in the utter misery of the one and ecstatic joy of the other, Methodists prayed that their worship would be occasions when God would act among them, convicting sinners, justifying mourners, sanctifying some believers, and enabling all the other "professors" to happily enjoy grace. They hoped and prayed that their public worship would be seasons of grace when poor sinners would cross from hell's misery to heaven's peace. In their own estimation, God's gracious presence was a frequent

58. Newell, *Life,* 139-40.
59. Snelling, *Life,* 114-15.

occurrence in their public worship, particularly in their quarterly meetings. For this they praised God.

And in this experience of grace they gathered separately for occasions of private or restricted worship. These rituals—at quarterly meetings most notably the love feast and Lord's Supper—were their rites of closer fellowship. Here heaven seemed to open even more fully in their midst. Here Methodists experienced not only the power of heaven to convert and sanctify, but the very quality of heaven itself: communion with saints, angels, and, especially, God.

CHAPTER 4

Private Worship at Quarterly Meetings: Love Feast and the Lord's Supper

"I was as in a little Heaven below, and believe Heaven above will differ more in quantity than in quality."
—comment after 1780 quarterly meeting love feast[1]

In addition to those services open to all, Methodists conducted certain rituals that were restricted in access, even to the point of overt exclusion. The necessity of restriction was an important feature in early Methodist polity, as expressed in their *Discipline*. The polity, inherited from Wesley, required that meetings of the societies themselves, the bands and classes, and the love feast be restricted to those who were current, active members. Individual exceptions were to be limited. After creation of The Methodist Episcopal Church in 1784 and the concomitant result of Methodist preachers being ordained to administer sacraments, the polity likewise included the Lord's Supper in this sphere of private—as opposed to public—worship.

Why would early Methodists be so concerned with limiting access to some of their meetings and rituals? Their answer was almost invariably the same: fellowship. In the meetings of the societies and classes and in the love feast and Lord's Supper, Methodists experienced their fellowship most intensely. The rituals especially served to express and reinforce the fellowship in Christ that Methodists shared. Indeed, the deep importance of this communal aspect in early Methodist worship stands in contrast to some contemporary portrayals

---

1. William Watters, *A Short Account of the Christian Experience, and Ministereal Labours, of William Watters* (Alexandria: S. Snowden, 1806), 75-76.

that represent early American evangelicalism as being tainted by rampant individualism.

So frequently intense and meaningful was the experience of fellowship in their restricted rituals that typically Methodists sought explanation for the experience not only in their ecclesiology but also in their eschatology. Simply put, Methodists believed that the quality of fellowship that they frequently experienced in their restricted rituals was nothing less than a foretaste of the quality of life in heaven itself. Their understanding of the church was thoroughly eschatological. That was why it was important to hold worship segregated from the nonmembers: it was there that heaven was most vividly revealed among them.

Love Feast Basics

Other than the quarterly meeting conference itself, a love feast was one of the earliest and most consistent features of quarterly meetings. The love feast found a regular place within the original liturgical scheme for quarterly meetings as Methodism emerged in America. As such, American accounts of quarterly meetings throughout the 1770s mention a love feast, almost without exception. Unlike watch nights, love feasts retained a prominent position in the liturgical activities of quarterly meetings even after the two-day, weekend format became dominant.

When this format originated in the 1770s and then spread through the states in the 1780s, the love feast acquired a rather invariable place in the structure of the entire weekend. While some exceptions did occur, the normal position was as the first act of worship on Sunday morning, most commonly at 9 A.M. The consistency with which the love feast held this position is uncommon in the fluid world of early Methodist worship.[2]

---

2. One notable exception occurred when the quarterly meeting had a very large number of Black Methodists attending. In this case segregated love feasts could be held. The practice seems to have occurred most frequently on the Delmarva peninsula, starting in the 1790s; few, in any, references to the practice outside of this area exist. Most frequently a separate love feast was held for the Blacks about sunrise with the second love feast starting around 9 A.M. Another variation was to hold the Black Methodist love feast on Saturday night. For examples of the sunrise love feast see William Colbert, "A Journal of the Travels of William Colbert Methodist Preacher thro' parts of Maryland, Pennsylvania, New York, Delaware, and Virginia in 1790 to 1838." Ts. United Methodist Church Archives-GCAH, Madison, NJ, 3:142, 4:25, 5:35; and Henry Boehm, Journal. Ms. Henry Boehm Papers, United Methodist Church Archives-GCAH, Madison, NJ. [Microfilm copy at Iliff Theological Seminary, Denver, CO.], 19 December 1800, 8 February 1801,

With respect to space, quarterly meeting love feasts were held in a variety of sites, just like public services. Homes, barns, as well as meetinghouses themselves, were used. If anything contrasted love feasts from public services, it was a stronger preference for an enclosed building of some sort, rather than an outdoor setting, in order to be able to restrict access and limit visibility by nonpartici- pants. Even the preference for inside space was not absolute, however; love feasts could be held outdoors, if necessary, due to the size of the assembly.[3] The love feast for an 1804 Baltimore circuit quarterly meet- ing, for example, was held in a field with women forming an inner circle and men an outer.[4]

The love feast ritual itself was little changed from its British roots. Generally, Americans conceived of the love feast as having essential- ly two parts, the food ritual and the testimonials. Summary references

---

5 December 1819. See also J. B. Wakeley, *The Patriarch of One Hundred Years; Reminiscences, Historical and Biographical of Rev. Henry Boehm* (New York: Nelson & Phillips, 1875; reprint, Abram W. Sangrey, 1982), 63. For examples of the Saturday night love feast see Colbert journal 4:68, 4:77, 4:151; and Boehm journal, 17 October 1801. The practice of separate love feasts extended at least back into the mid 1790s; see Richard Whatcoat, Journal. Ts. Garrett-Evangelical Theological Seminary Library, Evanston, IL, 20 July 1794, 3 August 1794, 10 August 1794, 21 September 1794, and 12 October 1794. Although racial attitudes were surely part of the reason- ing for segregation, it was apparently not these attitudes alone that caused the segregated love feasts; cf. Richey, "Chesapeake Coloration," 121-22. Segregated love feasts were not a strict rule in the region since integrated love feasts were held on these same Delmarva circuits during the same period. See, for example, Colbert journal 3:145 where a January 1801 love feast was inte- grated since smaller numbers were in attendance, perhaps due to weather. A significant con- tributing factor was the number in attendance at love feasts and, in particular, the size of Black attendance. A decade before the first indication of segregated love feasts in the region, some itin- erants were estimating that total attendance at love feasts at Delmarva quarterly meetings reached one thousand; see Robert Drew Simpson, ed., *American Methodist Pioneer: The Life and Journals of The Rev. Freeborn Garrettson* (Rutland, VT: Academy Books, 1984), 177-78, 207. Moreover, in both relative and absolute numbers Blacks made up a large part of Delmarva Methodism; see the statistical summaries in William Henry Williams, *The Garden of American Methodism: The Delmarva Peninsula, 1769–1820* (Wilmington, DE: Scholarly Resources, Inc., 1984), 111-12: in 1787, Blacks constituted 30 percent of Delmarva Methodist membership; in 1808, 38 percent; and in 1814, 43 percent. The impression given by the contemporary accounts is that a sizable Black congregation was often assembled for Delmarva quarterly meetings, cer- tainly to the extent that no one building could hold the entirety of Methodists gathered for the love feasts. Note especially the 1791 quarterly meeting in the Ezekiel Cooper journal (in Papers. Garrett-Evangelical Theoloical Seminary Library, Evanston, IL), 28 August 1791. On this occa- sion, the plan appeared to have been for an integrated love feast but the number of Methodists gathered forced a segregation of the members by racial lines. The segregated love feasts were held simultaneously. See also Colbert journal 5:37. Given the size of the crowds, separation might have been a necessity if privacy was to be maintained. Segregation could have been either along gender or racial lines. The latter was chosen.

3. See Boehm journal, 20 July 1800; Thomas Rankin, "The Diary of Reverend Thomas Rankin." Ts. Garrett-Evangelical Theological Seminary Library, Evanston, IL, 181; and especially Devereux Jarratt, *A Brief Narrative of the Revival of Religion in Virginia in a Letter to a Friend*, 3rd. ed. (London: J. Paramore, 1786), 34, which documents a love feast under an arbor.

4. Francis Asbury, "Extract of a Letter from Mr. Francis Asbury, to Mr. Zachary Myles," *MQR* 28 (January 1805): 47.

to a love feast often mention only these two parts, and many mention only the testimonials. The full liturgical structure, allowing for some variation, was more involved than that. As Nathan Bangs, a preacher who first itinerated in 1802, summarily described a typical love feast, it proceeded in this order: hymn, prayer, eating of bread and water, testimonies, monetary collection, hymn, prayer, benediction.[5] This order is essentially the same used by British Methodists (with one important exception soon to be noted).[6] In addition to this regular order, American love feasts could culminate with an invitation to mourners or with an eruption of the "work of God." Admission of new members was also a possible addition to the order.

The important exception to the typical British order was the location of the collection. Whereas descriptions of British love feasts locate the collection between food distribution and testimonials, in America the collection occurred at the end of the testimonials. One consequence in this, as will be discussed more fully below, is that Americans frequently used the collection as the point to fuse administration of the Lord's Supper to the love feast. In those instances the love feast was said to have closed with the sacrament.

Accounts of American love feasts give only the most scanty details about the bread and water and how they were used. Sometimes members brought the bread. At other times it appears the bread was purchased, since there are rare notes in quarterly meeting conference records of reimbursements for bread. Descriptions of how the food was handled are likewise sparse. It is most often mentioned that the bread and water were "passed around" or had "gone around" among the members.[7] Distribution of the bread may have involved breaking off pieces, handing them to others, and receiving the same in return.[8]

5. Nathan Bangs, *A History of the Methodist Episcopal Church*, 3rd ed. (New York: Mason and Lane, 1840), 1:249. The prayers were extemporaneous, since there was no written liturgical text for love feasts.

6. See Frank Baker, *Methodism and the Love-Feast* (London: Epworth, 1957), 15; C. R. Stockton, "The Origin and Development of Extra-liturgical Worship in Eighteenth Century Methodism" (D.Phil. diss., Oxford University, 1969), 121-24; Richard O. Johnson, "The Development of the Love Feast in Early American Methodism," *Methodist History* 19.2 (January 1981): 69; and William Myles, *A Chronological History of the People called Methodists* (London: Thomas Cordeux, 1813), 4.

7. James P. Horton, *A Narrative of the Early Life, Remarkable Conversion, and Spiritual Labours of James P. Horton, Who has been a Member of the Methodist Episcopal Church Upward of Forty Years.* (n.p.: Printed for the author, 1839), 85-86; Ezekiel Cooper journal in Papers. Garrett-Evangelical Theological Seminary Library, Evanston, IL, 12 June 1796; David Dailey, *Experience and Ministerial Labors of Rev. Thomas Smith, Late an Itinerant Preacher of the Gospel in the Methodist Episcopal Church* (New York: Lane & Tippett, 1848), 86.

8. Samuel A. Seaman, *Annals of New York Methodism being a History of the Methodist Episcopal*

The amounts received were small but that did not diminish participants' appreciation of the food. The bread and water were well-received symbols of a greater reality; in Methodist terms, they were "tokens" of Christian fellowship and love.[9]

Occasionally, for a variety of reasons, the bread and water were omitted entirely. Sometimes it was a matter of forgetfulness: no one brought or arranged for the food. Overcrowding of the space for the love feast could also prevent use of the food. The readiness to continue to call the ritual a "love feast" even though it did not use bread and water demonstrates the priority of testimonies in the ritual. The food could be omitted but—in the Methodists' estimation—if there were no testimonies (or only "cold" ones), there was no love feast.

Presumably the presiding elder officiated at a quarterly meeting love feast. This seems especially true if the love feast was connected with administration of the Lord's Supper, a very frequent occurrence. However a strict requirement for the presiding elder to officiate did not exist, since generally the *Discipline* did not connect this role to ordination. Most love feast accounts are silent about this aspect, as well as about others, such as the manner of recognizing those who desired to share their testimonies and of choosing the hymns to be sung.

Love Feast Testimonies

The heart of any love feast was its testimonies (see the examples in appendix E). These usually occupied the majority of time allotted to a love feast. Here again the importance of experimental religion among early Methodists is evident. Their spirituality emphasized subjective, discernible religious experiences. They believed that God had dealt with them in their mundane lives in ways that were transforming. Testimonies were their witnesses to the wealth of God's direct dealing with them.

Church in the City of New York from A. D. 1766 to A. D. 1890 (New York: Hunt & Eaton; Cincinnati: Cranston & Stowe, 1892), 484-85. Seaman disgustedly notes that sometimes the bread retained traces of the snuff that the members—even the women—had used. Use of tobacco during worship seems to have been a common practice among Methodists. See Coles journal, United Methodist Church Archives-GCAH, Madison, NJ, 22 January 1819; W. P. Strickland, *The Life of Jacob Gruber* (New York: Carlton & Porter, 1860), 91; and Frances Trollope, *Domestic Manners of the Americans*, 5th ed. (New York: Dodd, Mead & Co., 1927), 105.

9. See Thomas Ware, *Sketches of the Life and Travels of Rev. Thomas Ware, who has been an Itinerant Methodist Preacher for More than Fifty Years* (New York: Lane & Sandford, 1842), 63; John Littlejohn, "Journal of John Littlejohn." Ts. Transcribed by Annie L. Winstead. Louisville Conference Historical Society, Louisville, KY [Available on microfilm from Kentucky Wesleyan College, Owensboro, KY], 233; Simpson, *Freeborn Garrettson*, 211; and N. Bangs, *History* 1:279.

In fact, Methodists described this part of a love feast as "speaking their experiences" as easily as they used the term "testimonies."[10] The goal was similar to other Methodist liturgical speech: vividly articulating the affective dimensions of one's religious experiences in a way that would be moving to other people. A common way to say that someone had given a well-spoken testimony was to say that she or he had spoken "feelingly."[11] When love feast participants "sketched their experience" with "life and power," Methodists would remark on how "the heavenly fire burned within us."[12]

Like most other Methodist liturgical speech, the opportunity to testify was offered to all in attendance. No racial, gender, or age restrictions existed. Even in integrated love feasts, slaves were given liberty to speak and often gave the most striking testimonies. And it was considered unusual if women did not speak. As one itinerant marveled after a 1795 quarterly meeting love feast: "Lovefeast at 9 o clock the first that I remember being at that not one of our White Sisters Spoke!"[13] The same liberty was granted to young people who sometimes spoke with great power. Catherine Livingston Garrettson noted one "little boy" who spoke with such effect that he seemed "like a man of forty."[14]

The testifiers' lack of formal theological training or social standing did not detract from the power of their speech. If anything, a lack of formal training in a speaker added to the worshipers' appreciation of the testimony. Early Methodists considered this kind of grass-roots eloquence a demonstration of God's power. Even those who had been exposed to the best governmental rhetoric valued these testimonies more highly. As one presiding elder put it, he had grown tired of listening to legislative debate when stationed in Albany, New York, but attended love feasts weekly

10. Colbert journal 4:198; Ffirth, *Experience and Gospel Labors of the Rev. Benjamin Abbott; to which is annexed a Narrative of his Life and Death* (New York: Carlton & Phillips, 1853), 177-78, 234.

11. N. Bangs journal, 5 October 1805; Dailey diary, 8 June 1817; John Early, "Journal of Bishop John Early who lived Jan. 1, 1786–Nov. 5, 1873." Ts. Southern Historical Collection, University of North Carolina, Chapel Hill, NC, 26 December 1810; Catherine Livingston Garrettson diary, in Papers. United Methodist Church Archives-GCAH, Madison, NJ, 79; Colbert journal 4:77-78, 112; and Ffirth, *Benjamin Abbott*, 162.

12. David Lewis, *Recollections of a Superannuate: or, Sketches of Life, Labor, and Experience in the Methodist Itinerancy*, ed. S. M. Merrill (Cincinnati: Methodist Book Concern, 1857), 114. Compare Henry Smith, *Recollections and Reflections of an Old Itinerant* (New York: Lane & Tippett, 1848), 229.

13. Richard Whatcoat, Journal. Ts. Garrett-Evangelical Theological Seminary Library, Evanston, IL, 10 January 1795.

14. *Extracts of Letters, Containing some Account of the Work of God since the Year 1800* (New York: J. C. Totten, 1805; reprint, Barnard, VT: Joseph Dix, 1812), 32. See also Colbert journal 1:91.

where I hear men, women, and youth, most of whom make no pretension to eloquence or learning, speak in artless language, or broken accents, of God's goodness to them, and it is still interesting, affecting, and as it were, new to me every Sabbath.[15]

Slaves, too, often with no education at all, spoke "the wisdom from above." If they spoke from their hearts of their experience of a gracious God, any Methodist could speak "with wisdom and zeal and power."[16] Simplicity was an especially desirable quality in their testimonies.

The ability to offer testimonials seems innate to early Methodists. It was not unheard of for one who had never seen nor participated in a love feast before to show a proficiency in speaking their experience. At the first love feast held in Philadelphia in 1770, Joseph Pilmore was pleasantly amazed at how well the people participated.[17] A quarter of a century later, Ezekiel Cooper had a similar comment on the first love feast in Needham, Massachusetts. Although the people had never seen a love feast before and were newly converted, "they spoke very freely of their exercises & experiences."[18] Cooper was moved, remarking "I don't know that I have been in a better love feast for a year past." Thirty years later itinerant Joshua Glenn, appointed to the missionary station of St. Augustine, Florida, had similar comments after the first love feast held in that town.[19] This ready embrace of communal testifying to worshipers' religious experience shows how well suited the message of experimental religion was to the social classes among whom Methodism had appeal. And their innate openness was further groomed and drilled in weekly class meetings.

The content of testimonies was likely quite uniform. Most were probably variations on a common theme: how that individual had gone through the various stages to salvation. As such, testimonies

15. Elbert Osborn, *Passages in the Life and Ministry of Elbert Osborn, an Itinerant Minister of the Methodist Episcopal Church, illustrating the Providence and Grace of God* (New York: published for the author, 1847–1850), 52.

16. Colbert journal 5:35 and 1:165.

17. Joseph Pilmore, *The Journal of Joseph Pilmore*, ed. Frederick E. Maser and Howard T. Maag (Philadelphia: Message Publishing Co. for the Historical Society of the Philadelphia Annual Conference of The United Methodist Church, 1969), 40. Compare Freeborn Garrettson's experience in 1779 New Jersey in Simpson, *Freeborn Garrettson*, 164.

18. Ezekiel Cooper journal, 10 November 1793. A few months earlier, on 30 July 1793, Cooper held perhaps the first Methodist love feast in Boston. He was incredulous that "[as noted] as this great town has been for religion, nevertheless that apostolic & primitive custom of Love feasts, was never introduced here till now."

19. Joshua N. Glenn, "A Memorandum or Journal of the first part of my life to the twenty third year of my age." Ms. on microfilm. Library of Congress, Washington, D.C., 164.

would have shared many of the same details and had the same basic order. That commonality was itself part of the benefit and purpose of testimonies. In this way, individual after individual reaffirmed the common understanding of salvation and demonstrated that the grace of God was indeed experienced among people like themselves.

The shorthand ways in which early Methodists described the content of testimonies show their similarity. A very common description was to say that people had told their "experience of the goodness of God."[20] Generally, this sort of testimony consisted of reciting the details of one's conviction and conversion. The effect in listeners could be overwhelming, as one itinerant described after an especially moving love feast in 1789:

> Surely the Lord sent the angel of his presence, with a living coal from the altar, and applied it to every heart and tongue. . . . We stood as on the top of Pisgah and viewed the land which the Lord had said, "I will give you."[21]

Admittedly, not all love feasts and testimonies were so moving. The accounts sometimes complain of self-centered boasting masquerading as testimonies, incoherent testimonies, excessively long testimonies, and testimonies by those whose lives contradicted their words. On one occasion a testifier, who was known to be especially cruel to his slaves, had trouble speaking because of a coughing attack. A local preacher, seeing the man's difficulty, told him: "That's right, brother; cough up the [slaves] and then you'll have an open time."[22]

Those who heard moving testimonies reported a variety of benefits from doing so. One common benefit was the validation of one's own spiritual experience. Many would have agreed with Francis Asbury's sentiment after a quarterly meeting love feast when he reported that the testimonies had been very pleasing since he had "a correspondent witness of the same in my own breast."[23] For others the testimonies offered inspiration to remain on the path toward conversion or sanc-

---

20. Robert Ayres, "The Journal of Robert Ayres." Ts. United Methodist Church Archives-GCAH, Madison, NJ, 31; James B. Finley, *Autobiography of Rev. James B. Finley; or, Pioneer Life in the West*, ed. W. P. Strickland (Cincinnati: Methodist Book Concern, 1853), 186; Jarratt, *Brief Narrative*, 13-14; and Nelson Reed, "Diary of Rev. Nelson Reed." Ts. United Methodist Historical Society, Lovely Lane Museum, Baltimore, MD, 25 January 1779, where Reed was so moved by the testimonies that he "wanted a thousand tongues" to praise God.

21. Ezekiel Cooper, "A brief account" (also in G. Phoebus, *Beams of Light*, 95). Cooper's scriptural allusions are to Isaiah 6 and Deuteronomy 34.

22. Strickland, *Life of Jacob Gruber*, 121.

23. *JLFA* 1:167.

tification or both. For example, someone struggling with the assurance of his or her sanctification could have their residual doubts swept away by hearing others testify of their sanctifying experience and their confidence in it. Similarly, preachers wondering if they had misunderstood their own vocations, and others dealing with "trials and temptations," often came away from the love feast with a much greater sense of contentment and peace.

Testimonies at love feasts seemed to serve a specific role of reawakening participants to a sense of their distinctiveness as a church body, and leading them to recommit themselves to Methodist spirituality and mission. For example, Joshua Glenn, the itinerant preacher in St. Augustine, Florida, records his impression of the testimony of an African American member at the first love feast held there in 1823:

> One poor African got up and after telling how he was brought a way from his country and how he had got on since and the way he first came to hear me [the itinerant preacher] preach as also the manner of his conviction & conversion all of which he done in a few words—he then added and more if my Massa would give my freedom and all Augustine I would not turn back from my religion—and then he made a very humble request for an interest in our prayers.[24]

The itinerant preacher could hardly restrain himself in joy. Surely echoing the sentiments of others, he thought, "Glory to God for his unmerited goodness to us. I hardly knew how to contain my self. My very soul responds Glory Glory to God forever."[25] On a similar quarterly meeting occasion, another Methodist, after hearing the love feast testimonies, became so enamored of Methodism that he considered a sacrifice of "a thousand worlds" would not have been too great a price to pay for the enjoyment of his religion.[26]

For those on the thresholds of the saving experiences of justification and sanctification, hearing testimonies was essential to their own progress in grace. The benefits they received were several, the most basic being that hearing someone testify to justification or

---

24. Glenn journal, 164.
25. Ibid.
26. Coles journal, 4 April 1819. Compare Asbury's description of some love feast testimonies (*JLFA* 2:98): "many praised God for the instrumentality of the Methodists in their salvation." Sometimes the testimonies served to strengthen commitments to particular aspects of Methodist life. See Cooper journal, 18 September 1791, where one related the blessing of following Methodist discipline in freeing his slaves; Finley, *Autobiography*, 286, where the testimonies related the blessings of participation in prayer meetings; and N. Bangs journal, 5 October 1805, where many spoke favorably about the introduction of camp meetings.

sanctification validated the goal of their own spiritual pursuits. The testimonies also defined and shaped expectations for the experience of justification or sanctification. Moreover, hearing someone affirm that they had experienced either justification or sanctification offered hope that the experience was truly within reach. Those seeking that experience could see and hear peers saying the experience was obtainable. Therefore, the testimonies were sometimes immediate catalysts for the mourner or the one seeking sanctification to experience that aspect of grace. At one love feast held in conjunction with an Annual Conference, Benjamin Abbott began to speak of his experience of sanctification. Immediately one of the other preachers dropped down and did not rise until he too could profess that God had "sanctified his soul." Abbott reported that he was approached afterward by six worshipers who said they had experienced sanctification, and seven claiming justification.[27]

On occasion those on the threshold of a certain aspect of salvation used the time of testimonies to express their own distress and ask for communal prayer. One future bishop, John Emory, was converted in this way. Under deep conviction, Emory rose during a quarterly meeting love feast and "called upon God and angels, heaven and earth, and the assembly then present, to witness that he that day determined to seek the salvation of his soul."[28] After a prayer circle formed around him, Emory experienced justification.

Love Feast Privacy

To the non-Methodist the most visible aspect of holding a love feast was its restricted nature. Entrance into the love feast was normally closely guarded, due to the desire to limit participation to Methodists and a few specially permitted outsiders.

The criteria for admission to love feasts were part of Methodist polity. Affirming the propriety of restricting love feasts and defining terms for admission was one of the initial items for business at the first Annual Conference held in America in 1773. At that time, the preachers affirmed that no one was "to be admitted into our love-feasts oftener than twice or thrice unless they become members."[29]

---

27. Ffirth, *Benjamin Abbott*, 163-64. Abbott reported similar scenes at quarterly meetings.

28. [Robert Emory?], *The Life of the Rev. John Emory, D. D* (New York: George Lane, 1841), 26-28. Compare [Richard Sneath], "Diary," in *The History of Bethel Methodist Episcopal Church Gloucester County New Jersey 1945*, comp. Mrs. Walter Aborn Simpson (n.p., 1945), 45.

29. *Minutes/1773*, 5.

After creation of The Methodist Episcopal Church in 1784, American *Disciplines* outlined the restrictions in specific detail. In response to the question of how often strangers could be present at love feasts, the *Disciplines* answered: only a very few times ("twice or thrice") and only with the utmost caution.[30]

A doorkeeper was used to effect the actual restriction of access. Most frequently one of the itinerant preachers of the circuit assumed the responsibility for staying at the door and deciding who could enter. The responsibility could be shared by multiple itinerants or by local preachers knowledgeable of the circuit's members. If someone slipped by the doorkeepers, removal was not unknown, as in the case of one man removed by a "large, athletic" Irish Methodist who reportedly escorted the intruder to the door and ushered him out with the bottom of his foot while exclaiming, "There, go! and the blessing of the Lord go wid ye."[31]

Doorkeepers used a variety of criteria for admission. For love feasts held within a particular society, possession of a current ticket would guarantee admission.[32] But mention of these tickets at quarterly meeting love feasts is rare.[33] More common are references to acquiring special notes of permission that allowed admission at a particular quarterly meeting's love feast. Seemingly not required of members in good standing, these notes were provided by an itinerant to non-members upon their request. Granting these notes was not a foregone

30. *Discipline*/1785, 5; the 1787 *Discipline* (p. 32) added the reference to thrice. For the period under consideration, this provision had no other changes.

31. [Dan Young], *Autobiography of Dan Young, A New England Preacher of the Olden Time,* ed. W. P. Strickland (New York: Carlton & Porter), 1860, 105-6.

32. Originally these tickets, distributed quarterly by the senior itinerant in the circuit, were technically tickets of admission for class meetings. However, in America their function and name changed. First in an unofficial sense, the class tickets became love feast tickets. In 1820 the *Discipline* updated its language about renewal of tickets to recognize this. Cf. Frank Baker, "The Americanizing of Methodism," *Methodist History* 13.3 (April 1975): 6; and *Discipline*/1820, 39.

33. Evidence I have found of actual use of love feast tickets suggests that their use was more common in cities along the Atlantic coast, such as Wilmington, North Carolina (George G. Smith, *The Life and Letters of James Osgood Andrew* [Nashville: Southern Methodist Publishing House, 1882], 81); Boston (Joseph Snelling, *Life of Rev. Joseph Snelling, Being a Sketch of His Christian Experience and Labors in the Ministry* [Boston: John M'Leish, 1847], 19); Petersburg, Virginia (Allin Archer Account book for Petersburg, VA 1819–1850s. Ms. Fletcher H. Archer Papers. Special Collections Library, Duke University Library, Durham, NC); Durham, Connecticut (entry for 5 November 1825 in Durham [CT] Methodist Episcopal Church Records, 1816–1847. Ms. United Methodist Church Archives-GCAH, Madison, NJ); and Philadelphia (various receipts in Francis Tees, comp., "Book of Antiquities," St. George's United Methodist Church, Philadelphia, PA). See J. B. Wakeley, *Lost Chapters Recovered from the Early History of American Methodism* (New York: 1858), 412-25, for a history of different forms of love feast tickets in New York City. For a reference to use of tickets in 1830s quarterly meetings see James Erwin, *Reminiscences of Early Circuit Life* (Toledo: Spear, Johnson & Co., 1884), 16 and 222 (where the preachers had to use tickets too!).

conclusion, as in the case of a man who was required to follow the disciplinary provisions for holding his slave; namely, submitting the facts of the purchase to the quarterly meeting conference for its ruling on how long the slave could be held before manumission.[34]

Nonmembers lacking a ticket or note of admission were not always summarily excluded. Doorkeepers had some level of discretion. One common admission was when the nonmember, usually under some significant degree of awakening, had been invited by a member who presented the guest to the doorkeeper. Another common exception, at least during the strong expressions of unity at the beginning of the Second Great Awakening, was the inclusion of Presbyterians. Generally, doorkeepers had the discretion to admit members and those who were genuine, serious "seekers" of religion. In their terms, they admitted "all that had obtained peace with God, and all who were seeking it" or "the children of God and those that were seeking Jesus."[35] Questions that the doorkeeper might ask included whether the person had ever been in a love feast and how often. The goal was to allow only "proper characters," although sometimes members thought too many "wicked" had been admitted. In contrast, some doorkeepers acted in a very rigid manner. Members themselves could be excluded from the love feast, such as in the case of John Bangs, a Methodist who once brought the food for the love feast, stepped outside to tend to his horse, and then found that the door had been closed when he tried to enter again. Despite his protests, he was not granted entrance.[36]

Doorkeepers seemed to have a good amount of repartee with those seeking admission. Sometimes the latter were willing to try to barter their way in. On one occasion John Early was confronted by a group of genteel young persons whose curiosity about the love feasts led them to promise to follow Methodist rules against worldly dress by discarding their "ruffles, rings, and wreaths" right then.[37] Sometimes it was the doorkeeper who initiated the repartee. Some took the oppor-

---

34. Norman journal, 16 March 1799. The 1798 *Discipline* (p. 170) required that "if any member of our society purchase a slave, the ensuing quarterly meeting shall determine on the number of years, in which the slave so purchased would work out the price of his purchase. And the person so purchasing, shall immediately after such determination, execute a legal instrument for the manumission of such slave, at the expiration of the term determined by the quarterly meeting." Failure to comply was sufficient cause for dismissal from the Methodist societies, according to the *Discipline*.

35. Ware, *Sketches*, 63; and Dailey, *Experience and Ministerial labors of Rev. Thomas Smith*, 86.

36. John Bangs, *Auto-biography of Rev. John Bangs, of the New-York Annual Conference* (New York: printed for the author, 1846), 40-41.

37. Early journal, 12 September 1812.

tunity to exhort those entering to follow more closely the General Rules or even to quit enjoying the privileges of membership—admission to the love feast—unless they were willing to join. Some preachers used it as an opportunity to get pledges from people that they would join.

Not all quarterly meeting love feasts were so restricted, either by accident or by design. For example, if it rained, Methodists took pity on those standing outside. Either the love feast was canceled, changed into some public service like a prayer meeting, or conducted nonetheless. Some love feasts were de facto open services because of the poor condition of the meetinghouse, as in the case of a meetinghouse that had neither door nor shutters.[38] In other cases, love feasts were forced open by the unwillingness of those excluded to be left out. This was a frequent situation in New England where the idea of closed meetings seemed particularly distasteful.[39] If the site was a "union" meetinghouse—that is, one cooperatively built by several denominations—members of the cooperating, non-Methodist denominations sometimes were piqued for not being allowed entrance into "their" meetinghouse.

Some Methodist preachers themselves felt uncomfortable with limiting access. This minority of preachers argued that exclusion would be an "insult" to non-Methodists. Typically this view was opposed by more traditional preachers who replied that it was a false goal to want to be "popular," or that unrestricted love feasts were not nearly as beneficial to Methodists.[40] Itinerant Ezekiel Cooper, for example, was strongly convinced that he had "proof after proof" that private rather than public love feasts were more "profitable."[41]

In those love feasts that were successfully restricted, the act of excluding some created an interesting dynamic: it made two separate, clearly distinguishable groups. One was active in the love feast. The other included those limited to the role of bystanders, those who would stand outside, catching only hints of the testimonies, prayers, and hymns. Reactions varied. For some it was just an opportunity to be rowdy and oppose the Methodists. They might try to throw things,

38. [Richard Swain], *Journal of Rev. Richard Swain,* ed. and trans. Robert Bevis Steelman (Rutland, VT: Academy Books, 1977), 34.

39. Simpson, *Freeborn Garrettson,* 283; Lakin journal, 9 August 1810. For examples of New England discomfort see [Young], *Autobiography of Dan Young,* 105-6 and Finley, *Autobiography,* 287.

40. Lakin journal, 13 April 1811.

41. Cooper journal, 11 November 1787.

like hatchets, through the windows. Or they would pound on the doors and windows in an effort to break in, sometimes successfully so.[42] For others, the exclusion was their catalyst for being awakened. The experience of being excluded from the people whom they recognized as the people of God caused them to begin to grieve over their own status as being separated from God and the people of God. Overhearing the activities within the love feast, particularly if the "work of God" had broken out, could also accentuate the desire for experiencing salvation in those seekers who were outside. On these occasions, when the love feast was concluded and the door opened, the bystanders eagerly flooded into the space in order to experience the gracious power of God.

Early Methodists offered a variety of reasons why private love feasts were so important. The most obvious was the desire to safeguard the atmosphere so participants felt able to speak freely in testimony. Personal testimonies were nearly synonymous with the love feast itself, so creating the best atmosphere possible for speaking was a self-justifying goal. As the bishops noted in 1798, including unawakened persons could "cramp, if not entirely destroy . . . liberty of speech" in love feasts.[43] A particular concern was preserving the liberty of women members since some non-Methodists opposed women speaking in the church.[44]

The freedom to testify to Christian experience openly—and the concomitant Methodist understanding that God's presence was experienced anew in these testimonies—was closely tied to a more explicitly theological reason for restricting access to love feasts. Simply put, early Methodists considered that God was uniquely present and revealed in their midst when they gathered as God's distinct people. Mixture with unawakened outsiders voided the condition by which God was present and revealed. Methodists restricted admission to their worship because there they experienced the glorious presence of God.

The strongest statement of this was in the bishops' commentary in the 1798 *Discipline*. Explaining limited access to the love feast and to meetings of the society itself, the bishops noted:

---

42. William Jessop, Journal. Ms. United Methodist Church Archives-GCAH, Madison, NJ, 1788, 4 July 1790; Seth Crowell, *The Journal of Seth Crowell; containing an Account of His Travels as a Methodist Preacher for Twelve Years* (New York: J. C. Totten, 1813), 96; Finley, *Autobiography*, 280.

43. *Discipline*/1798, 73. See also Colbert journal 1:143.

44. See quote from the 1838 *Christian Advocate and Journal* in Richard O. Johnson, "The Development of the Love Feast in Early American Methodism," *Methodist History* 19.2 (January 1981): 75.

It is manifestly our duty to fence in our society, and to preserve it from intruders; otherwise we should soon become a desolate waste. God would write *Ichabod* upon us, and the glory would be departed from Israel.[45]

Two items are particularly interesting in the bishops' statement. The first is the reference to fencing the "society" and not just fencing "the table" or some other liturgical act or place. This reference implies that the bishops considered the preeminent place of God's revealed presence was in the fellowship and, second, in the liturgical acts of this fellowship. The other interesting item is the scriptural explanation given for this view. The biblical allusion is to a passage in 1 Samuel 4, the same chapter used to explain the "shout of the king in the camp" phenomenon. This common scriptural basis shows that early Methodists had fused the traditional aspects of their polity with their distinctly American form of Methodist spirituality, the shout tradition. Moreover, it demonstrates the role of polity in their understanding of ecclesiology: their discipline existed not just as provisions for existing as an institution, but so they could be a distinct people for God in whom God was uniquely manifest. By following the polity, Methodism showed itself as an exceptional fellowship in which God dwelled. The symbol of and the occasion for this manifestation was often a love feast.

The bishops' view was by no means exceptional for early Methodists. As in describing eruptions of the "work of God" in public venues, their language strained to capture the experience of God's presence in their private worship. Some resorted to staggering theological claims. Concerning one love feast, a participant noted: "it seemed as if the Lord Jesus had come down & visibly stood in the midst of us. The glory of God filled the house."[46] At another love feast, held "in token of the unity and fellowship of such as partook thereof," the participant noted that "the power of God [was] manifest in the assembly."[47] Others resorted to biblical allusions. For example, the presence of God among the people made one love feast a "Bethel" at which "the Lord made the place of his feet glorious."[48]

---

45. *Discipline*/1798, 154.
46. Jessop journal, 24 February 1788.
47. Emory, *Life*, 31.
48. Rankin diary, 181. The intensity of these descriptions contradicts the subtle implication found in some secondary material, namely that early Methodists appreciated love feasts only as some kind of poor substitute for the Lord's Supper—e.g., John Bishop, *Methodist Worship in Relation to Free Church Worship* (New York: Scholars Studies Press, Inc., 1975), 89. See also Robert Milton Winter, "American Churches and the Holy Communion: A Comparative Study in Sacramental Theology, Practice, and Piety in the Episcopal, Presbyterian, Methodist, and German Reformed Traditions, 1607–1875" (Ph.D. diss., Union Theological Seminary, 1988), 579.

Methodists also used a variety of terms to characterize those allowed into the love feast as distinguished from those excluded. Those allowed in were, as one hymn put it, "faithful followers of the Lamb" who were "the same in heart and mind / And think and speak the same." When at love feasts "all in love together dwell / The comfort is unspeakable."[49] Methodists gathered at love feasts were also the "good" in contrast to the "bad" or the "wicked."[50] These sorts of terms provided additional justification for restricting attendance at the ritual. One presiding elder, trying to answer why privacy was the best mode for love feasts, argued that the Scriptures told them not "to give that which was holy to dogs, or to cast our pearls before swine."[51] If "thoughtless and profane" people were mingled with the "devout," another itinerant argued, a love feast would be that in name only.[52] How much better, the Methodists thought, to have congruence between the symbols, the symbols used, and the loving fellowship symbolized. In other words, the bread and water were symbols of the society assembled and so should be used by the society—and not outsiders.

Lord's Supper Basics

Administration of the Lord's Supper in the setting of quarterly meetings can be traced to the earliest times of Methodism in America, even before creation of The Methodist Episcopal Church in 1784. From nearly the beginning of widespread Methodist activity in America, quarterly meetings were natural settings for the sacrament and, when possible, American Methodists celebrated the Supper at these gatherings.

Francis Asbury noted that as early as 1772 Methodists were clamoring for their preachers to administer the sacrament and that Richard Boardman, one of the first two (unordained) itinerants sent by John Wesley, succumbed to the pressure, serving the sacrament at a fall 1772 quarterly meeting in Maryland.[53] Administration of the

---

49. Thomas Haskins, "The Journal of Thomas Haskins (1760–1816)." Ts. Transcribed by Louise Stahl (Terre Haute, IN: Indiana State University), 22.

50. Lakin journal, 7 April 1811; Sneath, "Diary," 66.

51. Finley, *Autobiography*, 287. His argument alludes to Matthew 7:6.

52. Charles Giles, *Pioneer: A Narrative of the Nativity, Experience, Travels, and Ministerial Labours of Rev. Charles Giles* (New York: G. Lane & P. P. Sandford, 1844), 176.

53. *JLFA* 1:60.

sacrament in this setting throughout the 1770s appears sporadic, however, since most preachers remained faithful to the "old plan," that is, a refusal to administer the sacrament without ordination and a consequent reliance upon Church of England priests. There are accounts of a few sympathetic Church of England priests occasionally attending quarterly meetings during this period, apparently to administer the Lord's Supper.

If Methodist preachers did choose to administer the sacrament prior to 1784, quarterly meetings were a common setting. The most significant occurrence came after the 1779 Annual Conference of preachers from Virginia and North Carolina. Deciding to wait no longer, they designated themselves a presbytery and ordained some of their own number. This minor schism lasted only a year because, in response to a request of their northern counterparts in 1780, those ordained agreed to postpone sacramental administration. But during this year quarterly meetings were frequently the time when both the Lord's Supper and baptism were administered.[54]

With creation of The Methodist Episcopal Church in December 1784, in which Wesley provided the American preachers with an ordination that they considered fully legitimate, the connection between quarterly meetings and sacramental administration became so strong that the meetings came to be the most regular settings for the Lord's Supper. The connection started as soon as the newly appointed Superintendent Thomas Coke arrived from England in November 1784. Coke's first two weekends were spent traveling to quarterly meetings, where he administered the Lord's Supper and multiple baptisms.[55] When the preachers met a month later in a specially called conference in Baltimore and some were ordained as elders, the intent appears to have been for them to exercise their new sacramental authority in the context of quarterly meetings.[56] The regularity of administering the sacrament at quarterly meetings was reflected in Bishop Coke's description of American practices to a British audience, which noted that American quarterly meetings after 1784 had not only a love feast but also the Lord's Supper.[57]

54. Reed diary, 72-73, 86-87, 94.

55. Haskins journal, 42.

56. Thomas Ware, "The Christmas Conference of 1784." *MQR* 14 (1832): 98. Compare Wallace Guy Smeltzer, *Methodism on the Headwaters of the Ohio: The History of the Pittsburgh Conference of the Methodist Church* (Nashville: Parthenon Press, 1951), 55.

57. Coke, *Extracts of the journals of the Rev. Dr. Coke's five visits to America* (London: G. Paramore, 1793), 35.

American Methodists were exuberant about how they saw God immediately blessing administration of sacraments at quarterly meetings. Meetings in the first months after Coke's arrival were often exciting times when pent-up Methodist desire for sacraments was finally fulfilled with no qualms. The honeymoon had begun. Multitudes came to the meetings. New members joined daily. As one itinerant noted, the sacraments at quarterly meetings were "singularly owned of God." He noted too that no one could have enjoyed himself more than Coke, who delighted when thousands pressed around him for the sacraments.[58] For some preachers in England this American sacramental ecstasy of joy was a sure sign that separation from the Church of England was God's will.[59] Americans would not have disagreed.

The blessings experienced in celebrating the sacrament at quarterly meetings through the 1780s helped to establish it as a regular part of the weekend's liturgical activities. But, like other things in the fluid nature of Methodist worship, its inclusion was never absolute. Despite the regularity with which it was included, for various reasons—most of which are obscure—the Lord's Supper was sometimes not administered at quarterly meetings. The love feast retained a greater permanence than the sacrament.

Differing Settings for the Lord's Supper

With the solidification of its inclusion on the roster of activities at a quarterly meeting came the question of where to place the Lord's Supper within the weekend's events. Three typical arrangements emerged: attaching it to a love feast, administering it in the manner of a love feast itself, or following a preaching service.[60] Although the first arrangement was most standard, all were common. No foolproof criteria for predicting which arrangement would be used can be determined. While certain regions and individuals tended toward specific set arrangements, tendencies were exactly that, nothing more. Moreover, the Lord's Supper could occur on either Saturday or

---

58. Ware, *Sketches*, 115.

59. John C. Bowmer and John A. Vickers, ed., *The Letters of John Pawson (Methodist Itinerant, 1762–1806)* (World Methodist Historical Society, 1994), 1:53.

60. Like love feasts, administration of the Lord's Supper at quarterly meetings could also be racially segregated; see James Meacham, Journal. Ms. Special Collections Library, Duke University Library, Durham, NC, 15 July 1792.

Sunday, at any time of the day, although Sunday morning to early afternoon was apparently the most common time.

Attachment to the Sunday morning love feast was a very frequent place for the Lord's Supper in a quarterly meeting. In this case the Lord's Supper concluded the private worship on Sunday morning. One itinerant's journal description of a quarterly meeting can be replicated innumerable times: "Love feast began between 9 & 10 oClock which held till after 11 then the Sacrament of the Lords Supper was administerd—public preaching began after 12."[61]

A natural point of fusion for the two rites was a collection taken for the poor. Whenever the love feast or the sacrament are described independently, this collection is indicated as part of the regular order of each service. Nathan Bangs's description of typical early love feasts notes that they culminated with a collection immediately prior to a closing hymn, prayer, and benediction.[62] Meanwhile the eucharistic rite adopted by the American church in 1792 (an abbreviated form of the rite Wesley sent over in 1784) began with a collection. Structurally, it would have been a simple matter to fuse the sacrament's beginning point to one of the love feast's concluding acts.

Contemporary descriptions of the respective collections suggest that this fusion indeed took place. The *Discipline* officially designated the purpose of collections made at either love feasts or "sacramental occasions" as the same: "for the poor of our own society."[63] Local records reflect that the collections were indeed used for the poor, as well as to pay for certain immediate expenses like the actual supplies for the love feast and the sacrament. For example, the $8.12 gathered and recorded as a *love feast* collection at an 1807 quarterly meeting in Maryland was disbursed in two ways: $1.67 paid for the wine used in the sacrament and $6.45 to a woman whom the circuit helped on a regular basis.[64] This record implies that only one collection was made at a joint administration of the love feast and sacrament. Some other records reveal more clearly the fused nature of this one collection. The steward accounting for the collection made at a 1792 New Jersey love

---

61. Cooper journal, 10 February 1788.

62. N. Bangs, *History* 1:249.

63. *Discipline*/1787, 13. For background on this concern see Karen Westerfield Tucker, "Liturgical Expressions of Care for the Poor in the Wesleyan Tradition: A Case Study for the Ecumenical Church," *Worship* 69 (1995): 51-64.

64. Harford Circuit (MD) quarterly meeting conference records, 11 July 1807. Compare the accounting for 20 February 1785 in "Steward's Book for the New Mills Circuit (NJ)," 9. Frustratingly, there is no complete standardization of terms in these records, either between circuits or within the records for one circuit.

feast, for instance, simply entered one amount for a "Love feast & Communion Collection."[65]

Love feast/sacramental collections were distributed in a variety of ways. The money often went toward regular support of a few impoverished people. When the records name the recipients, women, who were likely to be widowed, are more prominent.[66] Perhaps Sally Callihan, a regular recipient of a portion of the Baltimore Circuit's quarterly meeting love feast/sacramental collection, was a widow.[67] Those receiving help were often Methodists themselves, as the *Discipline* recommended. Callihan was a Methodist as were Sisters Carnan and Williams, regular recipients of a portion of the quarterly meeting collection of another Maryland circuit.[68] The overall evidence, although irregular, suggests that the money was as likely to go to poor Methodists as to be given externally. Sometimes the money was used for specific charitable purposes. One circuit's records noted using one collection to pay a doctor's bill and another to buy a coffin.[69] Sometimes the collection did not go to the poor at all. One 1805 Ohio collection, after reimbursement for sacramental expenses, was used entirely to make up the quarterly salary and expenses of the itinerants.[70] In 1799, the Baltimore Circuit used its collections to help pay for an itinerant's horse in one instance and a stove for a meetinghouse in another.[71]

While the most typical arrangement was for the Lord's Supper to culminate the love feast, on some occasions the sacrament began Sunday morning activities. In this case the love feast culminated the sacrament. This arrangement can be illustrated by a 1793 quarterly meeting when the elder "opened the Love-feast by administering the

---

65. "Steward's Book for the New Mills Circuit (NJ)," 38. Compare page 34. The prevalence of these collections, under a variety of different names, in the different stewards' records contradicts the assertion by Johnson ("Development of Love Feast," 79) that love feast collections were rare.

66. "The Proceedings of the Quarterly Meeting 1789. Copied from the Original Stewards Book for Salem Circuit (NJ) 1789," 44-45.

67. See various entries starting 19-20 December 1795 in the Baltimore Circuit (MD) Steward's Book 1794–1815.

68. See the entries beginning 4 May 1805 in the Harford Circuit (MD) quarterly meeting conference records. "Sister" was the common way to designate a female Methodist.

69. "The Proceedings of the Quarterly Meeting 1789. Copied from the Original Stewards Book for Salem Circuit (NJ) 1789," 33, 35. In both cases the expenses seem related to assisting fellow Methodists.

70. Entry for 8-9 June 1805 in the Hockhocking Circuit (OH) Steward's Book. This is not a rare occurrence.

71. Entries for 22-23 June 1799 and 14-15 September 1799 in the Baltimore Circuit (MD) Steward's Book.

Lord's Supper," or by a 1789 meeting that started Sunday morning activities with the sacrament, after which the love feast began.[72] In this arrangement the Lord's Supper and the love feast would seem to retain their distinctive identities, unless, as is quite possible, the references to "love feast" in these situations refer only to a time of testimonials.

Particularly within the latter arrangement, it was only a short step from conjoined services to administering the Lord's Supper as a form of love feast—the third typical setting for the sacrament in a quarterly meeting. It is difficult to tell precisely how administration of the sacrament was changed in such a case. The easiest transformation involved substituting wine for water. In this case the Lord's Supper would have looked like a love feast: after the opening hymn, prayer, and perhaps initial statement by the presider, the bread and wine (instead of bread and water) were shared. The 1779 Fluvanna Conference minutes described a sacramental rite very much like this: the Lord's Supper was to consist of singing, prayer, exhortation, and then distribution of food.[73] The rite would have concluded with testimonies and the other final acts. A more minimal revision of the sacrament would be simply to add an extended time of testimonies, which were understood to be the essence of the love feast, after distributing the bread and wine. As one itinerant described such an occasion, on Sunday morning of a quarterly meeting the "sacrament was administered, & a number communicated, who afterwards spoke their experience."[74] This practice was very common and is widely attested.[75]

---

72. Colbert journal 1:143; Simpson, *Freeborn Garrettson*, 261.

73. 1779 ms. minutes in the Philip Gatch papers. These minutes are also reproduced in Jno. J. Tigert, *A Constitutional History of American Episcopal Methodism*, 2nd ed. (Nashville: Publishing House of the Methodist Episcopal Church, South, 1904), 106-7.

74. Nathaniel Mills, Journal. Ms. United Methodist Historical Society, Lovely Lane Museum, Baltimore, MD, 9 March 1806. Compare his entry for 3 November 1811: "We had the sacrament at 9, after which the friends spoke after the manner of Lovefeasts."

75. Norman journal, 23 April 1797; Colbert journal 2:79, 2:200-201, 3:55, 3:91, 4:75; Mann journal, 18 November 1805; Early journal, 6 January 1811, 25 October 1811; William Ormond journal. Papers. Special Collections Library, Duke University Library, Durham, NC, 29 August 1795; and *JLFA* 1:621, 695. The administration of the Lord's Supper at the 1791 Virginia Annual Conference climaxed with a severe prophetic rebuke given by Sister Whitehead, "a precious dear woman." Without any sense that it was unusual for a woman addressing those assembled for the worship of annual conference, the participant recorded her statement: she "begged the preachers to excuse her, she was weak and a poor woman, but she was awfully impressed with grief and that was almost more than she could bear up under. She said when she turned her eyes upon the young sisters and saw them catching after the modes of fashion of this world which passes away, backsliding from God and wounding his cause, she could scarcely bear up under her grief, and what was worse than all her poor dear young preachers, some of them would be following the fashions of the wicked world that ought to be examples of the flock. Numbers looking at them and justifying themselves by such and such preachers and something

The merger of the Lord's Supper and love feast into one rite, where the sacrament subsumed both the tone and elements of a love feast, is reflected in the use of an unusual term, "sacramental feast." Richard Whatcoat, a future bishop, wrote about such a rite in 1800: "the people spoke moderately at our sacramental feast."[76] Other itinerants' accounts use the same term: "the Sacramental feast was precious" and "The Sacramental feast began at 9 oclock it was a sweet time, during Love feast my Soul was deeply humiliated."[77] The last instance is particularly revealing—the term "love feast" is used to identify the testimonial time within a larger "sacramental feast."[78] The subtleness of this distinction allows for those occasional instances where "love feast" and "sacrament" are used synonymously: "Our lovefeast, or rather sacrament began at 9 oclock."[79]

The other typical setting for the Lord's Supper at a quarterly meeting was to attach it to a preaching service. Examples are numerous and were apparently not restricted to any one region or individual. Presumably, when the sacrament immediately followed a preaching service, the latter's conclusion was abbreviated so that it flowed smoothly into administration of the sacrament. The sacrament could begin with a collection since (as noted in chapter 2) "public" collections were a common event at quarterly meetings.

The intimacy of the connection between administration of the sacrament and the preaching service should not be stressed too strongly. Some examples of the manner in which the sacrament was administered suggest more autonomy for the sacramental rite. At one 1790 quarterly meeting the preaching service was followed by a fifteen-minute "intermission" before administration of the sacrament began.[80] On other occasions sacramental administration did immedi-

else added with. They would stand in the pulpit and explode the cursed practice of slavery, and then they themselves would marry a young woman who held slaves and keep them fast in bloody slavery. Members who have been professors of the religion of Jesus Christ for ten or twelve years would come to me and apparently be as happy as saints in Heaven, and follow them home and you will see their slaves in the field and kitchens cruelly oppressed, half starved, and nearly naked. O! my Lord, is this the religion of my adorable master Jesus? How can I keep grieving over these cruel oppressors who are in error? And I fear they will be slaves to the devil in Hell forever." See William K. Boyd, ed., "A Journal and Travel of James Meacham," *Annual Publication of Historical Papers of the Historical Society of Trinity College* 9 (1912); 10 (1914): 92-93.

76. Whatcoat journal, 27 April 1800.
77. Meacham journal, 9 October 1796 and 19 February 1797.
78. See Mills journal, 4 February 1816.
79. Ibid., 12 May 1811. See also 21 July 1811: it "continued to rain so that our love feast, or rather sacrament was small."
80. Jessop journal, 14 February 1790.

ately follow the preaching service, but only after the administration had been moved to another place. In one 1803 meeting, for instance, the presiding elder dropped his original plans for an outdoor administration after the preaching service, moving it back inside a Methodist's home after disruptive behavior by some of the preaching service participants.[81]

Lord's Supper Privacy

This presiding elder's ability to decide whether to administer the sacrament outdoors in a more public setting or indoors in a more private setting serves as a reminder that the Lord's Supper was understood most often as a restricted, private form of worship. The manner of restricting access for the sacrament was more fluid than for the love feast. The precise manner in which admission to the Lord's Supper was restricted in any particular quarterly meeting was directly tied to the setting in which it was administered.

When attached to a love feast, admission to communion was restricted by virtue of the privacy safeguards already in place for love feasts. The criteria and methods used to limit access were, then, the same as those employed at a love feast. In other words, admission to the love feast meant admission to the sacrament and vice versa. For example, at a 1788 New Jersey quarterly meeting, a minister from another church applied for admission to the Lord's Supper. "Having nothing against him & hoping of his sincerity," the Methodist granted him "liberty to enter love feast & take the Lord's Supper."[82]

When administered in connection with a preaching service, however, the restriction was not as tight. A different standard for admission was used. And, because noncommunicants were not excluded from the space, such a Lord's Supper had a higher degree of visibility to bystanders than did one within a love feast.

But whether administered in a public or private setting, early Methodism consistently maintained a sense that admission to actual communion should be limited. When the southern preachers formed a presbytery in 1779 and began to anticipate regular administration of the Lord's Supper, they defined who was eligible to commune as "those under our care and Discipline."[83] With the creation of The

---

81. Colbert journal 4:168. See also Simpson, *Freeborn Garrettson*, 284.
82. Cooper journal, 11 May 1788.
83. 1779 ms. minutes in the Philip Gatch papers (and Tigert, *Constitutional History*, 106-7).

Methodist Episcopal Church in 1784 the *Disciplines* continued this concern, although the polity tended to weaken the direct connection to Methodist membership implied in the 1779 requirement. The provision in the 1785 *Discipline* presumes that nonmembers will be communing with the Methodists and established as guidelines for admission: "Let no Person who is not a Member of the Society, be admitted to the Communion without a Sacrament-Ticket, which Ticket must be changed every Quarter."[84] In 1787 this provision for nonmembers was modified by adding a requirement for examination before communion and by changing the reference from "ticket" to "token."[85] But from 1785 on, the eligibility of members in good standing to commune is never questioned; their membership provided automatic qualification.[86]

While automatic, the connection between membership and eligibility to commune was not unconditional. This is best seen in polity guidelines for determining which nonmembers could be permitted to commune. The 1785 *Discipline* specifically disallowed from participating in the sacrament anyone who had been expelled or voluntarily withdrawn from the Methodist society for not complying with the rules concerning manumission of slaves. These persons were to be prevented from rejoining the Methodists or communing until they complied.[87] Although these passages were dropped in the following year's *Discipline*, a similar—albeit more general—provision was added in 1792: "No person shall be admitted to the Lord's Supper among us, who is guilty of any practice for which we would exclude a member of our society."[88] This passage is important not only for the

---

84. *Discipline*/1785, 17.

85. *Discipline*/1787, 29. Despite the fact that this passage remained unchanged in the *Disciplines* well into the nineteenth century, the exact nature of these sacramental tickets/tokens remains a mystery. The primary material for the period is virtually silent on their use and nature. Perhaps they were so commonplace that they never were mentioned. Perhaps the elders worked on a more ad hoc basis, as will be suggested by some material below, and did not strictly follow the disciplinary requirements in this respect. Perhaps the notes of admission granted for participation in one quarterly meeting's love feast would have enabled admission to the sacrament too, as suggested by changing "ticket" to "token."

86. Throughout this early period very little mention is made of immediate sacramental discipline for Methodists in order to be eligible for communion. John Bowmer's assessment of British practice ("A Converting Ordinance and the Open Table," *Proceedings of the Wesley Historical Society* 34 [1964]: 111-12), that the ongoing accountability of Methodist membership was a sort of continual sacramental discipline, seems likewise accurate for American Methodists. A hint is sometimes given in the accounts that Methodists participated in a Friday fast before Sunday communion; see Minton Thrift, *Memoir of the Rev. Jesse Lee. With Extracts from his Journals* (New York: Bangs & Mason, 1823), 207. Remember that the Friday before quarterly meetings was normally designated as a day of fasting.

87. *Discipline*/1785, 16.

88. *Discipline*/1792, 40.

cautiousness it reveals about which nonmembers should be allowed to commune—much greater cautiousness than found in modern Methodism—but also for the willingness it reflects to remove a current member's right to commune for sufficient cause. Indeed, from 1788 onward the one category of nonmember specifically identified by *Discipline* to be denied access to communion was any former member who had been tried and expelled from the society. That person lost not only the "privileges of society" but also admission to the sacrament.[89]

This double injunction was necessary because the criteria for admission to the love feast ("society") and the sacrament were not identical. Admission to the love feast was more closely tied to actual membership in a Methodist society, allowing very few exceptions. By contrast, membership was not required for admission to the sacrament, only a general sense of qualification for membership. And even this was stated in a negative manner that blunted its force: if one was somehow disqualified for membership, then admission should be denied. In practice, this gave those administering the sacrament great latitude in deciding whom to admit.

The accounts of the Lord's Supper in open, public settings give hints as to some of the unofficial standards used. On one occasion Bishop Coke granted permission to "any serious person of the congregation who desired it" to commune with the Methodists.[90] At another, Bishop Asbury preached that "true penitents and real believers" were proper communicants.[91] Other itinerants used similar criteria. At an 1823 quarterly meeting the invitation to commune was given "to the pious, & to all that were desirous."[92] And another time the elder administered the sacrament "in an open way & invited all Christians to come."[93]

Such latitude did not mean that elders placed no restriction on access, or that everyone in attendance communed. At a 1793 quarterly meeting the preacher specifically explained to the congregation

89. *Discipline*/1788, 41. Of course the necessity for such a provision implies that certain elders were considered too lax in who they admitted. Note the distinction in terms between "privileges of society" and "privileges of sacrament." In 1787, when a new section was inserted into the *Discipline* entitled "On the Privileges granted to serious Persons that are not of the Society," the polity discussed only admission to society meetings and love feasts. The implication is that the sacraments were not considered an inherent part of the "privileges of society" but were placed in a broader theological basis, as will be discussed below.

90. Coke, *Extracts,* 107.

91. *JLFA* 1:728.

92. Mills journal, 12 January 1823.

93. Ormond journal, 11 April 1802.

"who ought, and who ought not partake of the supper of the Lord" before it was administered.[94] This restrictive function could also be accomplished by sermons that sought to explain the Lord's Supper. Preached immediately prior to administration of the sacrament, such sermons could explore the question of who are proper subjects to receive the sacrament.[95]

The restriction could also be done on a more specific individual basis. At one quarterly meeting the presiding elder refused to admit a woman who had applied for admission because upon examination she was disclosed to hold views on the divinity of Christ that the elder considered heretical—namely, Arianism.[96] And sometimes the restriction was voluntary. Alfred Brunson, newly a Methodist, was surprised at his first Methodist communion to see his class leader not commune. When asked why, the class leader responded that he had an unresolved conflict with other Methodists and thus he could not receive without disobeying Christ's command.[97] With these various types of restriction, even when the sacrament was conducted outdoors in a very public setting with a very large congregation from a preaching service, the number of communicants could be a minority of those in attendance.

Accounts of the Lord's Supper in early American Methodism also indicate that some things were usually *not* required before admission. One was a previous conversion experience. Serious mourners were frequently welcomed, whether or not they were members. For example, a missionary elder in Nova Scotia caused a great stir when he admitted two unconverted female mourners. The shock of the townspeople was quieted only by seeing that "the Lord visited the souls of these two women whilst at the tables."[98] Recognizing the gracious activity of God during a sacrament even on the unconverted was commonplace in eighteenth-century Methodism, which traced its belief that the sacrament could be a "converting ordinance" back to Wesley himself.[99]

---

94. Colbert journal 1:150.

95. For an example, see the account of the 22 May 1814 quarterly meeting in the Early journal.

96. Giles, *Pioneer*, 240-42.

97. Alfred Brunson, *A Western Pioneer: or, Incidents of the Life and Times of Rev. Alfred Brunson, A.M., D.D., Embracing a Period of over Seventy Years* (Cincinnati: Hitchcock & Walden; New York: Carlton & Lanahan, 1872; reprint, New York: Arno Press, 1975), 1:58-59. Because Brunson had waited to follow his class leader forward to commune, he missed his opportunity too. At home that night Brunson, eagerly desiring to commune, conducted his own form of a sacrament using bread and water. Brunson justified his action by arguing "the *motive* justifies the act" and thus "I felt approved of God in so doing."

98. Simpson, *Freeborn Garrettson*, 130-31.

99. See the entries for 27-28 June 1740 in Wesley's *Journal* (*Works* 19:158-59) for an early use of

The accounts sometimes describe how a mourner's justification occurred at the very moment of communing. Bishop William McKendree once administered the sacrament to a mourner to whom "pardon was communicated" just as she tasted the wine.[100] Similarly, at a Delmarva peninsula quarterly meeting a mourner named Mary Broughten "was powerfully converted with the bread in her mouth" and fell to the ground. The itinerant assisting the administration by handling the wine began to leap joyfully and forgot to give her the wine. Broughten, after praising God for awhile, finally picked herself up off the ground and reminded the wine-handler that he had done but half his work.[101]

There is also evidence that baptism was not required in order to be admitted to communion. One New England presiding elder admitted two women although neither had joined the society or been baptized. When the presiding elder questioned why they had not been baptized, they said they preferred to be immersed but no good opportunity had arisen. The presiding elder immediately admitted them into the society as well as to the Lord's Supper at that quarterly meeting.[102]

Finally, membership in another church did not disqualify someone from communing with the Methodists. Examples of intercommunion—particularly by Presbyterians and particularly after the start of the Second Great Awakening—are numerous and are found in accounts of administration of the sacrament in a variety of settings, including quarterly meetings and Annual Conferences. The 1802 Kentucky Annual Conference, for example, had not only Presbyterians communing with Methodists but Presbyterian ministers assisting in the administration.[103] Less frequently, Baptists and

---

this concept. Wesley's understanding emerged in early disputes with Moravians about the role of the means of grace. The argument of some scholars that the American Methodists no longer saw the sacrament as a converting ordinance because they restricted access is not persuasive since they typically overlook the fact that a conversion experience was never the threshold for membership (cf. Kenneth B. Bedell, *Worship in the Methodist Tradition* [Nashville: Tidings, 1976], 53). One could be a Methodist member in good standing and still only be a mourner. Thus, even if admission to the sacrament was restricted to members only, there would have been opportunity for some to have experienced grace in it as a converting ordinance. Note that Wesley occasionally listed certain qualities necessary to receive the grace of the sacraments: "a mind well-instructed, a sound belief, and heart well inclined for that purpose" ("A Roman Catechism," Q. 54, *Works* [Jackson] 10:113) or "previous instruction, true repentance, and a degree of faith" ("Popery Calmly Considered," §IV.2, *Works* [Jackson] 10:149).

100. Finley, *Autobiography*, 401-2.
101. Colbert journal 4:14-15.
102. Newell, *Life and Observations*, 69-70.
103. H. Smith, *Recollections*, 85. Smith noted that "this is the ground which Protestant churches must meet, if they would evangelize the world." See also James Jenkins, *Experience, Labours, and Sufferings of Rev. James Jenkins, of the South Carolina Conference* (n.p.: printed for the author), 1842, 192.

Episcopalians also communed. The fairly frequent practice of inter-communion, particularly with Presbyterians, and the presence of Presbyterian proselytes to the Methodists probably explains the constant inclusion of a provision in the *Disciplines* to allow communion either by sitting or standing in addition to the traditional Methodist practice of kneeling.

To some outside observers, the differing standards of restriction for the love feast and the Lord's Supper appeared to be backward. Thus Baptists who practiced closed communion and were criticized by Methodists for the practice retaliated by arguing that the intense restriction normally applied to the love feast was just as exclusive and, when compared to the greater openness in a Methodist sacrament, was theologically nonsensical.[104]

One Methodist reply was to distinguish between the love feast and the sacrament as different types of means of grace. The love feast was classified as a prudential means of grace—one specifically given to Methodists and thus essential for Methodist nurture—whereas the sacrament was an instituted means of grace—one commanded of all Christians.[105] This distinction shows an important aspect of early Methodist doctrines of grace and the church. Extremely confident that God indeed worked graciously in their midst and had gathered them together as a distinctive people, Methodists nonetheless refused to deny the same status to other churches. The love feast showed the fullness of grace in Methodist fellowship; intercommunion could demonstrate that grace was not limited to the boundaries of Methodism.

Notwithstanding the relative open admission to communion when administered in a public setting like a preaching service, there were always some—sometimes a sizable majority—who did not commune. As in the case of love feasts, two groups were created: those who participated and those who watched and listened to the activities. With public communions this division could be markedly visible. Consider a quarterly meeting where the sacramental table stood in the green outside a barn where preaching was held. At the time of administration the congregation was divided into two groups: those who com-

---

104. Johnson, "Development of the Love Feast," 77-78.

105. Ibid. See also *Discipline*/1798, 120 where the bishops' commentary uses this distinction in connection with justifying sacramental privacy: caution is required in admitting nonmembers since, if they are unfit for prudential means, it would be inappropriate for them to partake of instituted means. Compare James B. Finley, *Sketches of Western Methodism: Biographical, Historical, and Miscellaneous*, ed. W. P. Strickland (Cincinnati: Methodist Book Concern, 1854), 81.

muned and the "spectators" who formed a ring around them.[106] This dynamic—spectators observing the gracious activity of God in the sacrament—occurred in many other Methodist sacramental administrations. One early itinerant described such a scene:

> The disciples of Jesus came forward with boldness and owned their divine Teacher in this holy ordinance, whilst hundreds of spectators were looking on with amazement to see the mighty display of God's power, for many were overwhelmed with the loving presence of God during this season of commemorating one of the greatest events ever exhibited to human view.[107]

In such a case the spectators were privy to a double manifestation of God's grace. They saw not only the symbols of the commemoration of Christ's death—the bread and wine—but also a fellowship that was the visible representation of the present beneficiaries of this act of love.

The spectators' ability to discern more acutely what they were seeing was assisted by extemporaneous speaking. Exhortation was sometimes offered during the administration. Even a short exclamation could trigger an experience of grace as at one quarterly meeting where the brief remark by the preacher distributing the bread, "O that we could see Jesus Christ set forth before us crucified and slain," brought a spectator in the gallery into mourning.[108] Less frequent but equally as moving were those times when some would testify to their experience of grace after the sacrament. At an 1804 Delmarva quarterly meeting, for instance, "some bore (before a gasing multitude) a feeling testimony of their sins being forgivn by Faith in Christ, and love of God shed abroad in their hearts by the holy Ghost."[109] For receptive spectators such testimonies made their social peers specific, visible representations of the grace Methodists said God shared in the sacrament.

Lord's Supper Administration

When attention turns to the actual administration of the sacrament it is clear that early Methodists preferred a short, unencumbered rite

---

106. Newell, *Life and Observations*, 135. An invitation was given to mourners after the sacrament, during which many "eagerly rushed forward."
107. N. Bangs journal, 5 October 1805. See also Finley, *Autobiography*, 304.
108. David Kilburn, Journal. Ms. United Methodist Church Archives-GCAH, Madison, NJ, 13.
109. Boehm journal, 17 June 1804.

with opportunity for extemporaneity. When the southern presbytery was formed in 1779, its minutes describe the ritual that should be used. In terms reminiscent of a love feast, the prescribed ceremony involved simply "singing praying & exhortation" after which "the preacher delivers the bread, Saying the body &c according to the Church Order."[110] The brevity of this rite contrasts sharply with the eucharistic liturgy that John Wesley sent over with Coke in 1784. Anticipating the needs of Americans once they had formally separated from the Church of England, Wesley revised the 1662 *Book of Common Prayer*, titling the revision *The Sunday Service of the Methodists in North America*. American Methodists waited eight years—conveniently one year after he died—to revise Wesley's rite in 1792.[111] Two aspects of this revision are particularly striking: the rite was sharply abbreviated in that everything prior to the offering was discarded except for one prayer, and a new concluding rubric made only the prayer of consecration absolutely necessary "if the elder be straitened for time." The American preference for brevity was clear in this revision.

Although no further official revisions to the eucharistic rite were undertaken in The Methodist Episcopal Church until the mid–nineteenth century, all other indications reveal the same tendency toward abbreviating the rite. One example was a rite for the Lord's Supper prepared in 1801 by a disgruntled group who had left the St. George's society in Philadelphia. Writing a new constitution for themselves, they included most of the texts for the rites of The Methodist Episcopal Church. Only the eucharistic rite underwent significant revision, with the splinter group further abbreviating the rite.[112] Of the eight items in the 1792 rite prior to the prayer of consecration, only three were retained. Of the four items after the act of commu-

---

110. 1779 ms. minutes in the Philip Gatch papers (and Tigert, *Constitutional History*, 106-7). Note, likewise, there the instructions for how to baptize: "short & extempore." What particular document was meant by "Church Order" is hard to tell since the allusion to the formula for delivery of the bread is exceedingly brief. Perhaps the Church of England's *Book of Common Prayer* was in view since, at this time in Virginia, many of the preachers would have had an Anglican background and were familiar with the *Book of Common Prayer*. See the statement by one of the preachers, Philip Gatch (in ms. autobiography), that he knew much of it by heart. However, given the adoption of a presbyterian polity at this conference, perhaps some Presbyterian document is being referred to.

111. The easiest way to compare the 1792 revisions to the rites in the *Sunday Service* is the chart in Nolan B. Harmon, *The Rites and Ritual of Episcopal Methodism* (Nashville: Publishing House of the Methodist Episcopal Church, South, 1926).

112. "[Constitution for the] United Societies 1801." Ms. 18 August 1801, in Francis Tees's "Book of Antiquities," St. George's United Methodist Church, Philadelphia, PA.

nion, only two were retained. Revision of the eucharistic rite by the schismatic Methodist Protestant Church in the late-1820s shows a similar marked tendency toward abbreviation.[113]

In practice, American Methodists needed to look no farther than John Wesley himself for an example of an authority who abbreviated the communion service. Wesley openly admitted that he frequently abbreviated the administration of the Lord's Supper. When someone brought a charge that he had left out the confession from the communion rite, Wesley replied simply "Yes, and many times since. When I am straightened for time, . . . I begin the Communion-service at, 'We do not presume to come to this thy table'."[114]

American Methodists frequently followed Wesley's example in abbreviating this service. Many communion celebrations likely included little more than an extemporaneous prayer of consecration. The possibility for extemporizing in prayer during the Lord's Supper was one of the most significant additions John Wesley made to the rite from the *Book of Common Prayer*, although his rite provides for such prayer only after the Gloria and prior to the final blessing.[115] Given the predilection American Methodists had for extemporaneity, the higher esteem in which extemporaneous prayer was held, and the limited time available for administration in some circumstances, some elders probably prayed extemporaneously almost every time they administered the sacrament. The practice was common enough to cause one Methodist to note in 1807 that Methodism's ritual texts, including the one for the Lord's Supper, were "increasingly disused" and "generally omitted."[116] Particularly in a quarterly meeting situation where the sacrament was appended to the end of a love feast, the congregation had already been worshiping for several hours and

113. This revised rite can be found in The Methodist Protestant Church's *Constitution and Discipline of the Methodist Protestant Church* (Baltimore: Book Committee of the Methodist Protestant Church by John J. Harrood, 1831), 75-82.

114. Wesley, "Some Remarks on Mr. Hill's 'Review of All the Doctrines Taught by Mr. John Wesley'," §30, *Works* (Jackson) 10:411.

115. A noteworthy example of a presiding elder offering an extemporaneous closing prayer was the situation noted above in which a woman accused of Arianism was turned away from the table. As everyone knelt while the elder began the closing prayer, "the before-mentioned Arian woman came into remembrance, and I prayed for her, personally, that she might be delivered from error, and be brought into the truth; that she might behold the glorious character of her Redeemer, who is *'the true God—the mighty God—the Lord from heaven—the Creator of all things.'* " At that moment the "work of God" erupted and the communicants all began to pray aloud, too. The "work" continued for an hour. See Giles, *Pioneer*, 240-42.

116. George Bourne, *The Life of the Rev. John Wesley, A.M., with Memoirs of the Wesley Family. To which are subjoined, Dr. whitehead's Funeral Sermon: and a Comprehensive History of American Methodism* (Baltimore: George Dubbin and Murphy, 1807), 340, 344.

public preaching of some duration would be expected to follow. In addition, the presiding elder's heart might be deeply moved by the testimonies and so would allow them to continue at length. In this situation, limiting administration of the rite to a short, extemporaneous consecratory prayer was not seen as a "reduction" but as a very suitable expression of their experience of God.

This sort of extemporaneity was surely what eventually led to grumbling about a lack of uniform practice, beginning around the end of the first quarter of the nineteenth century. A committee at the 1824 General Conference complained in its report that printed texts for the rites were used by some, "mutilated" by others, and wholly neglected by still another group.[117] Not surprisingly, that year the *Discipline* began to mandate invariable use of the printed ritual text, such mandates being, as some have said, "probably good evidence that it was not" used.[118] Individual leaders also encouraged preachers to use the printed texts, the implication being that doing so was novel. One elderly preacher noted disparagingly in 1826 that some preachers conducted the Lord's Supper, baptisms, and weddings extemporaneously.[119] In all probability, what had changed by this time was not extemporaneous practice in sacramental administrations but the perception of it. With greater social acceptance, increased levels of ministerial education, and clearer self-recognition of being a church rather than a group of societies, some Methodists were becoming more concerned about proper use of prescribed textual forms.

Another striking aspect of the Lord's Supper in quarterly meetings was a form of "concelebration." After the monetary collection and before the presiding elder began praying, all the preachers—itinerant and local, ordained and unordained—would gather in the chancel around the table. The first rubric in the Methodist Protestant rite highlighted this act of assembly by noting that "all the ministers and preachers present, shall be invited to assemble within the communion rail."[120] Participation by the preachers was apparently not optional. Consider Robert Boyd, who received a local preacher's license at an 1814 quarterly meeting when he did not really want one. He attended the Lord's Supper on the last day of the meeting, taking his regular

---

117. *JGC/1824*, 1:298. A good example of what an extemporaneous consecratory prayer might have been like is the one printed in the 1831 *Discipline* of The Methodist Protestant Church.

118. *Discipline/1824*, 72; James F. White, *Protestant Worship: Traditions in Transition* (Louisville: Westminster/John Knox, 1989), 159.

119. Simpson, *Freeborn Garrettson*, 395-96.

120. *Constitution and Discipline of the Methodist Protestant Church* (1831), 75.

spot among the people. But the administration was stopped so that two preachers could escort Boyd to his proper place with the other preachers.[121] At large meetings, like quarterly meetings and Annual Conferences, the chancel could become quite crowded. At one 1791 Annual Conference, fifty preachers crowded around the table.[122] If ministers from other denominations were present, they too could help administer the sacrament and, presumably, gather with the preachers inside the railing.

Methodist Spirituality in the Lord's Supper

Early American Methodists were frequently staggered by the graciousness of God they experienced in the sacrament and by the overwhelming sense of God's presence. As one itinerant named the Lord's Supper, it was "that awful, solemn, heavenly institution."[123] Some of the most melting sacraments were those at quarterly meetings. This was true for William Colbert, first an itinerant circuit preacher and then a presiding elder in the 1790s and 1800s. Amazing demonstrations of God's power and presence in the Lord's Supper were regularly part of his descriptions of the sacrament for the period. Reflecting thankfully on the experiences, Colbert used a constant refrain in regard to the sacrament: "It was an awful time."[124] While traveling the Albany (New York) District as its presiding elder in the early 1800s Colbert summarized his perception: "The times of administering the Lords supper, and the Love feast I have found in this Country times of great power."

Colbert's opinions were by no means unique. On some occasions Methodists' desire to commune was so great that the ministers had to ask them not to crowd so around the railing but to be patient and wait for their turn. A missed opportunity to commune caused a great sense of loss and remorse. When Benjamin Lakin's business forced him to leave the 1809 Annual Conference in Cincinnati early and miss administration of the sacrament, he reproved himself that he "should so lightly esteem the ordinance of the Lord."[125] After one quarterly

---

121. Robert Boyd, *Personal Memoirs: Together With a Discussion upon the Hardships and Sufferings of Itinerant Life; and also a Discourse upon the Pastoral Relation* (Cincinnati: Methodist Book Concern, 1868), 56-57.

122. W. Boyd, "Journal and Travel of James Meacham" (1914): 92.

123. Emory, *Life*, 30.

124. Colbert journal 2:189, 3:40-41.

125. William Warren Sweet, *Religion on the American Frontier 1783–1840*, vol. 4, *The Methodists* (Chicago: University of Chicago Press, 1946), 4:234.

meeting a woman who missed an opportunity to commune wept until she could no longer speak.[126]

The more articulate Methodists expressed their eucharistic piety in intense terms. Methodist preacher Richard Allen, a former slave and future bishop, once demonstrated his awe and expectation at the sacrament in a sort of private creed entitled "Acts of Faith":

> I believe, that Thou hast instituted and ordained holy mysteries, as pledges of Thy love, and for a continual commemoration of Thy death; that Thou hast not only given Thyself to die for me, but to be my spiritual food and sustenance in that holy sacrament to my great and endless comfort. O may I frequently approach Thy altar with humility and devotion, and work in me all those holy and heavenly affections, which become the remembrance of a crucified Saviour.[127]

The deep appreciation early Methodists brought to the sacrament was part of a broader phenomenon of evangelical Protestantism in the late–eighteenth century.[128] In this period an evangelical experience led *to* greater desire for the sacrament, not away from it. The evangelical experience itself often had a sacramental tone. Consider Benjamin Abbott's conversion in the early 1770s, which took place before he was introduced to Methodism. Dreaming of spiritual realities one night, Abbott awoke and

> saw, by faith, the Lord Jesus Christ standing by me, with his arms extended wide, saying to me, "I died for you." I then looked up, and by faith I saw the Ancient of Days, and he said to me, "I freely forgive thee for what Christ has done." At this I burst into a flood of tears, and with joy in my heart, cried and praised God, and said, O! that there were a minister to give me the Lord's Supper! Then by faith I saw the Lord Jesus come to me as with a cup in his hand, and he gave it to me, and I took it and drank thereof: it was like unto honey for sweetness.[129]

---

126. Marjorie Moran Holmes, "The Life and Diary of the Reverend John Jeremiah Jacob (1757–1839)" (master's thesis, Duke University, 1941), 103-4.

127. Richard Allen, *The Life Experience and Gospel Labors of the Rt. Rev. Richard Allen* (New York: Abingdon, 1960), 42-43. Allen, a Philadelphia Methodist, was founding bishop of the African Methodist Episcopal Church. His statement is about as close to a formal definition of eucharistic theology as can be found among American Methodists for the period.

128. The centrality of the Lord's Supper in early British Methodism has been noted in J. Ernest Rattenbury, *The Eucharistic Hymns of John and Charles Wesley,* American ed. (Cleveland: OSL Publications, 1990), 1-5; and John C. Bowmer, *The Sacrament of the Lord's Supper in Early Methodism* (Westminster: Dacre Press, 1951), 187-205.

129. Ffirth, *Benjamin Abbott,* 18. Compare the experience in Catherine Livingston Garrettson, "Autobiography," 4.

Some were fortunate enough not to have to rely upon a visionary communion but were able to find a sympathetic human minister. One such minister was Devereux Jarratt, an Anglican priest in southern Virginia, who noted that one of the fruits of his evangelical preaching was greater crowds. When he began his ministry Jarratt could only count on a "few of the more aged" communing. By 1773 he was exulting in sacramental administrations with up to a thousand communicants.[130] Organized Methodist activity began in the region about this same time; many of its first members were drawn from these evangelicals, especially those with a sacramental bent.

This is the setting in which popular clamoring for the sacraments from the hands of Methodist preachers emerged, a clamoring finally satisfied only with the creation of The Methodist Episcopal Church in 1784. In the meantime, the temptation of the preachers to succumb to the desire of the people was strong. In 1777 one itinerant estimated that he could add one hundred members in his Virginia circuit in six months if he was willing to administer the Lord's Supper. The people told him that they were unwilling to receive it from the hands of Church of England priests since many were engaged in what the evangelicals considered immoral activity:

> In Albermarle the M [Minister] loves strong drink. In Louisv. the M Fights, Fiddles, & dances. In Hanover upper parish is a gamester, in ye lower they have none. In Caroline the M Games & incourages dancg in Hensico he is much the same in chart [character] & in Goughland they seldom have one.[131]

The people clamored for Methodist sacramental administration because they desired to be faithful to the command of Christ—a central aspect of Wesley's eucharistic spirituality—but their desire conflicted with their opportunities since they were reluctant to seek it from seemingly "ungodly" priests.[132]

---

130. Jarratt, *Life*, 102. Compare the ratio of communicants to total worshipers in the congregations served by the nonevangelical Anglican priest Charles Woodmason in South Carolina and North Carolina in the late 1760s; see Richard J. Hooker, ed., *The Carolina Backcountry on the Eve of the Revolution: The Journal and Other Writings of Charles Woodmason, Anglican Itinerant* (Chapel Hill: University of North Carolina Press, 1953), 26, 48. The proportion never exceeded 10 percent and in many cases, out of a congregation of several hundred, there were only one or two communicants.

131. Littlejohn journal, 48.

132. For a discussion about the distrust of Church of England priests, see the corresponding thoughts of the contemporary British itinerant John Pawson who argued that, because the Bible said that "the prayers of the wicked are an abomination to the Lord," God would not answer the prayers of an ungodly priest in a eucharistic rite; Bowmer and Vickers, ed., *Letters of John Pawson*, 1:115.

One recurring aspect in American Methodists' accounts of administration of the Lord's Supper is a strong affirmation of God's presence. Rather than saying early Methodists had a "high" *doctrine* of sacramental presence, it is more accurate to say they had a "high" *sense* of it because the categories that they normally used to describe divine presence were drawn from the intensely affective nature of their piety. As one itinerant described the experience of communion in a 1792 Methodist service, "the presents of the Lord was powerfully felt. Almost every heart was melted into love."[133] Or, as another described the sacrament at a 1789 quarterly meeting, "the Lord met with us in Maraculous Manner, a time of refreshment from his presence."[134] Such encounter with the presence of God in the sacrament could be understood as an experience that transposed the Methodist fellowship: "our good God was pleased to meet us at his table."[135] At times the intense sensibility of God's presence led Methodists to experience what they called "raptures" or "ecstacies" of joy in the sacrament.[136]

Early Methodists were not unaware of the seeming irony in these sorts of claims. Not generally well thought of—at least through the first part of the nineteenth century—and sometimes meeting in the most humble of circumstances, Methodists thought it consistent with their theology of Christ that God would amazingly meet with them in such circumstances. This sense comes through clearly in William Colbert's description of the first time he administered the sacrament (at a 1793 quarterly meeting in New York State):

> For the first time in my life [I] administered the Lords Supper, this meeting was held in the Widow Bidlacks barn. The LORD confines not himself to the heaven's or to Temples built with hands but it to be found by all the faithful followers of him who left a Celestial Pallace [to] be born in an earthly manger, in what ever place he is sought with cencerty.[137]

Although the circumstances and the people themselves might have been humble, Methodist affirmation that God was present in their sacrament was often connected with a notion of God's power. If God was present, then God was present in power. This linking was fre-

---

133. Cooper journal, 2 December 1792.
134. Meacham journal, 25 January 1789. See also Myles Greene, Journal. Ms. Special Collections Library, Duke University Library, Durham, NC, 4-5 July 1789.
135. Thrift, *Memoir of Jesse Lee*, 277.
136. See Cooper journal, 13 September 1789 and *Extracts of Letters*, 110.
137. Colbert journal 1:124-25. See a similar reflection in Lakin journal, 2 January 1803.

quently made in explicit terms. Writing after an 1802 Kentucky quarterly meeting, the presiding elder noted that "the Lord was powerfully present; the place was so awful, that the looks of the bystanders visibly proclaimed, 'God is here and we are afraid'."[138] Other accounts make God's presence synonymous with God's power by noting that during the sacrament, "the power came down."[139] Sometimes the presence of God in power and the resultant outbreak of the "work of God" forced an interruption in distribution of the bread and wine, as in the case of a 1789 quarterly meeting.[140] Methodists could also describe the powerful presence of God in the idiom of their shout tradition:

> I administered the Lord's Supper to near 100 precious souls, and the power of the Lord came down in a wonderful manner. . . . The flame soon increased, and spread from heart to heart, and glory be to God! The shout of a King was heard in our Camp.[141]

Early Methodists understood the power of God's presence to be purposeful: when God was present, God was present to save. Thus a Kentucky itinerant described a 1788 quarterly meeting in this manner: "the work of sanctification amongst the believers broke out at the Lord's Table; and the spirit of the Lord went through the assembly like a mighty rushing wind."[142] God's saving work was not confined just to those seeking sanctification. When "the Lord made bare his arm" at another Lord's Supper "sinners were convicted, backsliders were reclaimed, mourners were converted, and many brought to struggle for full redemption in the blood of Jesus."[143]

There was a clear connection between American eucharistic spirituality and that of British Methodism—particularly as found in John

---

138. *Extracts of Letters,* 41. Please note that while the perception of divine presence was consistently affirmed by Methodists, almost no consideration is given to theological details of how God is present.

139. Colbert journal 4:14-15. Compare the comments by Bishop Asbury in 1789 (*JLFA* 1:597): "At sacrament especially, the Lord's power and presence were great indeed."

140. Sweet, *Methodists* 4:83. The interruption lasted two hours. See also Reed diary, 72-73, where the power of God was acutely present in a 1779 quarterly meeting. The administrant on this occasion was Philip Gatch, one of the members of the presbytery organized by the 1779 southern annual conference.

141. Jessop journal, 14 February 1790.

142. [James Haw], "An extract of a letter from James Haw, elder of the Methodist Episcopal church in America, to Bishop Asbury: written from Cumberland near Kentucke, about the beginning of the year 1789," *AM* 13 (1790): 203.

143. *Extracts of Letters,* 53; see also page 48. "Struggling for full redemption" is another way of saying that someone desired the experience of sanctification.

and Charles Wesley. Generally, the writings and sacramental hymns of Americans show a definite continuity with the Wesleys' thought, even if the sophistication and breadth of their thought are not as evident.

Expressions of Wesleyan eucharistic spirituality were known and appreciated on this side of the Atlantic. In particular, the major source of Wesleyan eucharistic thought—the hymns on the Lord's Supper—was known and used in America. When the nascent church printed its own edition of Spence's *Pocket Hymn-Book* in 1786 it added a new sacramental section containing nine hymns from the Wesleys' *Hymns on the Lord's Supper*.[144] The table of contents in later editions of this hymnal listed an additional four hymns as "sacramental."[145]

Beyond this official resource, there is evidence that American Methodists were otherwise familiar with the entire corpus of Wesleyan eucharistic hymnody. The papers of Philip Gatch, an itinerant in the 1770s who was a member of the 1779 schismatic presbytery, contains a manuscript sermon outline book in which fifteen Wesleyan eucharistic hymns are written out by hand.[146] Some bear the hymns' numbers in a British edition of the eucharistic hymnal. Gatch made some attempt to edit the hymns for use; for example, verses from different hymns with the same meter were combined to form a new hymn. Significantly, Gatch's collection of Wesleyan hymns was not dependent upon the *Pocket Hymn-Book* since only one hymn is duplicated between the two collections.

144. See hymns #222-230 (pp. 217-23) in *Pocket Hymn-book* (1786). The first lines of these hymns, in order, are "In that sad memorable night," "Let all who truly bear," "Rock of Israel, cleft for me," "Author of our salvation, thee," "O thou, who this mysterious bread," "Jesu, at whose supreme command," "Who is this, that comes from far," "Jesu, dear redeeming Lord," and "Jesu, we thus obey." For the relationship between this hymnal and that of Robert Spence, a British Methodist, see Carlton R. Young, *Companion to the United Methodist Hymnal* (Nashville: Abingdon, 1993), 100-106. A collection of the entire 166 Wesleyan eucharistic hymns was apparently never published as a whole in America until recently. I am indebted to the research of a former student, Darren Elin, at this point.

145. See *Pocket Hymn-book* (1800). The first lines of these four hymns are "Behold the Saviour of mankind," "Arise, my soul, arise," "He dies, the friend of sinners dies," and "Alas! and did my Saviour bleed?" These four can be found in the 1786 edition but were not listed as "sacramental" there.

146. The first ten hymns appear to be in Gatch's own handwriting based on comparison with other materials in the papers. The last five are written in a different ink and, perhaps, in a different hand as well. The fifteen hymns incorporate material from the following hymns in *HLS*, in order of appearance: 86, 90, 67, 65, 72, 1, 7, 47, 81, 40, 6, 51, 55, and 151. After he ceased from itinerating, Gatch was a well-respected local preacher, first in Virginia and then in southwest Ohio. If Gatch appreciated these Wesleyan eucharistic hymns, he would have had ample opportunity to spread this appreciation to other Methodists such as Bishops Francis Asbury and William McKendree, both of whom were frequent visitors to his home.

Other key sources of Wesleyan thought were known and respected. The 1812 reprinting of a book first published in 1805 as *Extracts of Letters, Containing some Account of the Work of God since the Year 1800* ended with an extract from Wesley's sermon on constant communion as well as a eucharistic hymn of unknown origin.[147] The inclusion of the sacramental material in this reprint is significant in that the book purportedly focused on Methodist evangelistic activity, including the emergence of camp meetings. Contrary to the opinion in some secondary material that sees early Methodism's evangelistic concern, expressed by camp meetings, as negating a "true" Wesleyan sacramentality, American Methodists seemed not to have divorced the two.[148]

If there is any discontinuity between Wesley's eucharistic spirituality and that of early American Methodists, it is in hints that American thought did not possess the same breadth and complexity as Wesley's. For instance, it is striking that of the hymns in the two American collections of Wesleyan eucharistic hymns (the *Pocket Hymn-Book* and Gatch), only one comes from outside the first two divisions in which Wesley organized his hymns ("As it is a Memorial of the Sufferings and Death of Christ" and "As it is a Sign and a Means of Grace"). What this suggests might be lacking in the American Methodist understanding of the sacrament is the Wesleyan emphasis (in other divisions) on eucharistic sacrifice—both the sacrifice of Christ and that of the believing community.

But these are only hints that Americans did not have the same breadth of thought as Wesley; they should not be overemphasized. It is helpful to remember that Wesley's eucharistic thought was not entirely distinctive in its own right. It belonged to larger evangelical sensibilities in the eighteenth century. The American emphases, evidenced in the limited reproduction of Wesleyan hymns, were also tied into this larger evangelical world. It is not that the American Methodists disagreed with the broader eucharistic themes in Wesley. They simply chose to emphasize the two themes in Wesley—living

---

147. *Extracts of Letters*, 118-20.

148. Some scholars have argued that the emergence of camp meetings should be understood in connection with a strong sacramental piety. See Keith Watkins, "The Sacramental Character of the Camp Meeting," *Discipliana* 54.1 (spring 1994): 2-19; and Leigh E. Schmidt, *Holy Fairs: Scottish Communions and American Revivals in the Early Modern Period* (Princeton: Princeton University Press, 1989), 59-68.

The hymn, along with several others found in American primary material can be found in appendix F.

commemoration of Christ's redemptive suffering and the Lord's Supper as a "sign and a means of grace"—which were most broadly shared in the eighteenth-century evangelical world.[149]

Moreover, there was fluidity in Wesleyan and American Methodist spirituality about what exactly constituted a "sacramental" theme. Certain common themes in the Wesleyan hymns, like the visibility of the crucified Christ and his ongoing intercession in heaven, can be found in many hymns (Wesleyan and otherwise) that are not explicitly "sacramental." Themes that appear in explicitly eucharistic material in Wesley might appear elsewhere in American Methodism or, conversely, Wesleyan hymns like "Arise, My Soul, Arise" could be labeled as "sacramental" by American Methodists. Thus the initial hint that Americans lacked the breadth and complexity of Wesleyan eucharistic spirituality must not be overly stressed.

Many of the explicit Wesleyan themes about the Lord's Supper do occur in American eucharistic contexts. As Wesley began his discussion of the sacrament's meaning by defining it as a memorial of the sufferings and death of Christ, so did American thought. At the sacrament, American Methodists gathered "to celebrate the scenes of Gethsemane and Calvary" or "commemorate his dying love."[150]

More specifically, American Methodists frequently emphasized the visibility of the commemoration of Christ's passion, as did Wesley and other contemporaries.[151] Good examples are the hymns listed as "sacramental" in the index of the 1811 hymnal printed by permission of the Virginia Annual Conference.[152] These hymns repeatedly speak of viewing Christ's sufferings. Generally lacking explicit eucharistic

149. For placement of Wesley within the context of eighteenth-century Anglican evangelicals, see Christopher J. Cocksworth, *Evangelical Eucharistic Thought in the Church of England* (Cambridge: Cambridge University Press, 1993), 61-78. Some of Wesley's sacramental themes can be traced back to late-sixteenth- and early-seventeenth-century Anglicanism. See Cocksworth, 44: prior to Wesley "several writers introduced the motif of the eternal offering of Christ as a way of relating the past sacrifice of Calvary to the present moment." Compare the theological themes and similar spirituality among Presbyterians in Schmidt, *Holy Fairs*, 69-114.

150. Finley, *Autobiography*, 304, 401-2. Compare G. Smith, *Life and Letters of James Osgood Andrew*, 86; Norman journal, 23 April 1797; and especially Boehm journal, 25 September 1815. "Commemorating the death and passion" is Boehm's constantly repeated shorthand phrase for the Lord's Supper.

151. Karen B. Westerfield Tucker, " 'In Thankful Verse Proclaim': English Eucharistic Hymns of the Seventeenth and Eighteenth Centuries," *Studia Liturgica* 26.2 (1996): 247. Indeed, Schmidt in his discussion of contemporary Presbyterian sacramental theology labels one of his chapters "A Visible Gospel" (Schmidt, *Holy Fairs*, 69-114).

152. Stith Mead, *A General Selection of the Newest and Most Admired Hymns and Spiritual Songs, Now in Use. The second edition revised corrected and enlarged, and published by permission of the Virginia Conference held at Raleigh, (N.C.)* (Lynchburg: Jacob Haas, 1811). Mead was an itinerant preaching in this conference.

reference, they instead seem to be generally "sacramental" because they talk about viewing the redemptive sufferings of Christ. The first line of one, "When on the Cross, My Lord I See," expresses this sentiment succinctly.[153]

This sentiment was pervasive among American Methodists of the period. One South Carolina Methodist noted such an experience while the consecratory prayer was said: "I had such a view of my Saviour hanging on the cross, that my flinty heart was broken in pieces, and my soul filled with joy unspeakable."[154] Others noted that the entire body of communicants could have the same sort of experience: "how sweetly was the slaughtered lamb exhibited to them . . . in sacrament Jesus was set forth before their eyes."[155] This piety parallels the sentiments of the Wesleyan hymns: "Christ revives His sufferings here/Still exposes them to view" and "Crucified before our eyes/Faith discerns the dying God."[156] In similar manner, an American hymn writer could sing

> Thy body broken for our sin
> Upon the Cursed tree
> When we behold the bread and wine
> With eyes of faith we see

and

> Our souls by faith in Raptures gaze
> Upon the bleeding Lamb
> We round thy table sing thy praise
> Thy Dieing love proclaim.[157]

Moving to a second parallel, as Wesleyan spirituality emphasized the bread and wine as effectual means of grace, American Methodists

---

153. Ibid., 161.
154. Jenkins, *Experience*, 42.
155. Sneath, "Diary," 63, 71.
156. *HLS*, #3, #5.
157. From hymn 47, "Sacramental" and hymn 48, untitled, in Ebenezer Hills's ms. hymnal. Both of these hymns are provided in full in appendix F. Notice that 47 even used the same paradox frequently found in the Wesleyan hymns: God died in the crucifixion. This hymn also contained an image common in the Wesleyan hymns: a vision of Christ's eternal intercession on behalf of sinners made present in the sacrament. That contradicts the assertion by Paul S. Sanders ("The Sacraments in Early American Methodism," *Church History* 26.4 [December 1957]: 355-71. Reprinted in *Perspectives on Early American Methodism: Interpretive Essays*, ed. Russell E. Richey, Kenneth E. Rowe, and Jean Miller Schmidt [Nashville: Kingswood, 1993], 368) that there is no evidence of this aspect of eucharistic theology among American Methodists.

frequently spoke of experiencing the grace of God in their use. Although the Wesleyan hymns might be quite specific in this regard ("The sign transmits the signified/The grace is by the means applied"),[158] American sensibilities were not out of line with the Wesleyan appreciation. "I felt much melting of heart while partaking," one Methodist wrote after a quarterly meeting sacrament.[159] Echoing the words of the eucharistic rite, another noted "we surely partook of the Lord Jesus Christ by faith with thanksgiving."[160] Others emphasized that experiencing grace in using the means was God's doing: "during the administration the Lord was pleased to break the bread of life" or simply "God owned his ordinance."[161] Little concern was paid to the details of how use of the elements might be a true means of grace. It was better just to marvel at the mystery: at the Lord's Supper at one quarterly meeting "the Simbols were Swollowed up in the Substance" when the power of God came down.[162]

Finally, American Methodists understood an eschatological aspect in their communion, just as affirmed in the Wesleyan hymns. Americans would have agreed that the sacrament was a "pledge of heaven," as another collective category in *Hymns on the Lord's Supper* was titled. The sacramental banquet was an "antepast of heaven."[163] Thus they could sing at the Lord's Supper:

> But when we rise to worlds of love
> In shineing robes of white
> To praise our God who reigns above
> In uncreated light
>
> With holy Angels joyn the train
> And this the glorious song
> The Lamb is worthy that was slain
> To him all praise belong.[164]

158. *HLS*, #23.

159. Catherine Livingston Garrettson diary, 129.

160. Cooper journal, 20 April 1794. Compare Mills journal, 29 October 1787.

161. Glenn journal, 85-86 and Sneath, "Diary," 82. See also the ms. letter from Amos G. Thompson to Henry Waters, 26 August 1787: "The Lord was with us in a peculiar Manner at our Q meeting . . . at the sacrament the Lord caused his word to run with a softening Quickening influence."

162. Whatcoat journal, 27 July 1794.

163. Enoch Mudge, *The American Camp-Meeting Hymn Book. Containing a Variety of Original Hymns, Suitable to be Used at Camp-Meetings; and at Other Times in Private and Social Devotion* (Boston: Burdakin, 1818), 100.

164. Hymn 48, Ebenezer Hills's ms. hymnal. Contra Sanders ("Sacraments," 367) who states that there is no evidence of "any conscious relation between communion and eschatology" in American Methodism.

In this respect, the sacrament was presently a communion of saints both in earth and heaven:

> Saints on Earth, and Saints above
> Celebrate his dying Love,
> And let every ransom'd Soul,
> Sound His praise from Pole to Pole.[165]

Methodists noted the eschatological dimension of their sacramental experience. As one gloried during the sacrament: "we did set in heavenly places in Christ Jesus."[166]

Heavenly Fellowship

As suggested by this eucharistic hymn, the early Methodists experienced a strong eschatological dimension in their worship. Among a myriad of images that they used to explain what happened when they worship, the eschatological one recurs constantly. Whatever Methodists lacked in sophistication in their theology at this point they made up for in insistence. Perhaps more frequently than any other metaphor, Methodists referred to their worship as an experience of heaven. This assertion was made about all their worship, not just their particular rituals of fellowship, such as the love feast and Lord's Supper, although they perceived these as unique manifestations of paradise. This notion of heavenly manifestation was a dominant, recurring motif in their description of worship at quarterly meetings, and elsewhere. Indeed, early Methodist worship cannot be understood without recognizing the role the image of heaven played in their theology and piety.

It would be wrong to portray Methodist fascination with heaven as a merely individualistic hope, just as it would be wrong to portray

---

165. *Extracts of Letters*, 120. Note *HLS*, #53 and #55. Interestingly, some of these hymns (#162 and #166) contain passing references to heavenly shouting, inspired by the eschatological passages of 1 Thessalonians 4:16 and Revelation 19:6. Compare also hymn 709, "Come, Let Us Join our Friends Above," in *The United Methodist Hymnal* (Nashville: The United Methodist Publishing House, 1989), which uses technical Methodist societal terms ("friends") and a reference to shouting to discuss eschatological communion. More study is needed on the influence of the book of Revelation in early Methodist spirituality. Reading their journals, one is struck by the relative frequency at which texts from Revelation are chosen for preaching. In addition, each of the components of "a *shout* of the *King* in the *camp*," including a reference to the ark of God, can be found in the book of Revelation.

166. Thrift, *Memoir of Jesse Lee*, 207. Compare hymn 5 in appendix F, which speaks of drinking Christ's blood and eating Christ's flesh as heavenly activities themselves.

their participation in worship as an individualistic activity. Some secondary material has strayed in that direction, perhaps fooled by the intensely personal nature of reports of their experiences of justification and sanctification.[167] But there was a broader communal nature to both their understanding of heaven and their experience of salvation. Specifically, they had an experience of Christian fellowship that anticipated and shaped their understanding of eschatological fulfillment. Their fellowship, specifically in worship, revealed the power and promise of heaven; it was a participation in heaven in the here and now. Thus their experience of fellowship was the source of their power and desire to evangelize. Inclusion in their fellowship was the goal of the evangelization. Participation in their fellowship was a joy-filled experience of heaven itself. This thought, traceable to the Wesleys, was of critical importance to early American Methodism.[168]

Methodists described how heaven was manifested in their worship in several ways. One was to emphasize the coming of God in saving power as being the opening of heaven. They used phrases such as the opening of the "gate," "door," or "windows of heaven." As one itinerant described a 1792 quarterly meeting: "in time of preaching the Lord opened the windows of heaven and poured down blessing upon us. Sinners were struck as with hammer and fire."[169] This sort of reference was often made in speaking about the outbreak of the "work of God." It was used equally for public and private worship services.

Methodists could shift the emphasis in this initial image in order to focus better upon the human enjoyment of the gracious coming of God. To do this they used metaphors that emphasized worship's ability to refresh God's people. If God opened heaven to pour out blessings upon worshipers, then these worshipers could be said to have eaten of "heavenly manna" or to have been "refreshed with the Dew of Heaven." They could be said to have drunk of the "Sweet

---

167. See, for example, Sanders, "Sacraments," 360 and, especially, Paul S. Sanders, "An Appraisal of John Wesley's Sacramentalism in the Evolution of Early American Methodism" (Th.D. diss., Union Theological Seminary, 1954, Sanders), 250, where he argues that Methodists "held the dominant evangelical conviction, nourished in a pietistic and sectarian environment, that salvation is solely a matter of personal relationship between God and the individual."

168. See, for instance, the phrase "antedate the joys above/Celebrate the feast of love" in stanza 1 of Hymn 505 in Wesley's *Hymns* (*Works* 7:695). This hymn was included in *Pocket Hymn-book* (1786), 188.

169. Cooper journal, 19 February 1792. See also Rankin diary, 109, 119, 120-21; Colbert journal 1:124; and especially Giles, *Pioneer*, 86, speaking of a New York quarterly meeting: "the place seemed like the gate of heaven; though the building in which we worshipped was only a rough barn, it was honoured with the presence of God."

Refreshing Wine of Heaven's Eternal Love" or even to have fed on "Angels' food."[170]

Another way that Methodists explained the manifestation of heaven in their worship was to emphasize the revelatory quality of their communion together. Specifically, they saw the unity they felt when they loved each other as being a participation in the life of heaven itself. As one noted, "how like heaven it is to be where Christians love each other."[171] Therefore, whenever the loving bonds of their fellowship became obvious, Methodists would speak of their vivid—even if proleptic—enjoyment of the fellowship of heaven. On 9 August 1789 in Baltimore, Maryland, for example, Ezekiel Cooper spoke of quarterly meeting love feast participants approaching eternity, dwelling, as it were, in the "suburbs of heaven":

> Love-feast began at 8 o'clock, and a feast of love it was. The flame kindles through the church, as though every heart had brought the fire of love burning with them. . . . It was as a Penticost indeed, and like unto the very suburbs of heaven. . . . The love, joy and power which we felt exceeds what human language can fully express.[172]

It was their love—it was a "feast of love indeed"—which had brought them to the suburbs of heaven. The intensity of the loving fellowship demanded a point of reference beyond earth and normal human existence. Not surprisingly, most of these types of references were linked to private Methodist services: the Lord's Supper and especially the love feast.

There were several commonly recognized elements to eschatological revelation: love, peace, unity, and harmony. These words appear countless times in summaries of Methodist assemblies, which had gone well. Their use was almost formulaic—"All was peace and love"—and they could be applied to a variety of meetings, including General Conferences, Annual Conferences, the meeting of a society, a class meeting, and heaven itself.[173] Despite its subtlety, a definite

---

170. Respectively: Boehm journal, 24 May 1800; Whatcoat journal, 15 November 1795 and 22 February 1795; and [John Smith], "The Journal of John Smith, Methodist Circuit Rider, of his Work on the Greenbrier Circuit, (West) Virginia and Virginia." In *The Journal of the Greenbrier Historical Society* 1.4 (October 1966): 34, 38.

171. Sneath, "Diary," 92.

172. Cooper, "A brief account" (also in G. Phoebus, *Beams of Light*, 95). Compare Ezekiel Cooper, "An Account of the Work of God at Baltimore, in a Letter to *****," *AM* 13 (1790): 409-11.

173. See Boyd, "Journal and Travel of James Meacham," (1914): 100; Jessop journal, 23 September 1790; Simpson, *Freeborn Garrettson*, 297; Strickland, *Life of Jacob Gruber*, 19; Cooper journal, 27 May 1794. A General Conference is the national legislative meeting held every four years.

eschatological reference was intended. One presiding elder, describing a quarterly meeting love feast in his district in 1819, used them in this way:

> Our souls mingled together as water, in the bands of peace and charity. Old Brother Bostwick, an old presiding elder, seemed to be like Moses on Pisgah, and spoke as on the margin of his inheritance. It was heaven on earth.[174]

For some, it was the presence of these eschatological qualities that set the stage for revelation. "God was in the assembly!" Catherine Livingston Garrettson exulted after one quarterly meeting, "There is a very great degree of simplicity, love & zeal among the people of God in this place."[175]

To Methodists, the manifestation of heaven within their worship was not only a sense of fellowship with each other but also of communion with God. They went beyond using earthly images to describe their worship, not only because of the intensity of the Christian fellowship, but also because of their frequent experiences of being overwhelmed with an almost palpable sense of God's presence. Surely only life in heaven itself could exceed the joy of their ecstatic perceptions of God's presence here on earth. Overwhelmed once by a "powerful, solemn sense of a present and gracious God," Francis Asbury speculated on what this experience would be like in heaven "where a much deeper sense of the Divine presence is eternally enjoyed, without interruption or cessation!"[176]

The final way in which Methodists spoke of the manifestation of heaven in their worship was to note the eternal quality of the act of worship itself. Worshiping God is the essential, eternal activity of heaven. The worship Methodists participated in now anticipated the adoration saints and angels continually offered to God in heaven. William Jessop, reflecting on other Methodists who had died, looked forward to meeting them again in heaven "where loud HALLE-

---

174. [James B. Finley], "Extract of a letter from the Rev. J. B. Finley, to the Editors, dated Mount-Pleasant, June 30, 1819," *MQR* 2 (1819): 309. Note the similarity to the Cooper passage above. See also Boehm journal, 29 May 1813; and Colbert journal 4:110, where a version of the formula was applied to the quarterly meeting conference. See also *Extracts of Letters*, 9-10 where Shadrack Bostwick used the formula to describe the unity in his district among members and preachers alike.

175. Catherine Livingston Garrettson diary, 72.

176. *JLFA* 1:280. Compare the thought of Kentucky itinerant Benjamin Lakin in Sweet, *Methodists* 4:228 where Lakin noted the sporadic nature of this sort of experience on earth and decided that this sense would be "proper and perpetual" in heaven.

LUJAHS shall be our employ."[177] Specific aspects of their worship were seen as being revelatory of heaven. As Jessop's quote implies, loud praise was known as "heavenly shouting"; shouting was the normal mode of liturgical discourse in heaven, even for angels.[178] Likewise, praise generally was the "language of heaven."[179] Methodist singing and prayer also reflected heavenly worship and manifested that realm on earth. Sometimes it was just the sheer vividness of the corporate experience itself that conjured up impressions of heaven.

The unity of the Methodists' fellowship was reinforced by terms they often used for each other. The terms can be grouped in two types: familial or friendship. The first is seen in the universal use by Methodists of the term "brother" or "sister" for another Methodist man or woman. These terms were used to designate both an individual Methodist—"that man is Brother Jones," for example—and groups of Methodists—as when someone would designate all the women within a society as the "Sisters." The terms were also used in direct address between Methodists. A few people received the honorific "Father" or "Mother." These terms were not necessarily connected to formal office within the church but were related to widespread recognition of a person's spiritual influence. For example, the charismatic (in both senses of the word) Benjamin Abbott, who never rose to being more than an itinerant preacher, was widely called "Father Abbott."[180] While part of this designation might have been due to Abbott's age, some of it was due to the popularity and respect that Abbott commanded among Methodists. In like manner, women well respected for spiritual acumen were designated as "mothers in Israel."[181]

The other intrasocietal designation was "Friend." This term, gender-neutral in contrast to the familial terms, was used in approximately the same way. It could be applied to individual Methodists or collectively.

---

177. Jessop journal, 21 January 1790.

178. Mann journal, 5 August 1810. See hymn 5 in appendix B: "May they shout Hallelujah like the angels above." See also the hymns in Richard A. Humphrey, comp., *History and Hymns of John Adam Granade: Holston's Pilgrim-Preacher-Poet* (n.p.: Commission on Archives and History, Holston Annual Conference, The United Methodist Church, 1991), 99, 135, 156.

179. Finley, *Autobiography*, 290.

180. Ffirth, *Benjamin Abbott*, 74, 80. See especially page 85 where Abbott is called "Daddy Abbott." Compare the account of the 1800 Pennsylvania quarterly meeting where Methodist itinerant William Colbert (journal 3:11) mentioned that "Dadda Boehm" was present. Most probably this was Martin Boehm, one of the originators of The United Brethren and the father of Methodist itinerant Henry Boehm, whose material has been used extensively in this dissertation.

181. Wigger, *Taking Heaven by Storm*, 151-72. Note that the phrase was used by the Wesleys too. See *Hymns*, #52, "On the Death of a Widow," *Works* 7:144: "A mother in Israel is gone!"

As one itinerant wrote in the early 1800s, "Our quarterly meetings have been rendered singularly useful . . . this year, and our friends seem much united, both to their preachers, discipline, one another and to their Lord."[182] Use of this term made Methodism its own sort of a "society of friends."

Universal use of these standard designations served to heighten the Methodists' sense of belonging to each other, as well as creating a sharpened sense of being distinct from outsiders. As Russell Richey accurately pointed out concerning Methodist use of the familial terms, they "distinguished those with whom one shared intense Christian bonds from those with whom one did not."[183] To a non-Methodist they could serve as windows into a fellowship made attractive by love. Dining with a group of Methodists, one outsider was struck by their calling each other brother and sister. Afterward he said, "This is Bible religion—it is all love."[184]

Methodists used these intrasocietal designations not only to increase their sense of internal fellowship but also to express their connection to heaven. Richard Allen's description of the communal aspect of heaven is rich in the use of these technical Methodist terms. To him, heaven is a continuation of the Methodist societal fellowship he knew. In heaven, Methodist societal "friends" joined a society in which angels and apostles, among others, were also considered "friends":

> When, therefore, we shall leave this impertinent and unsociable world, and all our good old friends that are gone to Heaven before us, shall meet us as soon as we are landed upon the shore of eternity, and with infinite congratulations for our safe arrival, shall conduct us into the company of patriarchs, prophets, apostles and martyrs and introduce us into an intimate acquaintance with them, and with all those brave and generous souls, who, by their glorious examples, have recommended themselves to the world; when we shall be familiar friends

---

182. *Extracts of Letters*, 9-10.

183. Richey, *Early American Methodism*, 6. Richey also correctly nuances Methodist use of the terms by noting the special relationship itinerants had for each other (pp. 6-7) and the sense of fraternity in other evangelical groups for the time (p. 103 n. 11). For more on the special intensity of fellowship among the itinerants see Wigger, *Taking Heaven by Storm*, 62-64. Wigger's suggestion that the liminal social status of the itinerants created their vivid sense of belonging to each other and could be applied equally to Methodism as a whole, particularly in its early stages.

184. Ellwood H. Stokes, *A Pilgrim's Foot-Prints, or Passages in the Life of Rev. John Hancock, of East Madison, N.J., who Labored for 50 Years as a Local Minister in the Church of Jesus Christ* (New York: Dix & Edwards, 1855), 37.

with angels and archangels; and all the courtiers of heaven shall call us brethren and bid us welcome to their Master's joy, and we shall be received into their glorious society with all the tender endearments and caresses of those heavenly lovers; what a mighty addition to our happiness will this be![185]

The familial terms could be used in the same way. For Charles Giles, a "sacred bond of unity extends from earth to heaven, connecting the children of God to God, their heavenly Father, and runs from heart to heart throughout the whole heavenly family." Thus Giles preached that "Christians are all brethren in a proper, high, and perfect sense."[186]

The very rhythms of assembling within quarterly meetings reinforced worship as a manifestation of heaven. Two distinct rhythms were involved: gathering and dispersing. The Methodist circuit, the typical organization of Methodists, was a church in diaspora. Only at quarterly meetings did the entire circuit actually assemble as a circuit. Methodists recognized the distinctness in this assembly by noting their process of gathering in the joy of pilgrimage and dispersing in the pain of parting. Both the gathering and the dispersing were portrayed in reference to heaven.

The gathering was not only at the location for the quarterly meetings but also occurred gradually as groups of Methodists converged closer to their destination. It was a pilgrimage of a sort: not a pilgrimage, necessarily, to a place, but to be a worshiping assembly, as Henry Boehm described an 1800 quarterly meeting. Starting on a Friday to make the meeting's beginning on Saturday, Boehm noted that his small group had traveled about ten miles when they met some more friends. He continued, "I think then was about 21 altogether. We then came on singing and praising the Lord."[187] A similar experience by another Methodist caused him to note: "how pleasant to travel in company with those who are also travelling to heaven."[188]

This association of the Christian life with a pilgrimage to heaven made gathering for quarterly meetings revelatory of a deeper reality. Fellow Methodists were "Zion travelers," with Zion being under-

185. From "A Short Address to the Friends of Him Who Hath no Helper" in Allen, *Life Experience,* 87.

186. Giles, *Pioneer,* 187.

187. Boehm journal, 1 August 1800.

188. Cooper journal, 19 April 1794. See also Holmes, "The Life and Diary of the Reverend John Jeremiah Jacob," 161.

stood as the heavenly city.[189] The pilgrimage of walking together along a road to attend a quarterly meeting, at which one would dwell in the "suburbs of heavens," was a concrete manifestation of a shared spiritual journey, the pilgrimage to heaven. The connection was so obvious to early Methodists that they created a way to make the image fit even when they were not traveling on land to quarterly meetings. Thus the thought came to William Jessop, traveling with thirty-two people in three boats to a quarterly meeting held on an island, that their watery pilgrimage was "as if we were then launching out in the ocean of eternity & were heaving in sight of the sweet Haven."[190]

Even more than the act of gathering, parting at the end of quarterly meetings had a direct connection in early Methodists' minds with their hope and experience of heaven. Innumerable accounts exist of the pain they felt when they had to say farewell. Their honest tears at saying good-bye told them that the manifestation of heaven that they experienced in their worshiping fellowship was not yet permanent. Their taste of eschatological fulfillment in worship made the dispersing more painful and served to sharpen the nature of their eschatological hope.

Their worship experience specifically caused them to envision heaven as a place where they would never have to part with their Methodist brothers and sisters again. The reunion they anticipated in heaven was not primarily portrayed as being with actual family—although this was a part—but with their Christian family, their society of friends. "I never knew till now what Christian fellowship could do," Kentuckian Benjamin Lakin said after a 1795 quarterly meeting, "I was unable to converse . . . by reason of sorrow of heart to think of seeing them no more in time, may the Lord bring us to meet in heaven where parting is no more."[191]

The reunion in heaven would be wonderful, they thought. As one Methodist speculated on heavenly joys, the only thing he could think

---

189. Boehm journal, 28 November 1801. Compare the similar terms in William Cowan letter to Edward Dromgoole, 20 December 1777 (Edward Dromgoole papers); and Daniel Grant letter to John Owen, 3 September 1790. See also the hymn entitled "The Zion Traveller" in Humphrey, *History and Hymns of John Adam Granade*, 43-44.

190. Jessop journal, 25 February 1788.

191. Sweet, *Methodists* 4:209. See similar statements in Wakeley, *Patriarch,* 153; Colbert journal 1:35-36; Cooper journal, 24 August 1788, 15 November 1790, 27 May 1794; Meacham journal, 27 March 1789; Edward Dromgoole letter to Philip Gatch, 27 October 1813; and Mary Avery Browder letter to Edward Dromgoole, 2 December 1777. See also Asbury's statement after parting with Thomas Coke once (*JLFA* 2:118): "Strangers to the delicacies of Christian friendship know little or nothing of the pain of parting."

of that could add to the joy of communing with God was the joy of Methodist fellowship:

> I have thought that if any thing can add to the Joys of happy Souls above Except the Imediate presence of God & our blessed Redeemer it will be the delight of our souls to meet our Dr departed friends relations & fellow worshipers.[192]

Of special attraction to this Methodist was the purpose of this reunion: worship. The joy of this fellowship would be "especially in that happy uniformity of mind which will then possess the whole heavenly Quire both of Saints & angels."

Early Methodists did not understood their worship as being some individualistic experience of God, or even being narrowly focused on God alone. They worshiped and in this corporate activity God and heaven were made manifest. Consequently, they saw their worshiping fellowship as a true anticipation of the eternal worshiping fellowship of all God's people. They longed for the fulfillment of their proleptic experience:

> Our hearts by love together knit
> Cemented mix'd in one
> One hope one heart one mind one voice
> Tis heaven on earth begun
> Our hearts did burn while tears spake
> And glow'd with sacred fire
> We stop'd and talk'd and fed and bless'd
> And fill'd the enlarge Desire

Corus

> A Saviour let creation sing
> A saviour let all Heaven ring
> He's God with us we feel him ours
> His fullness in our souls he pours
> Tis almost done tis almost oer
> We are joining them that gone before
> We then shall meet to part no more
> We then shall meet to part no more.[193]

---

192. Daniel Grant letter to Chisley Daniel, 27 October 1791.

193. Untitled, undated hymn in the Bradford ms. hymnbook. Notice that Wesley's *Hymns* has seven hymns on the subject of parting. Note too that the reuniting of Methodist friends is a recurring theme in the funeral hymns written by Charles Wesley. See Charles Wesley, *Funeral Hymns* (First Series), 7th ed. (London: Paramore, 1784), 3: "There all the ship's company meet,/who sailed with the Saviour beneath,/with shouting each other they greet,/And triumph o'er trouble and death."

Prose could express the same sentiments:

> Our love feast was one of the best I ever was in. We sat together in heavenly places; and to express myself in the words which I immediately wrote down, I was as in a little Heaven below, and believe Heaven above will differ more in quantity than in quality. Our eyes overflowed with tears, and our hearts with love to God and each other. The holy fire, the heavenly flame, spread wider and wider, and rose higher and higher. O! happy people whose God is the Lord, may none of you ever weary in well doing. May we after having done the work alotted us, meet in our father's Kingdom to tell the wonders of redeeming love, and part no more.[194]

Conclusion

There was no official requirement for Methodists to include their private services in the liturgical scheme of quarterly meetings. There were neither far-reaching legislative mandates nor episcopal dictates making the love feast and Lord's Supper mandatory components. But these services consistently were included, especially the love feast.

The reason Methodists included these services must be found in the nature of quarterly meetings themselves. This setting alone allowed the average Methodist to participate in a Methodist fellowship fuller than the one he or she normally experienced weekly. While the experience of local class meetings and society meetings was gratifying in its own right, a quarterly meeting was the occasion when the average Methodist "brother" or "sister" could participate in a fuller way in the Connection, the Methodist term for the wider fellowship of the denomination and its organization. The Methodist Connection was normally a church in self-imposed diaspora. Its typical system of preachers itinerating within a circuit joined people across a wide area under a traveling ministerial leadership. Quarterly meetings were the few, regular occasions when the itinerants did not come to the people, but the people came to the itinerants. And in this act the fellowship of the Connection, as found in a single circuit, was made visible and real. The assembling of this Connectional fellowship at quarterly meetings probably made the celebration of love feasts and the Lord's Supper natural.

Methodists insisted that a greater manifestation often took place

---

194. Watters, *Short Account,* 75-76.

when they assembled in this manner. Their voices were hurried with excitement and rich with the exuberance of an overwhelming spiritual experience. Although they almost never attempted an explanation of how it happened, they were confident that in their private worship God was present among them with gracious saving power, and that the very essence of heavenly existence truly shone in their humble, loving midst. Their Connection, assembled in a unique manner at a quarterly meeting, became an avenue to greater spiritual realities.

CHAPTER 5

Grace and Worship in Quarterly Meetings

"The Lord then made bare his holy arm in the sight of all the people."
—summary of worship at 1804 Kentucky quarterly meeting[1]

"Enter, and find that God is here."
—line from early Methodist hymn on admitting new members[2]

Early Methodists were seldom content to recount bare details about their worship at quarterly meetings. Mixed in with facts about who preached, what text was read, how many were justified and sanctified, and where services were held, their accounts almost inevitably include some sort of theological assessment. Where was God and what was God doing? were among questions asked and answered. Although theological assessment was sometimes subtle, very often the accounts are explicitly theological, even if the categories used derive more from their piety than from a formal theological vocabulary.

The first epigraph above comes from an account of Sunday morning preaching services during an 1804 quarterly meeting, held simultaneously in a meetinghouse and a barn. In its entirety this account reads: "As the preaching in the barn was over at the same time, the two congregations met in the yard. The Lord then made bare his holy

---

1. J. B. Wakeley, *The Heroes of Methodism, containing Sketches of Eminent Methodist Ministers, and Characteristic Anecdotes of their Personal History* (New York: Carlton & Porter, 1857), 114.

2. *A Pocket Hymn-book, designed as a Constant Companion for the Pious. Collected from Various Authors*, 5th ed. (New York: W. Ross, 1786), 191.

arm in the sight of all the people. Sinners were cut to the heart."[3] The first part provides a simple fact. The second highlights a theological understanding of what really happened: God was present in saving power; thus sinners became aware of their state before God.

Modern readers should not be surprised by this approach to telling history by early Methodists. Theological assessment was so common that to find an account without it is exceptional. Methodists were drawing upon a certain kind of Protestant spirituality, rooted in both Puritanism specifically and Protestant Pietism generally, which immersed itself in trying actively to perceive God's providence.[4] For Methodists, all history—and particularly their own—was sacred history. To recount the story of their own activities and experience was to recount the dealings of God with humanity. From this perspective, any history of their lives, activities, and growth as Methodists by necessity carried implicit theological weight. In particular, their sense of God's participation in worship was so strong and self-evident that it seemed completely natural to move from reciting facts to explicit theological claims: "the Lord then made bare his holy arm in the sight of all the people."

Any adequate history of quarterly meetings must recognize this theological dimension in sources that describe the meetings. Their theological claims are typically so explicit that they cannot be easily ignored, nor should they be. Simply put, early Methodists constantly asserted that people—sometimes in numbers so great as to constitute a revival—experienced the grace of God during worship at quarterly meetings.

The previous chapters have tried to present early Methodism by using its own terms as much as possible. This commitment now demands that the sources' inherent theological claims be acknowledged and dealt with in some legitimate manner. At a minimum, one should presume the veracity of the claim that people experienced grace in worship at quarterly meetings. Given this presumption, I want to probe how experiencing God's grace within the arena of their worship shaped the early Methodist understanding of the nature of God's gracious activity. The testimony of early Methodists stressed that the communal dimension of their worship was crucial in peo-

3. Wakeley, *Heroes of Methodism*, 114.
4. Russell E. Richey, "Methodism and Providence: A Study in Secularization," in *Protestant Evangelicalism: Britain, Ireland, Germany, and America c. 1750–c. 1950* (Oxford: Basil Blackwell, 1990), 55.

ple's experiences of grace. The individual's experience of grace normally occurred in the context of his or her interaction with the Christian fellowship known as Methodism. Individual experience was dependent upon Christian community, and God offered saving grace in and through this community.

Fellowship as the Dominant Aspect of Early Methodist Ecclesiology

Toward the end of his life, the venerable Methodist bishop, Francis Asbury, wrote a "Valedictory Address" to the newest Methodist bishop, William McKendree. In it Asbury gave a short recounting of Methodist history, including an account of how American Methodism became a church. While Asbury rightly pointed to 1784—the year in which a specially called conference in Baltimore adopted the name of The Methodist Episcopal Church, began to ordain some of its itinerant preachers for sacramental ministries, and generally assumed other aspects of an episcopal government—Asbury also noted that before this time American Methodists had begun to recognize themselves as a church, although with some ambiguity:

> At this time [pre-1784] the Methodists were, among others, not organized and had not the ordinances among us. As some in pleasantry said: "We were a Church, and no Church."[5]

This statement embodies the heart of the complexity of early Methodist ecclesiology. Formally, Asbury and other Methodists accepted that they were not a church before 1784: they had neither a proper organization nor the sacraments. But at another level their hearts told them something different: "We were a Church." Their hearts spoke from their experience of Methodism as fellowship. Although they recognized that they lacked many external marks of a church, their intense unity and love, expressed in common piety and mission, overwhelmed them with a sense that their internal fellowship was God-given and rightly equated with the essence of the

---

5. *JLFA* 3:475-92. Reflecting on the official organization of the church, Richard Allen once described sympathetically a pamphlet published at the time that stated "that when the Methodists were no people [before 1784], then they were a people; and now they have become a people [after organization of The Methodist Episcopal Church] they were no people." See Richard Allen, *The Life Experience and Gospel Labors of the Rt. Rev. Richard Allen* (New York: Abingdon, 1960), 22. The scriptural allusion is to 1 Peter 2:10.

word, "church." In other words, *fellowship was the dominant aspect of early Methodist ecclesiology.* The 1784 conference did not create Methodism as a church out of nothing but fulfilled in Methodists' eyes the best aspects of their previous ecclesiological experience by adding marks of organization and sacrament.

The centrality of fellowship in early Methodists' understanding of themselves as a church is clear in their writings, although almost never stated in formal theological terms. In a wide variety of ways they constantly reaffirmed that in their disciplined love and unity in Christ they had experienced what it meant to be a church. The images were frequently rich and powerful. But their very breadth of expression hindered early Methodists in trying to articulate clearly their ecclesiology.

Methodists had trouble defining themselves as church (among other issues) because of their competing "languages" or vocabularies.[6] Their experience of ecclesial fellowship went beyond the limited formal theological language they had: the Articles of Religion adopted from the Church of England. But their other sources for ecclesiological terms—their evangelical, biblical vernacular and their societal, polity language—were difficult to use with theological precision. It was not always clear then (or now) how to harmonize the different languages. The Articles of Religion spoke of a visible church as a congregation of the faithful with preaching of the Word of God and due administration of sacraments, while the common ecclesiological terms derived from their piety spoke of the church as "Zion" or an "ark" with fellow Christians as "friends," or "brothers and sisters."[7] Additionally, their polity gave them terms for the church like society, circuit, class, and Connection. Against this background the relative theological imprecision that marked the ecclesiology of early American Methodists should come as no surprise. They were probably better theological poets and ecclesial engineers than writers of theological prose.

---

6. I am indebted on this point to Russell Richey. He argues that Methodists spoke four different "languages," the tensions between which were not always reconciled. These "languages" were evangelical pietism, Wesleyan societal polity, an episcopal vocabulary derived from Anglicanism, and republican political terms; see Richey, *Early American Methodism,* (Bloomington: Indiana University Press, 1991), 14, 94-95; and his earlier discussion in "Ecclesial Sensibilities in Nineteenth-Century American Methodism," *Quarterly Review* 4.1 (spring 1984): 33. The same tensions continue unabated in forms of modern Methodism.

7. On "Zion," see Richey, *Early American Methodism,* 43 and 95. On "ark," see David Dailey, *Experience and Ministerial Labors of Rev. Thomas Smith, Late an Itinerant Preacher of the Gospel in the Methodist Episcopal Church* (New York: Lane & Tippett, 1848), 154, where "ark" is used as a synonym for church, with probable allusion to Noah and the flood story.

While Methodist ecclesiological claims may have lacked precision, they seldom lacked evocative power. One particularly powerful, frequent way in which Methodists emphasized the importance of their fellowship was by eschatological references. As noted in the previous chapter, early Methodists were often so caught up in the wonder of their worship fellowship that they sought reference to heaven generally or to the heavenly city specifically. In these references they intended to highlight how their worshiping fellowship revealed both the quality of heavenly life and God's saving power. Again, poetic imprecision was common as different emphases were played off one another. The quality and power of heaven were dual aspects of a single reality manifest and experienced in their worshiping fellowship.

When Methodists achieved the intensity of fellowship that this spirituality valued, comparisons to heaven were evoked. A particularly frequent occasion for such intensity was love feast testimonials, one of the regular forms of worship at quarterly meetings. Fellowship was typically at its most intense during the sharing of testimonies, as individual after individual spoke of the goodness of God experienced within his or her experience of Methodism. Here, during a "feast of love indeed," fellowship fed on itself through the bonds of loving unity that worshipers felt with God and each other. The phenomenon was not unique to love feasts or sacramental administrations, it was also a common feature of class meetings and even business sessions.[8] Out of the intense intimacy created by testimonies of their experiences with God, Methodists felt a deeper sense of unified fellowship with each other. This unifying quality to testimony is attested universally.

At most quarterly meetings the locus for this intense fellowship was private worship on Sunday mornings. There, at the love feast or sacrament or the two combined, their fellowship was an occasion for the manifestation of God. Their typical image was of fire: the presence of God ignited a few hearts, which began to burn more intensely until fire spread through the entire fellowship. One presiding elder portrayed an almost palpable or visible quality to this fellowship nourishing itself in the presence of God:

> In the morning our love-feast began, and God was with us: the fire burnt higher and higher, till it burst forth in a flame, so that the

8. Richey, *Early American Methodism*, 75-79; and Richey, *The Methodist Conference in America: A History* (Nashville: Kingswood, 1996), 40.

rejoicing and prayers of many were heard through the town. The church windows were open—many spectators were around, and many, who were not members, within. The power was so great and genuine that the whole seemed to be awed: I do not recollect to have seen a smile on one face. The power continued through the love-feast and sacrament.[9]

This "fire" often spread contagiously. Kindled within the fellowship of believers, it could quickly cross over to seekers present at the private worship. God's power seemed to so fill the fellowship that the building itself could not contain it; those waiting outside were often swept up in the fire. Henry Boehm described the process at an 1802 meeting:

> Our lovefeast began about nine, many spoke feelingly. The fire of God's love began upon the believers herts, it reacht the unconverted and caused them to crye for mercy. Believers praisd Jesus with their tongs, hands and feet, particularly among the poor opresed Africans. the power of God reacht the hearts of many out of Doors.[10]

At some quarterly meetings, fellowship was so intense that it "melted" those present even prior to private worship. Richard Garrettson described such a quarterly meeting in Virginia. To him the sight of Methodist fellowship was astonishing: "the saints struck my mind with the deepest views of heaven, and the love of God to man." According to Garrettson, the fellowship spontaneously combusted. Before a single preacher had arrived, the power of God had so come on the fellowship that

> when the people met (sometimes before they spoke) the sight of each other caused their eyes to melt in tears, and the cups ran over; so that they broke out in loud praises to God. Others, when they met, would hang on each other, and weep aloud, and praise God. Others, when they began to talk of what God was doing, were melted down, and the flame ran through the whole company.[11]

The power of fellowship to "melt" the gathered worshipers was not accidental but heightened by structures of polity and liturgical rubrics

---

9. *Extracts of Letters, Containing some Account of the Work of God since the Year 1800* (New York: J. C. Totten, 1805; reprint, Barnard, VT: Joseph Dix, 1812), 32.

10. Henry Boehm, Journal. Ms. Henry Boehm Papers, United Methodist Church Archives-GCAH, Madison, NJ. [Microfilm copy at Iliff Theological Seminary, Denver, CO], 3 January 1802.

11. R. Garrettson, "An Account of the Revival of the Work of God at Petersburg, in Virginia," *AM* 13 (1790): 302.

that evolved in early Methodism. One key aspect of Methᵊ ecclesiological "engineering" was the custom of holding some meeᴛings where nonmembers were excluded, allowing members to come together separately. This act of separating Methodists for certain kinds of worship was key to creating a sense of visible identity for the fellowship and an atmosphere in which worship could re-create and nurture fellowship. Far beyond their ability to articulate formally their theological reasons for liturgical separation, Methodists perceived that, by separating their fellowship, God flooded their worship with an outpouring of grace. Even if they had been better trained in precise theological formulations, perhaps their rich, poetic imagery better suited the overwhelming nature of their experiences.

Because of the typical intensity of fellowship it allowed, Methodists gathered at quarterly meetings considered maintaining the distinction between private and public worship to be a grace-filled act, not a sign of disdain for nonmembers. They understood that the act of joining together in private services had a powerful effect on those excluded. They realized that even as they experienced the essence of their fellowship in the love feast and sacrament, while gathered in a house or barn with windows and doors closed, this experience of liturgical exclusion also affected the crowd waiting outside. At times outsiders seemed moved by overhearing the proceedings within, or perhaps just by an awareness of Methodists gathered for worship. At one Delaware love feast, for instance, as the preacher brought the service to a close, he looked out the pulpit window and saw a crowd of several hundred "bathed in tears, smiting their breasts and crying for mercy."[12]

When love feasts were moved outside because the meetinghouse could not hold the Methodists, the impact of seeing the presence of God within the Methodist fellowship could be accentuated. At another Delmarva quarterly meeting the "strangers to the work" who were standing around as spectators to the love feast were astonished "with great solemnity in their countinance" as they watched the Methodists exhibit their fellowship in testimonies, praise, and cries for more grace.[13] In both cases, experience of witnessing—but not being allowed to participate in—Methodist fellowship provided the context for the public preaching service that followed. In other words, contact

---

12. Dailey, *Experience and Ministerial Labors of Rev. Thomas Smith,* 101.
13. Boehm journal, 20 July 1800.

with Methodist fellowship separated in private worship provided the background to the evangelical purpose of public worship.

In traditional thinking for the period, Methodists argued that the separation was not only useful but strictly necessary to maintain their nature as a graced fellowship. The bishops argued vehemently for the practice, maintaining that it was a "manifest duty" lest Methodism become a "desolate waste" devoid of the glory of God's gracious presence.[14] The argument, and concern, was a long-standing one. Thomas Rankin, the general assistant sent by John Wesley, had become concerned soon after his arrival in America that Methodist discipline had not been kept properly. For Rankin, at stake was not only Methodists' enjoyment of their own fellowship but fidelity and effectiveness in Methodist mission. In his opinion, because some itinerants had been inattentive to discipline and had opened love feasts and meetings of society to nonmembers, "a more glorious work in many places of this continent" had been forestalled.[15] In other words, the opportunity for people to experience grace through Methodist activity was dependent upon Methodists maintaining their distinction as a graced and disciplined fellowship. Or, to put it in the prophetic idiom of one early Methodist, "if ever our church loses the life of religion, it will be for want of discipline."[16]

Methodist Fellowship as Context for Experiencing Grace

By failing to account for the centrality of fellowship in early Methodism, other scholars have not always recognized the essential communal context for individual experiences of grace. Focusing perhaps on the intensely personal terms these people typically used to

---

14. *Discipline*/1798, 154.

15. John Telford, ed., *Wesley's Veterans* (London: Charles H. Kelly, 1913): 6:174. See also Rankin diary, 98, 108. From this viewpoint, a caricature of Rankin as a harsh disciplinarian seems unfair and misses the complexity of Methodist ecclesiology. See also Ezekiel Cooper journal (in Papers. Garrett-Evangelical Theological Seminary Library, Evanston, IL), 23 March 1793, where Cooper was greatly troubled by the failure of an experienced fellow itinerant to enforce separate meetings. Cooper seemed astonished that the necessity was not obvious and overwhelming to his fellow preacher.

16. Joseph Everett, "An Account of the most remarkable Occurrences of the Life of Joseph Everett [In a Letter to Bishop Asbury]," *AM* 13 (1790): 608. Of course, in addition to separate meetings for members, Methodist discipline ideally involved active, internal accountability for members administered through their classes, including the possibility of having membership cut off. This aspect of discipline, too, was often connected to the broader notion of maintaining the graced nature of Methodist fellowship. Such was the precise context for Everett's statement that explained how the "power of religion" had been on the decline in a circuit but was again kindled by "culling the societies and keeping up proper discipline in the church of GOD."

describe their threshold experiences of justification and sanc
some scholars have failed to notice the broader communal coɪ﹍
such experiences. For example, Paul Sanders, who did seminal work
on the role of the Lord's Supper in American Methodism, once
described Methodist soteriology in this way: "They held the dominant evangelical conviction, nourished in a pietistic and sectarian
environment, that salvation is solely a matter of personal relationship
between God and the individual."[17] His mistake, like that of other
scholars, was to make the notion of an intensely *personal* experience
synonymous with an intensely *individualistic* experience.

In actuality, the exact opposite of Sanders's description was the
case. Methodists saw their fellowship as being graced by God's presence and as the normal arena in which people received such grace.
This fellowship was the normal context for an individual's experiencing of grace. They saw a communal, corporate dimension inherent
to personal experience. To use Sanders's words, early Methodists
acknowledged that salvation was indeed "a matter of personal relationship between God and the individual" but denied vehemently
that it was "solely" so. Methodist fellowship provided the context for
individual experience of grace in several ways.

One important aspect of this communal experience of grace was
renewed piety. Another was an increase in zeal that Methodists chan-
neled into ministering to those who had yet to experience grace. One
fruit of the intense spirituality that often marked Methodist worship—
most acutely seen in quarterly meeting love feasts—was a spontaneous eruption of shouted praise, exhortation, and prayer. The latter
two were directed to those still needing to appropriate God's grace. In
other words, Methodists' experience of the gracious presence of God
in their fellowship motivated their evangelistic ministries to others.

The notion that one's experience of graced fellowship naturally
leads to willingness to offer grace to others is a clear element in many
accounts of quarterly meeting worship. The directional aspect—from
within the fellowship to outside it—was often quite pronounced. An
account of one New England quarterly meeting began with a typical
description of the dynamics of private worship: while the Methodist
fellowship was gathered for a Sunday morning love feast, a crowd
"thronged" outside.[18] After the "work of God" broke out within the

17. Paul S. Sanders, "An Appraisal of John Wesley's Sacramentalism in the Evolution of Early
American Methodism" (Th.D. diss., Union Theological Seminary, 1954), 250.

18. Abel Stevens, *Memorials of the Early Progress of Methodism in the Eastern States* (Boston:
C. H. Peirce and Co., 1852), 132.

love feast fellowship, one preacher stood at the window and exhorted those standing outside. For an attentive spectator the dynamic would have been striking. Initially excluded from the private assembly, this bystander now saw a member of the fellowship speaking from that assembly and extending an offer of God's grace. The gracious offer literally emerged from the midst of the worshiping fellowship.

Other accounts accentuate even more strongly the emergence of gracious ministry from an experience of fellowship. At another quarterly meeting, for instance, preacher James Horton slipped into a vision as the bread and water were passed around at a love feast.[19] In his vision Horton heard God speak to him, "Behold, dear child, none but the pure in heart can come here." As he looked around in heaven, Horton saw a congregation of millions gathered around God's throne. When the vision ended, he found himself standing on his chair with his hands uplifted. As Horton looked around at the Methodist fellowship in worship, he noted that to him "they looked like the shining ones in whose company I seemed to be the moment before in the heavenly world."

Horton could not be silent. First he began to speak to the love feast participants. Then he went to the window and exhorted those outside. Given leave by the presiding elder to go outside to "do your duty," Horton continued his exhorting among the bystanders. His experience of liturgical fellowship provided the zeal and the content of his exhortation. He ministered against a vivid, visible backdrop of separated Methodist fellowship, of which the spectators were aware. To conclude his account of this episode, Horton noted that he would lean against the church whenever he felt exhausted in exhorting. His phrase can have both a literal and figurative meaning: not only did he physically rest against the church building, but his reawakened sense of grace through the love feast fellowship provided support for his ministry to those outside the fellowship. Theologically, God offered grace through the ministry of those who first experienced grace themselves in their liturgical fellowship. Grace came through fellowship.

And grace came within fellowship too. That assumption was inherent in the traditional way Methodists viewed membership in their societies. Specifically, by setting the "one condition" for membership as "a desire to flee from the wrath to come, and to be saved

___
19. The full account can be found in Horton, *Narrative*, 85-86.

from their sins" and not as an actual experience of salvation itself, whether justification or sanctification, they presumed that their societal fellowship would provide the normal context for individual experience. Innumerable accounts report exactly that happening. Individuals wished to join the Christian fellowship that had awakened their desire for salvation; their desire for salvation was fulfilled after joining.

Some early Methodists reported needing divine assistance in overcoming their hesitation to join before having a saving experience. That assistance came for Ebenezer Newell after he was admitted to a love feast while under conviction. Newell marveled at Methodist worship; to him it seemed "a type of Heaven."[20] His conviction was increased, as was his desire to use the means of grace for salvation. At that moment Newell reported that the Holy Spirit spoke to him and said, "Join the church." He resisted, arguing that he was not yet fit for heaven and thus not fit to join the church. According to Newell, the debate was not over. A question came to him: "Where would you go to learn the French language?" Newell replied that he would go live with French people. The Spirit questioned him again: "Where would you go then in order to learn the language of Canaan and the doctrines of Christ?" Newell then realized that the church was a form of school and, if he wanted to learn the heavenly "language," he needed to join. He joined the Methodists; later he experienced justifying grace. In this case, the school metaphor for Methodist fellowship underscores both a processive and communal nature to Newell's individual experience of grace.

So closely intertwined were the notions of membership, worshiping fellowship, and individual experience that it became standard for American Methodists to associate opportunity for joining as a fitting conclusion for their worship. Specifically, their two most central restricted rituals of fellowship—the love feast and the Lord's Supper—frequently served as occasions when new members were enrolled at quarterly meetings. On a broader level, Methodist quarterly meetings often culminated with granting admission into membership. Methodists gloried in large numbers—both mourners and newly converted—joining on those occasions.

A standard Methodist term for this time was "opening the doors."

---

20. Ebenezer Francis Newell, *Life and Observations of Rev. E. F. Newell, who has been more than Forty Years an Itinerant Minister in the Methodist Episcopal Church* (Worcester, MA: C. W. Ainsworth, 1847), 37-38.

When they extended the invitation to join their fellowship, Methodists said they had "opened the doors for admission."[21] A precise origin for the term is probably unrecoverable but it is strongly reminiscent of the actual dynamics surrounding restriction of access to private Methodist fellowship meetings. When gathered for the Sunday morning love feast and sacrament the doors and windows were often closed. Only at the end, when the private worship had culminated, were the doors opened and people invited to come in for another worship service. Thus, calling the ritual of joining the Methodists "opening the doors" suggests that in a very important way one's new membership granted access to the most intimate gatherings of Methodist fellowship. For those nonmembers granted admission to the love feast, the parallel was even clearer. The literal open door for admission into the love feast was followed by the figurative open door for admission into the Methodist fellowship.

If Methodists "opened the doors" to their fellowship, then they can be said to have "opened the windows" too. As Russell Richey has aptly suggested, a third way existed in which Methodists understood their fellowship as context for individual experiences of grace: exhibiting fellowship as the catalyst for individual experience. Richey argues that at quarterly meetings "Methodism dramatically opened its community, opened its windows, to attest the sincerity and dependability of the grace promised and so freely assured."[22] In other words, quarterly meetings demonstrate the essentially communal nature of early Methodism, which frequently occasioned individual experiences of grace.[23]

Richey uses a variety of verbs to highlight the revelatory quality of communal worship at quarterly meetings. At quarterly meetings, Methodism *expressed* itself, most particularly in the private worship of Sunday morning or in the private conference where an intense communal spirituality was cultivated. In this setting Methodism *modeled* and *offered* its fellowship as a new form of community, a God-given and God-centered alternative society to the one in which people

---

21. See, for example, *Extracts of Letters*, 49; Benjamin McReynolds diary, 31 May 1823; and [T. L. Douglass], "Account of the Work of God in the Nashville District," *MQR* 4 (1821): 192.

22. Richey, *Early American Methodism*, 26. See also his discussion on pages 4-5, 14, 19, 25-29, 55, 62-63, 69-71, and 95. I am much indebted to his argument.

23. Richey paints this question in very broad strokes by focusing on the relationship between quarterly meetings and revivals. To make my theological assessment more generally applicable, I focus on individual experience of grace, whether the number of those affected was small—as in most quarterly meetings—or large—as when a quarterly meeting resulted in revival. Despite the difference in scale I see a basic agreement between our assessments.

belonged by birth. In like manner, quarterly meetings were an *enactment* of Methodism as church, a realization of the gospel in its communal, ecclesial dimension.

Through his vocabulary, Richey emphasizes the vitality of Methodist fellowship at quarterly meetings. He calls them "ecclesial dramas." At quarterly meetings, Methodism vividly and fully dramatized the grace-filled nature of the gathered community as church. There its most essential ecclesial qualities were embodied in, or made manifest through, a specific Christian assembly. In the worship and business sessions of quarterly meetings, Methodists literally acted out the grace-filled nature of a Christian people. At quarterly meetings, the unity, intimacy, and corporate spirituality that distinguished Methodist fellowship generally became acute and visible.

In particular, by the way they assembled and the message they proclaimed, Methodists acted out the catholic nature of grace and the church. They demonstrated this catholicity in worship in which they typically overturned the racial, gender, and age barriers that stood in the world outside. The breach of these barriers must have seemed particularly striking in quarterly meetings, given the number of Methodists involved and the number of spectators observing this drama.

The catholic nature of grace and the church was likewise dramatized in a common practice at quarterly meetings: preaching sermons against popular Calvinism of the time.[24] In these sermons Methodists offered free grace, often cast as a doctrine collectively and distinctively held by Methodism. To those listeners who held a form of Calvinism, this preaching frequently sounded like an almost unbelievably gracious offer. Previously convinced by Calvinists that they were "reprobate" and beyond the reach of God's salvation, these listeners now heard that they too could experience God's grace and be included in God's people. If such a listener was able to gain admission to the love feast, no doubt he or she would have seen an even more vivid dramatization of this doctrine as various Methodists testified of their own journey from supposed "reprobate" status to God-given assurance of a place in the heavenly Zion.

Another aspect of the ethos of Methodist fellowship at quarterly meetings was its dramatic discontinuity with contemporary cultural

---

24. For examples see William Colbert, "A Journal of the Travels of William Colbert Methodist Preacher thro' parts of Maryland, Pennsylvania, New York, Delaware, and Virginia in 1790 to 1838." Ts. United Methodist Church Archives-GCAH, Madison, NJ, 2:164 and 4:122.

norms. In particular, in a culture that valued "honor and deference," Methodists emphasized the liberty of grace in their worship:

> It must have seemed that Christian community quite literally offered itself in public. After ordering and nourishing themselves, those Methodists who seemingly loved one another opened their community to the public.[25]

At quarterly meetings, early Methodist discomfort with the ethics of the surrounding culture was obvious. Not surprisingly, quarterly meeting conferences often dealt extensively with matters concerning Methodism's alternative ethic. Ethical standards were spelled out, trials were held for wayward local preachers and exhorters, and other members tried and expelled from their local societies and classes could appeal to a quarterly meeting. In addition, a quarterly meeting conference determined crucial ethical matters such as the amount of time a Methodist could own a slave before manumission and the resolution of conflicts over debt.[26] At its best, this consideration of communal moral matters was just another dimension of the unity that Methodists claimed for their fellowship and from which they expressed liturgically in their private worship.

What happened when the quality of Methodist fellowship at quarterly meetings was clearly and vividly exhibited? Revival occurred! People in large numbers were drawn to the "infectious quality" of the fellowship's corporate spirituality whose intensity could "elicit religious experience."[27] Some causal connection between the graced fellowship that Methodists cultivated and experienced at quarterly meetings and the widespread experience of the grace of God among non-Methodists seems clear. Quarterly meetings were the times for Methodism to dramatize itself as a vessel of grace. When fellowship

---

25. Richey, *Early American Methodism*, 25. See also pages 4, 5, 57, and 63.

26. For examples of manumission adjudication see ms. records for the Accomack (MD), Baltimore (MD), Harford (MD), Madison (KY), and Tar River (NC) circuits; and for Baltimore City Station (MD). For examples of debt adjudication see records for the Harford (MD), Paint Creek (OH), and Tar River (NC) circuits. Other ethical resolutions adopted do not seem nearly as critical to modern observers, but in their cultural context were important for early Methodists. See Ormond journal, 21 November 1801, concerning a resolution against using stud horses on Sunday (the "Sabbath"), and the entry for 19 August 1809 in the Hockhocking Circuit (OH) "Book of Records" concerning attendance at "barbacues and Drinking of toasts" on the Fourth of July. In both cases the quarterly meeting conference disapproved of the activities.

27. Richey, *Early American Methodism*, 79. In his more recent work (*Conference*, 32-33) Richey describes the spiritual attractiveness of quarterly meetings in this manner: "The time and space of Methodism's meeting gradually assumed a very special quality which we might call gravity. By it we refer to the sacral character of conference itself, its spiritual weightiness, the powerful revivifying pull it made on those within its orbit. This quality characterized both the annual and quarterly conference (meeting)."

was strong it was part of the gracious message that Methodists offered to the world. When people responded, "revival was Methodism being blessed in consequence of being itself."[28]

If quarterly meetings were a kind of "ecclesial drama," then some form of staging was necessary. Indeed there was a very visible staging for exhibiting Methodist fellowship: the dynamics created by division of worship services into public and private. By limiting access to certain services, a visible distinction among those attending quarterly meetings was made: those in the assembled fellowship and spectators to this fellowship. Accounts of quarterly meetings are full of reports of various dynamics created by this division.

This distinction involved a limited porous nature between the groups, a particularly important dynamic. In several key ways, spectators were able to obtain a good view of the assembled fellowship. Methodist fellowship was never completely hidden at quarterly meetings; indeed, its separation—even behind closed doors and windows—called attention to it as an object for observation.

This porousness between the two groups was expressed in part by the access to private worship granted to a limited number of nonmembers. For those granted admission, observing the fellowship in Sunday morning worship at quarterly meetings was often the pivotal element in their experiencing of grace. For example, Benjamin Paddock's observation of a love feast at a quarterly meeting staggered him by means of the fellowship's heavenly quality and the worship's angelic nature. The resulting attraction to Methodist fellowship created a resolve in him that had two complementary aspects: desire to be part of Methodism and desire to accept the God Methodists worshiped. Paddock writes: "This people shall be my people, and their God my God."[29] The centrality of the fellowship dimension in Paddock's ongoing spiritual experience cannot be denied. Although most of his newly adopted Methodist brothers and sisters were total strangers to him, Paddock insisted that "his soul was so knit to them that they were dearer to him than any earthly relations."

Even those forced to remain outside as spectators had some opportunity to overhear and oversee Methodist fellowship at worship. Given

---

28. Richey, *Early American Methodism*, 28-29.

29. Zechariah Paddock, *Memoir of Rev. Benjamin G. Paddock, with Brief Notices of Early Ministerial Associates* (New York: Nelson & Phillips; Cincinnati: Hitchcock & Walden, 1875), 48. His phrase is an allusion to Ruth 1:16.

the rather poor condition of some buildings used for worship and the rather loud nature of Methodist worship, those outside often could catch glimpses of Methodist praise, prayer, and testimony. Perhaps more important, spectators' awareness of Methodists gathered as a separate worshiping fellowship often made a most basic statement about that fellowship: Methodists claimed to be a distinctive people for God, and spectators knew they were not part of this people.

Finally, the distinction between separated fellowship and bystanders was porous in that the staging of quarterly meetings normally had private worship immediately followed by public. When the private worship was over on Sunday morning, the doors and windows were thrown wide open and bystanders outside gained immediate knowledge of the result of the fellowship's worship of God. The fellowship's experience of the grace of God carried over into the public worship that followed. Initially excluded as spectators, non-Methodists now could see and hear in the public service's preaching, exhortation, singing, and prayer, the grace that the Methodist fellowship had just experienced privately. Sometimes the intensity of God's gracious presence in the private worship left the fellowship in such a condition that it could not begin public worship. In those times spectators were invited in to see the fellowship in this state.[30] Moreover, if a spectator came under intense conviction during the public worship, he or she would be literally surrounded by the Methodist fellowship itself in a prayer circle.

This clear, visible quality of separated Methodist fellowship at quarterly meetings often created a certain tension in the spectators that seemed to move them toward an experience of grace. Assembled Methodist fellowship had a dual quality to an outsider: it seemed like an assembly of her or his peers, yet was more. Methodists were recognizably familiar but retained a distinctive quality. Their fellowship seemed very accessible, yet claimed an eschatological character that placed it in the next world. This dual nature of the fellowship, often noted and accepted by nonmembers, created a disharmony or internal tension that propelled non-Methodists to explore their own faith or lack thereof.

For some nonmembers the plain fact that they were visibly excluded from this fellowship's private worship created a personal dilemma

---

30. See John Ffirth, *Experience and Gospel Labors of the Rev. Benjamin Abbott; to which is annexed a Narrative of his Life and Death* (New York: Carlton & Phillips, 1853), 234; and Colbert journal 4:77-78.

about their own spiritual state. Recognizing a special status of grace among those active in Methodist fellowship, some spectators experienced a deep sense of conviction that often led to a desire to join the Methodists and to seek justification. For some this sense of separation from the people of God had a particularly eschatological note: a realization of one's danger of being cut off from God's people at the upcoming judgment.

More commonly, exposure to Methodists in worship led to an optimism about the possibility of experiencing grace. At quarterly meetings those who had not experienced either justification or sanctification could see Methodists who claimed to have benefited from grace in either experience. Seeing such an example of grace experienced would awaken hope that grace was readily available. Countless seekers found hope by seeing peers who, in all respects, were like themselves yet could testify to the transformative power of God's grace in their own lives. Imagine the response from seekers of grace at one 1804 quarterly meeting. After a preacher spoke on "we know that we have passed from Death unto life because we love the Brethren," the Lord's Supper was administered. Immediately, many of the Methodists bore before a gazing multitude "a feeling testimony" of forgiven sins and of hearts filled with the love of God.[31] The worship itself became a recognizable face of grace experienced.

Seekers who recognized the graced status of their Methodist peers also more readily accepted Methodist proclamation of the gospel. A surprised reaction was common when first attending Methodist worship. To many seekers and mourners, Methodist messages in preaching, exhorting, testifying, singing, and praying articulated their own thoughts. Their accounts often spoke of their astonishment that the Methodists seemed to know the specific nature of their fears, sins, and desires. For example, John Langdon, who walked from Vermont to Connecticut to attend his first quarterly meeting, was amazed that the prayers and hymns of even the most common Methodists replicated the language of his own heart.[32] The result was a desire to unite with the Methodists, out of which came fruitful Christian experience for Langdon and a planting of Methodism in Vermont.

---

31. Boehm journal, 17 June 1804. The text for the sermon was 1 John 3:14.

32. Laban Clark, *Autobiography about his early life from 1778–1804: Circuit Rider for the Methodist Episcopal Church*, ed. E. Farley Sharp (Rutland, VT: Academy Books, 1987), 4; similar examples in chapters 2, 3, and 4. Note especially Daniel De Vinné, *Recollections of Fifty Years in the Ministry* (New York: Tibbals & Co., 1869), 9-12 where De Vinné's similar reaction to a Methodist exhortation was an inspired impression that "these are the people you have been looking for."

Another type of individual crisis involving grace came about by way of the conflict between accessibility and inaccessibility of Methodist fellowship. An outsider might have recognized the graced nature of Methodist fellowship, but may have been repulsed by the fellowship nonetheless. For many the tension was caused by accepting that Methodism was grace-filled, but also realizing that Methodists as a group were often despised. This tension created a desire for God's grace but an unwillingness to accept the cost of associating with the Methodists. As David Lewis later admitted, his initial enjoyment of Methodist fellowship was tempered by greater concerns: "My relations are all opposed to them—the world despises them, the devil hates them, and the pride of my heart keeps me back."[33] These sorts of accounts made explicit the connection between Methodist fellowship and an individual experience of grace. Such narratives typically describe individuals advancing in grace only to halt because they could not accept being associated with the despised Methodists.

"Comfortable Exercises of Grace": The Experience of William Keith

In 1806 an average Methodist from New York State, William Keith, published his short spiritual autobiography entitled *The Experience of William Keith. [Written by Himself.] Together with Some Observations Conclusive of Divine Influence on the Mind of Man.* In this book Keith maintains dual goals. At one level he was concerned with telling his experience of the grace of God through Christ. He wanted his readers to know about the wonder of forgiveness of sins he had obtained through Jesus Christ. At another level Keith desired to write an apology for the graced nature of Methodism. He wanted his readers to understand that his own story about experiencing grace was also a story about his perception of the authenticity of Methodism as a strand of Christian piety. As he stated in his preface, he was aware that many opposed the Methodists. Therefore he wanted to write his autobiography in a way that demonstrated how his own "experience

---

33. David Lewis, *Recollections of a Superannuate: or, Sketches of Life, Labor, and Experience in the Methodist Itinerancy*, ed. S. M. Merrill (Cincinnati: Methodist Book Concern, 1857), 36-37. See also George Brown, *Recollections of Itinerant Life: Including Early Reminiscences* (Cincinnati: Carroll & Co., 1866), 88, where Methodists were still considered a "sect everywhere spoken against" even in the second decade of the nineteenth century in Virginia.

and observations serve to shew that GOD owns these people."[34] Consequently, Keith's constant concern was to show how his own religious experience was integrally bound to his participation in Methodist fellowship. Because of this goal and because quarterly meetings played a key role in Keith's experience, his autobiography provides a useful example of the general theological propositions discussed above.

In many personal details Keith's story seems unexceptional for his time. He was born outside Easton, Massachusetts, in 1776. He lived in Massachusetts for his first sixteen years, acquiring a form of Calvinism from the "professors" of religion that he knew in that state. After he turned sixteen, Keith went to live in Litchfield, New York. Keith reported few details of his life there other than to detail his increasingly intense spiritual struggles, centered on pursuing various religious options. Keith noted religious anxiety caused first by his own Calvinism, then a belief in the universal salvation of all people, and finally "deism." The first left him frustrated with a sense that his sinfulness was inevitable, that he could not be saved, and that God was to blame. His foray into universalism was a variation of his Calvinism: instead of believing that God had eternally decreed some to be saved and some lost, Keith decided to believe that God had ordained all to be saved. A close encounter with a bear one night in the woods shattered Keith's shaky assurance, leaving him with a specific dread of dying. Finally, under the label of "deism," Keith tried to convince himself that there simply was no hell. His own unrelenting sense of guilt over sin, a constant feature through his entire narrative, never allowed him any ease in this position.

Sometime in 1793 Keith heard a Methodist preacher for the first time. Subsequently he often attended the Methodist preaching regularly appointed for his neighborhood. In May 1794 Keith attended a quarterly meeting in New Hartford, New York, a few miles outside of Utica. During this meeting he was justified at the love feast, to which he had obtained permission to attend. Keith returned home, joined a Methodist society, and began regularly attending class meetings.

William Keith progressed in grace and in status among the Methodists, although the path forward was not without interruption. Eventually he became a class leader. Later he received licenses as both an exhorter and local preacher. Starting in 1798 he itinerated briefly

---

34. William Keith, *The Experience of William Keith [Written by Himself.] Together with Some Observations Conclusive of Divine Influence on the Mind of Man* (Utica: Seward, 1806), 5.

on the Albany circuit, quitting in April 1799. Apparently he returned home, giving few details about his subsequent occupation.[35]

Keith structured his book around an astute and crucial theological question: Since Jesus Christ is no longer bodily present in this world, how can people now experience the grace he once offered? Keith's book raises this question twice, the first in the context of his early life. As a child Keith loved to read biblical stories. However, these same stories often left him dissatisfied:

> I often wept because I did not live in the days of the incarnation of Christ, that when he took children in his arms and blessed them, I might have cast myself at his feet and begged a blessing too.[36]

Later, after Keith developed a sense of sin and guilt, he began to incorporate these elements into the same basic question. Now instead of seeking a general "blessing" from Christ, Keith became more concerned about how he might experience the forgiveness Christ had once offered in the flesh:

> I thought that the Son of God had power while on earth, in human flesh, to save such as came to him with a sincere heart; but how a guilty sinner could now be brought into favor with God, was a mystery beyond my reach.[37]

This concern—how people can now experience the favor or grace of God—dominates Keith's entire narrative. His answer was to detail his own spiritual growth in the context of Methodist worship and fellowship. Among and through the Methodists, William Keith described how he had been saved by the grace of God in justification and sanctification and had continued to grow in grace beyond these threshold experiences. In addition to the basic facts of his life, Keith consciously wove together descriptions of his different experiences of grace with discussion of his relationship to the Methodists, in which quarterly meetings played an important role.

Throughout his story, Keith emphasized that the answer to his question of how one can experience God's grace in the present age has a communal dimension. For example, the background for his con-

---

35. After publication of his book, Keith once again itinerated. He died in 1810 while stationed in New York City. See his obituary in *Minutes*/1811, 193-94.

36. Keith, *Experience of William Keith*, 6.

37. Ibid.

version experience hinges on a fulfillment of a dream with a communal connection. Immediately after he had wondered "how a guilty sinner could now be brought into favor with God" Keith fell asleep and dreamed that the "enemy of souls" was carrying him away. Someone "whose form was like the Son of God" rescued him and carried him to a field where Keith saw six men clothed in white, sitting on white horses, and blowing the most melodious of music from trumpets. "Let me go with them!" Keith cried in his dream, but his guide responded, "Not now, but remember this." In the time that followed, Keith sought to fulfill his growing religious aspirations among Presbyterians but, because their preaching was more "pedantry than the plain gospel of Jesus," he did not find with them the fellowship that his dream had led him to desire.[38] His unfulfilled desire for fellowship was paralleled by continuing discomfort over the problem of his sin.

The fulfillment of his dream came at a May 1794 quarterly meeting in New Hartford, New York. When he saw the presiding elder, Thomas Ware, his dream came to mind and he realized that the six Methodist preachers he had heard by then—Ware was the sixth—"bore an exact resemblance" to the six horsemen he had envisioned.[39] Not surprisingly, that quarterly meeting was full of spiritual intensity for Keith, culminating in an experience of justification during love feast testimonials on Sunday morning.

Keith's description of that quarterly meeting featured all of the standard liturgical features, portrayed in a way that highlighted Methodist fellowship as the backdrop for his own experience. All day Saturday during worship it seemed to Keith that everything that was said directly addressed his own condition. Keith's perception that "the preacher knew all my heart" and that "the people . . . knew that I was the person pointed out by the preacher when he described the sinner" was made more acute by his realization that he did not belong to this fellowship. At the Saturday night prayer meeting, his distance from Methodist fellowship was readily apparent to him as he was the only one who did not kneel during prayer. The content of the Methodists' prayers underscored his lack of belonging as "they prayed for that sinner who was too proud to kneel."[40]

The climax came on Sunday morning. After arriving in time for the

38. Ibid., 6-7.
39. Ibid., 11.
40. Ibid.

love feast, Keith appealed to the doorkeeper to get in. When he was examined, Keith stated that his only qualification was being a "poor sinner" and was admitted because of his sincerity. The doorkeeper replied as he let Keith pass, "Christ came into the world to save sinners." Keith reported that, although he knew this biblical phrase, never had it held the meaning it did as he was admitted into the private worship of the Methodists.[41] Not surprisingly, like many others, Keith was converted as he witnessed firsthand the unity and love of this Methodist fellowship exhibited through the love feast testimonies. According to Keith,

> I went in to the lovefeast, and while they were telling the feelings of their hearts, I sensibly felt a change in my feelings. My load of guilt was removed, and every thing about me seemed to be changed.... I saw such a sufficiency in the savior's merits that I thought I was not afraid to die. There seemed such a union subsisting between Christ and my soul, that I thought I should love and praise him if he sent me to hell.[42]

In the midst of the most intense manifestation of Methodist fellowship at a quarterly meeting, while acquaintances and others testified to the grace of God, William Keith reported he had his own transforming experience. His journey toward a sense of assurance that God could save him—and indeed had saved him—from sin and toward full participation in Christian fellowship culminated at this love feast. After this quarterly meeting, Keith joined the Methodists and began regular participation in class meetings.

This same theme—that the experience of salvation is made available in the context of Methodist fellowship—is repeated throughout Keith's book. His exposure to Methodists before this quarterly meeting seems to have augmented the connection between Methodist fellowship and Keith's individual experience. For instance, the common internal tension caused by disharmony between the Methodists' familiarity and their unfamiliarity was felt by Keith. His initial response to the Methodist society in his home contained both attraction to this fellowship—they seemed more "devout" than other Christians he had known—and, at the same time, a discomfort with their being "too strict."[43] The same tension was at work as Keith listened to them in public worship. One exhorter's address to Keith to

41. Ibid., 12.
42. Ibid.
43. Ibid., 10.

"turn to the Lord" was well received as a word from God because of the dynamics between familiarity and nonfamiliarity. Keith had known this exhorter before he was a Methodist and accepted that grace had changed the man since he had become a Methodist. Accordingly, when this man exhorted him, Keith accepted his message as delivered with "no other motive than the good of my soul" and thus let himself become "resigned to the force of conviction."[44]

The same connection between participation in Methodist fellowship and experiencing grace continued after this quarterly meeting. In its most direct form, Keith linked his ongoing participation in Methodist fellowship with how well he seemed to enjoy the grace of God. On the one hand, in a period when he withdrew from societal life he noted that "in general I was in a dark state of mind."[45] On the other hand, when he joined the Methodists again he noted: "I felt a return of the favor of God, and could truly say, My Jesus is mine and I am his."[46] For Keith to make this direct connection was not surprising, given his description of gracious experiences while he was active in Methodist fellowship. One day in class meeting a few weeks after the May 1794 quarterly meeting, for example, his faith became more firmly established as again God seemed to pour out grace: "I obtained such an assurance of God's love, that I could no longer doubt. I could truly say, My Jesus is mine and I am his; or like Thomas, my Lord and my God."[47] Similarly, Keith's experience of sanctifying grace came during a lively prayer meeting a day after another quarterly meeting.

The final connection Keith made between his own experiences of grace and Methodist fellowship was the way he presented attacks to his spiritual status. Twice he reported being tempted by the arguments of others who tried to convince him to leave the Methodists. In the first instance, the attack came specifically on the basis that Methodists allowed the "unconverted" to join. Keith resisted this argument, partly on the basis of drawing a parallel to Jesus' practice of having fellowship with sinners. In this way Keith reconciled himself to the traditional Methodist threshold for membership and its corollary presumption that active participation in Christian fellowship was the normal way to experience saving grace. The second attack was in a way more insidious, as Keith realized that continued

44. Ibid., 11.
45. Ibid., 21.
46. Ibid., 22.
47. Ibid., 12. The scriptural allusion is to John 20:28.

association with Methodists would be a "cross to bear" due to their generally poor reputation. He ended his book with an acceptance of this cost of grace-filled fellowship and with a bold note to Methodist detractors. Quoting the apostle Paul in one of his trials, Keith declared

> "But this I confess, that after the manner which the world called heresy, so worship I the God of my fathers; believing in the prophets," and apostles, and in the methodist discipline and articles of faith.[48]

Having begun his theological portrayal of Methodism with the question of how people could still experience God's grace, given the bodily absence of Jesus Christ, by the end of his discussion Keith's answer was clear, at least for himself: one experienced grace through the Methodist fellowship at worship. While never addressing whether this claim was exclusive to Methodism, Keith consistently affirmed how characteristic it was of Methodism by telling of his own experience with the Methodists. Not surprisingly, the worship at quarterly meetings played a prominent role. By emphasizing the communal background to his experience, Keith's account helpfully exemplifies the dynamics of liturgical fellowship as the context for individual experiences of grace.

Conclusion

American Methodists officially became a church at the Christmas Conference toward the end of 1784. From that time forward The Methodist Episcopal Church grew steadily in prominence among American Protestant churches. To use this date as the beginning of Methodism in America, however, is misleading. In some crucial ways American Methodism had already acquired an ecclesial consciousness and self-identification before 1784. Emphasizing fellowship as the key ecclesial characteristic, and feeling as if their experience of Methodist fellowship was so wonderful that it had to be God-given and thus heavenly, Methodists had already begun to think of themselves as God's people before 1784. As some said in pleasantry, "We were a Church, and no Church."

A focus on the events of 1784 is also misleading if one allows it to

---

48. Ibid., 22. The quote is from Acts 24:14.

color too much what Methodists understood themselves to be as a church after this official transition. Even though they now had bishops, ordination, sacraments, and other external marks of a church, they were still a Connection of United Societies in the way they understood and conducted themselves at the local level. Their local consciousness—the level at which the average Methodists lived and believed—remained thoroughly societal. To read a journal or diary that begins before Christmas Conference and continues through creation of The Methodist Episcopal Church shows how pervasive this societal perspective was. At the local level—where classes met, where preachers itinerated on their circuit, where mourners under conviction were admitted as probationary members, where "professors" struggled for the second rest of sanctification—the Christmas Conference was no more than a small, although welcomed, blip on a screen. At this level, Methodism was still a connection of societies and classes linked together on a circuit served by itinerant and local preachers. Conspicuously absent was the notion of local Methodism as parishes and itinerant preachers as pastors.

Not surprisingly, Methodists seemed slow to use the word "church" to describe their embodiment in a local context throughout the remainder of the eighteenth and the beginning of the nineteenth centuries. For the most part they remained a society of "friends," and thus spoke most often of this society, or of the friends, or of Methodist brothers and sisters. And rightly so. Until the proliferation of itinerant elders locating, which happened in the late-eighteenth century, and the proliferation of stations, which began to happen in the nineteenth century, most Methodists were not confronted weekly with a full range of ordained ministries or liturgical rites and services. Depending on the number of available local preachers, many Methodists did not even have opportunity for regular worship on Sundays, as long as they remained on a circuit. For the average early Methodist there was little parish consciousness and almost no use of the word "church" to describe the Methodism he or she knew on a local level.

Indeed, as Russell Richey has perceptively suggested, the word "church," when applied to early Methodism on a smaller scale, is perhaps best used not for individual classes or societies but for the regular meeting of the entire circuit—the quarterly meeting.[49] There Methodism most intensely and visibly exhibited itself as an eschato-

---

49. Richey, *Early American Methodism*, 14, 20, and 28-29.

l fellowship within this world. Since fellowship was the central
t in their understanding of church, Methodists were not surprised when God graced their quarterly meetings with convictions,
justifications, sanctifications, and revivals. Simply put, a typical quarterly meeting was early American Methodism in its concentrated—
and fullest ecclesial—form.

Among early Methodists there was a phrase that intimately connected this relationship between grace and church fellowship: "social
grace." This short term suggests much about the essential communal
context for individual experiences of God. God's grace was *social*
grace, linked to one's experience of Methodist fellowship, particularly as experienced in worship. Thus one Wesleyan hymn declares:

> Let us join ('tis God commands),
> Let us join our hearts and hands;
> Help to gain our calling's hope,
> Build we each the other up.
> God his blessing shall dispense,
> God shall crown his ordinance,
> Meet in his appointed ways,
> Nourish us with social grace.[50]

For early American Methodism, quarterly meetings vividly and
repeatedly demonstrated the veracity of this claim. Often when
Methodist fellowship revealed itself in worship, a feast was set out
before the gathered people and many were nourished from the boun-
ty of God's "social grace."

---

50. *Hymns* #507, "The Love-feast," stanza 1, *Works* 7:698. This hymn was originally designated as a love feast hymn.

CHAPTER 6

A New Way to Be Church: The Decline of Quarterly Meetings as Liturgical Festivals

"Alas! the old-fashioned quarterly meeting is henceforth to be but a thing of history."
—*an itinerant preacher reminiscing about quarterly meetings*[1]

By the mid–nineteenth century Methodists could be found reminiscing sentimentally about the previous role of quarterly meetings in America. David Lewis, an itinerant preacher in New York State, reflecting upon the quarterly meetings he had known in the early part of the century, found it necessary to interpret their importance for a new generation:

> Methodists would go forty and fifty miles to quarterly meetings. These were our great festivals. Here we renewed our covenants with God and his people, obtained encouragement and strength in our souls, and rejoiced together in the salvation of God. . . . Truly our fellowship was with the Father, and with his Son Jesus Christ.[2]

One detects a note of sadness in Lewis's refrain: quarterly meetings *were* great festivals, but they are no longer.

Several of Lewis's contemporaries made similar comments. "The fame of our Quarterly meetings in former times," opined Orange Scott in 1835, "has come down to us from the fathers . . . they [the meetings] used to create a great interest among the people."[3] For

---

1. [James V. Watson], *Tales and Takings, Sketches and Incidents, from the Itinerant and Editorial Budget of Rev. James V. Watson* (New York: Carlton & Porter, 1857), 373.
2. David Lewis, *Recollections of a Superannuate: or, Sketches of Life, Labor, and Experience in the Methodist Itinerancy*, ed. S. M. Merrill (Cincinnati: Methodist Book Concern, 1857), 61.
3. Orange Scott, "Quarterly Meetings," *Zion's Herald* 6 (14 January 1835), 8. I am indebted to

centenarian Henry Boehm, former traveling companion for Bishop Asbury, "modern" quarterly meetings were emblematic of a fundamental change in the Methodism he knew. Not wishing to be identified with the "croakers" who flooded the mid- and late-nineteenth century with complaints about Methodist decline, Boehm nonetheless remarked that later Methodists might be shocked by earlier quarterly meeting revivals:

> What would we do if we could witness such a scene (of revival) at a modern quarterly meeting? There was a power among the fathers, both in the ministry and laity, that we do not possess. The ministers moved the masses as the wind does a field of wheat, and they mowed them down as the scythe does the grass.[4]

The memory had grown so faint for some by the mid-nineteenth century that preachers had to explain the features of an early quarterly meeting. Part of Abel Stevens's "memorials" of early New England Methodism was a description of the regular pilgrimage made by Methodists throughout the circuits to attend the meetings where "sinners must be converted, and believers sanctified."[5] Similarly, Charles Giles was eager to help Methodists understand the importance of earlier quarterly meetings: "They were made the theme of conversation long beforehand, and all necessary preparations were made to attend them" for "quarterly meetings then were accounted great seasons, not only by our own church, but by many others in community."[6]

By the latter half of the nineteenth century this kind of quarterly meeting was becoming a thing of the past. As Methodism continued to evolve, the nature of the typical quarterly meeting underwent a fundamental transformation. Passing from the scene were the quar-

---

Russell Richey for this quote as I am, generally, for his perceptive analysis of the evolution of quarterly meetings in his book *The Methodist Conference in America: A History* (Nashville: Kingswood, 1996).

4. J. B. Wakeley, *The Patriarch of One Hundred Years; Reminiscences, Historical and Biographical of Rev. Henry Boehm* (New York: Nelson & Phillips, 1875; reprint, Abram W. Sangrey, 1982), 140. For a discussion of "croakers" see John H. Wigger, *Taking Heaven by Storm: Methodism and the Rise of Popular Christianity in America* (New York: Oxford University Press, 1998), 180-90. For a more specific history of nineteenth-century Methodism see A. Gregory Schneider, *The Way of the Cross Leads Home: The Domestication of American Methodism* (Bloomington: Indiana University Press, 1993).

5. Abel Stevens, *Memorials of the Early Progress of Methodism in the Eastern States* (Boston: C. H. Pierce and Co., 1852), 297.

6. Charles Giles, *Pioneer: A Narrative of the Nativity, Experience, Travels, and Ministerial Labours of Rev. Charles Giles* (New York: G. Lane & P. P. Sandford, 1844), 212-13.

terly meetings that had grown into great liturgical festivals, subsuming the business component within a larger whole that commonly lasted a weekend. Taking their place were quarterly meetings that were stripped down to the business sessions of local leaders (i.e., the quarterly meeting conferences), with at most some brief "religious exercises" to call the meetings to order.

In a way, quarterly meetings came full circle from the mid–eighteenth to the mid–nineteenth centuries. Originally created in British Methodism solely to be business meetings, they were now returning to that status. The change was not universally welcomed, if the tone of George Coles's 1852 description is any indication:

> [Now] there are more quarterly conferences on the district than there are Sabbaths in the quarter. The old-fashioned quarterly meeting was a real religious festival, and very profitable. A quarterly-meeting conference now held on some evening in the week, is a mere business meeting, without sermon, love-feast, or sacrament.[7]

The changes in quarterly meetings' character and role were neither sudden nor intentional. The nineteenth century witnessed a slow unraveling of the strands that had made quarterly meetings so important and prominent as liturgical settings in early Methodism. There was no single fatal blow, nor a sole cause that dethroned the model of extended quarterly meetings.

One of the contributing factors in the decline of extended quarterly meeting with its multifaceted worship was competition from other Methodist innovations. Two innovations that became increasingly influential in nineteenth-century Methodist life were camp meetings and "two days' meetings." Both of these were spin-offs of the worship/revival dimension of extended quarterly meetings, and as their frequency grew, the need diminished for quarterly meetings to fulfill these functions. Revival could now, it was thought, be scheduled by the promotion of a specially planned protracted meeting. And business could be isolated to a quarterly meeting conference.

Another contributing cause to the reshaping of quarterly meeting was the increasing dissolution of active itinerancy and the tendency throughout the nineteenth century to split circuits into stations. This proliferation of stations brought greater "parish consciousness" to Methodism. With a larger number of ordained preachers in constant

---

7. George Coles, *My First Seven Years in America* (New York: Carlton & Porter, 1852), 82.

residence in their stations, sacraments, pastoral rites, and love feasts were available on a more regular basis in one's parish, a less connectional setting than a circuit. Accounts of quarterly meetings in the mid- and late-nineteenth century shows that quarterly meetings' two-day, multiple-service format—which had been virtually universal in American Methodism at the beginning of the century—survived primarily among circuits and not stations. Even in those circuits that continued the earlier format, accounts of the meetings read rather blandly. The excitement of these great liturgical festivals had largely worn off by the end of the nineteenth century. As the self-imposed diaspora caused by an active itinerant system progressively dissipated in this century, so did the earlier role of quarterly meetings. With this displacement of quarterly meetings as crucial liturgical setting, American Methodism was finding another way to be church.

From Quarterly Meetings to Camp Meetings

Early Methodists always aspired for a revival brought by God. Their bishops were no different. By the last part of the eighteenth century Bishop Francis Asbury was eagerly praying for a major revival of religion across America. Comparing the number of revivals he could count in British and American Methodism, Asbury hoped the time was ripe for another one in America:

> Mr. Wesley lived to see two general revivals of religion—one at the beginning, the other about thirty-six years ago; though, doubtless, they had generally a gradual growth of religion. We also have had two revivals—one at the beginning, the other about seven years ago [ca. 1787–1788]. The third revival has now taken place in England, and I hope ours will soon follow.[8]

Within a few years Asbury's hopes were realized. Beginning as early as 1796, reports began to come to him from across the nation with brief glimmers of an emerging revival. What began as a trickle of stories with encouraging numbers of converts and accessions to membership rapidly became a deluge after the turn of the century. The revival that scholars have called the Second Great Awakening— which Asbury called a new "work of God"—was in full bloom.[9] As he

---

8. *JLFA* 2:43. The entry is from Asbury's journal for 1795.
9. The Second Great Awakening was not limited to Methodism. Remember that this use of the

wrote in 1802, "I have a variety of letters, conveying the pleasing intelligence of the work of God in every State, district, and in most of the circuits in the Union."[10] Asbury was exultant that his hopes and prayers were fulfilled: "The Lord appears glorious upon our continent."[11]

Methodist reports about the emergence of this revival not only rejoiced that it was occurring, they highlighted where it was being manifested. While specific accounts of the eruption of this "work of God" might note any of several points of epiphany, frequently the emphasis was upon quarterly meetings as occasions for revival.[12] This was not a new role for quarterly meetings, and the focus given them as locus for revival surprised no Methodist at the time.

This focus was particularly true for reports written early in the revival. By the end of 1802 the spotlight began to shift, at first slowly, to the camp meeting. By 1812, camp meetings most frequently took center stage in Methodist accounts. Although not pushed into total obscurity, quarterly meetings were eclipsed. Whereas an itinerant's journal in the 1780s would inevitably place quarterly meetings at the heart of a "work of God" on his circuit, by the end of the first decade of the nineteenth century this limelight was usually captured by accounts of his camp meetings. If Methodists had gone to school at quarterly meetings to learn how to combine worship and evangelism in a large extended setting, camp meetings showed that they had graduated to something larger within a few years after the emergence of the Second Great Awakening.

Reports from Delaware in the early nineteenth century provide an

---

term "work of God" is the second of its possible meanings. Not only was the term applied to the particular manifestation of God's saving presence at one worship service, it was also used to describe the broader nature of God's activity, as intended here. It is not my intention to give a full history of the Second Great Awakening but only to use it to establish the context for the question immediately in view: the relationship of quarterly meetings to camp meetings. For more information on the Second Great Awakening see William G. McLoughlin, *Revivals, Awakenings, and Reform: An Essay on Religion and Social Change in America, 1607–1799* (Chicago: University of Chicago Press, 1978), 98-140; and Richard Carwardine, *Trans-Atlantic Revivalism: Popular Evangelicalism in Britain and America, 1790–1865* (Westport, CT: Greenwood Press, 1978), 3-58.

10. *JLFA* 2:340.

11. Ibid., 2:300.

12. For an example of multiple points of eruption in several common elements of Methodist life see the 1803 letter from local preacher John Jeremiah Jacob of western Maryland in *Extracts of Letters, Containing some Account of the Work of God since the Year 1800* (New York: J. C. Totten, 1805; reprint, Barnard, VT: Joseph Dix, 1812), 65-67. The initials for Jacob's name were mis-printed as "I. I." in the book and its reprints. The revival also had multiple geographic points of eruption. See Ruth, "A Little Heaven Below," 193-99 for a critique of other literature that too closely links the awakening with western regions.

excellent example of the shift from quarterly (and other meetings) to camp meetings. By the summer of 1805 the "work of God" had been ongoing for nearly five years on the Delmarva peninsula. Some of the best early manifestations were in extended meetings: Annual Conferences (particularly in 1800 at Smyrna, Delaware); "annual meetings" held outside Dover, Delaware, from 1801 to 1804; and the regular rhythm of quarterly meetings. The Delaware district's presiding elder had been zealously engaged in the work.[13] But, amazingly, the peninsula had not had a so-called camp meeting before that summer, although at other meetings participants had begun to camp out instead of traveling home each night.[14]

The presiding elder scheduled the first one for the end of July 1805. In his estimation it was a stunning success. It was not this district's only manifestation of revival that summer. In an account of the three months leading up to and climaxing with the camp meeting, the presiding elder detailed the "work of God" in ten separate quarterly meetings he had held.[15] Although the presiding elder, William Chandler, was pleased with the quarterly meetings, he was clear in his account that his and the district's focus of attention was on the camp meeting. Indeed he had used opportunities to speak at quarterly meetings in order to draw the people's hopes, prayers, and expectations for God to work beyond the quarterly meetings toward the camp meeting: "I made it a point, to call the attention of the people, at all the quarterly meetings; and explain to them, our intention and expectation [for the camp meeting]."[16]

The shift of focus embodied in this first called camp meeting in Delmarva was replayed throughout Methodism. Although quarterly meetings remained important settings for American Methodist worship and evangelism for some time, an important transition had begun. Ever increasingly, camp meetings became the times when revival was expected and planned for. They gave an opportunity to distill certain aspects that had been part of an integrated whole at

---

13. Kirk Mariner, "William Penn Chandler and Revivalism in the East," *Methodist History* 25.3 (April 1987): 135-46.

14. According to George Coles (*The Supernumerary; or, Lights and Shadows of Itinerancy. Compiled from Papers of Rev. Elijah Woolsey* [New York: Lane & Tippett, 1845], 85-86), the 1803 annual conference in Delaware was held with a large encampment of tents. The business session itself was in a nearby Quaker meetinghouse and the preaching in the Methodist meetinghouse. See also *JLFA* 2:389.

15. [William Chandler], *A Brief Account of the Work of God on the Delaware District, Since the Sitting of Conference, in May, 1805; in Which is Included an Account of the Camp-Meeting, Held in the State of Delaware, July 25, &c. in a Letter to Francis Asbury* (Dover, DE: n.p., 1805), 5-13.

16. Ibid., 13.

quarterly meetings—the liturgical and evangelistic aspects—and to place them in a setting not connected to the administrative aspect.

Indeed, camp meetings became *the* tool by which Methodists sought to extend and sustain the Second Great Awakening. The promotion of camp meetings was aggressively pursued for these ends in the first decade of the nineteenth century.[17] Bishop Asbury led the way. Having prayed for the arrival of a major revival for years and then having seen the role of encampments or "camp meetings" in this revival, Asbury encouraged the holding of these meetings as strongly as he could. Writing to the presiding elder of the Pittsburgh District in December 1802, for instance, Asbury urged:

> I wish you would also hold campmeetings; they have never been tried without success. To collect such a number of God's people together to pray, and the ministers to preach, and the longer they stay, generally, the better—this is field fighting, this is fishing with a large net.[18]

Asbury spent most of the next several years promoting adoption of camp meetings by writing letters, reading others' letters that gave accounts of the work of God, and (presumably) publishing several dozen of these letters in 1805 as *Extracts of Letters, Containing some Account of the Work of God since the Year 1800*. Before long camp meetings had become an unofficial institution for the seeking of revival across American Methodism.[19] They became times to schedule revival.

17. A comparison of the origins of quarterly and camp meetings as liturgical settings reveals the process by which liturgical innovations emerged and became standardized in early Methodism's evangelical ethos. There were three stages: spontaneous emergence of the practice, naming of the practice, and then active promotion of the practice under its name. For camp meetings, the emergence of the practice of camping (the truly distinctive part) began to be done sometime in the late 1790s or early 1800s, the widespread use of the term "camp meeting" per se occurred among Methodists in 1802, and active promotion began immediately afterward. See Lester Ruth, " 'A Little Heaven Below': Quarterly Meetings as Seasons of Grace in Early American Methodism" (Ph.D. diss., University of Notre Dame, 1996), 211-17 for an extended discussion of this process. A fourth stage should probably be added: as innovations matured and became standard, familiar practice, they were often supplanted by another innovation, as quarterly meetings were by camp meetings.

18. *JLFA* 3:251. Asbury should not be seen as the sole promoter of camp meetings. One of the Southern presiding elders, Stith Mead, was also instrumental—first by scheduling quarterly meetings in Georgia and then in Virginia, and second by keeping Asbury constantly informed in a flood of letters that Asbury read publicly and published.

19. A relevant issue at this point is the whole question of what defines a camp meeting. Some recent scholars have noted that the question of the origin of camp meetings eventually comes to a matter of definition (cf. Russell E. Richey, *Early American Methodism* [Bloomington: Indiana University Press, 1991], 105 n. 3; and Kenneth O. Brown, *Holy Ground: A Study of the American Camp Meeting* [New York: Garland, 1992], 4-5, 11). In particular, Brown takes to task the

Unforeseen and unintended was the eventual effect on the role of quarterly meetings. The emergence and promotion of camp meetings as a concentrated form of quarterly meeting helped set the path in the nineteenth century for returning quarterly meetings to an exclusive devotion to administrative business. By institutionalizing and externalizing the revivalistic dimension to camp meetings, the way was open for quarterly meetings' festivity and intensity to wane in the face of increasing administrative responsibility.[20]

There is great irony in the displacement of quarterly meetings by camp meetings since the latter were a direct derivative of the former. Not only were most camp meeting practices anticipated in several decades' worth of quarterly meetings, but many of the first meetings specifically called "camp meetings" were merely quarterly meetings with the added dimension of camping. To extend a quarterly meeting by a day or two by inviting the participants to come ready to house themselves and provide their own provisions was a very frequent way in which Methodists introduced camp meetings into a region. Surely that was the case in William McKendree's district in Ohio, Kentucky, and Tennessee; his four-day quarterly meetings in 1802 were indistinguishable from camp meetings.[21]

In fact, the line of demarcation between a quarterly meeting and an early so-called "camp meeting" is not clear. Many of the earliest Methodist camp meetings were quarterly meetings held as an encampment, nothing more. Some scholars, ignoring this fact, have thus overstressed the uniqueness of early camp meetings by failing to recognize their connection to already well-established patterns of church life.[22] In many instances, the first intentional camp meeting in an area—even if the name itself was not used—was a regularly scheduled quarterly meeting for which the itinerant preachers instructed the people to come ready to camp.

influential discussion by Charles Johnson in *The Frontier Camp Meeting* (Dallas: SMU Press, 1955), who so directed the definition of camp meetings that none of the antecedents could properly be considered camp meetings. I share Brown's opinion. As should be obvious, my own definition uses a very limited criteria: a camp meeting is one with widespread camping among the participants, who consequently are providing their own provisions. Camping defined a camp meeting, nothing more. The focus on camping, with concomitant self-provision, allows one to accept as camp meetings both meetings with other names that included camping (some Methodist quarterly meetings and Presbyterian sacramental meetings) as well as meetings scheduled as camp meetings per se.

20. Richey, *The Methodist Conference in America*, 61.

21. *Extracts of Letters*, 40-42.

22. This critique is not new. Leigh E. Schmidt (*Holy Fairs: Scottish Communions and American Revivals in the Early Modern Period* [Princeton, NJ: Princeton University Press, 1989]) raises a similar complaint by tracing camp meetings back to Presbyterian sacramental meetings. For exam-

The accounts from the Carolinas and Georgia, regions in which intentional camping occurred very early for Methodists, show that many of the first camp meetings were quarterly meetings planned as encampments.[23] At least one of the fall 1802 quarterly meetings in central North Carolina was intentionally held as a camp meeting. Beginning on Friday, 17 September, a five-acre camp with tents was laid out with multiple stands built for outdoor preaching.[24] Likewise, the presiding elder in Georgia noted that "the first general camp-meeting that I attended, in the Georgia district was at a quarterly Meeting held for Little River circuit" in October 1802.[25]

For itinerants who wanted to introduce the practice of camping, quarterly meetings were an attractive occasion to do so, as Henry Smith did in his Virginia circuit in 1803. Having successfully introduced the practice, a year later he was able to schedule an explicit camp meeting within the circuit.[26] Scheduling one of a circuit's quarterly meetings as an encampment became so commonplace that the practice became nearly universal, becoming one of the most standard ways to hold camp meetings for the various circuits.

In addition to such quarterly meetings held with a camping format, Methodists in some regions were scheduling full-fledged camp meetings, separate from any quarterly meeting, by the end of 1802. Over the next several years the practice spread so that by 1805 camp meet-

---

ples of works that highlight the role of camp meetings in the Second Great Awakening see Johnson, *Frontier Camp Meeting*; Dickson D. Bruce Jr., *And They All Sang Hallelujah* (Knoxville: The University of Tennessee Press, 1974); Bernard A. Weisberger, *They Gathered at the River: The Story of the Great Revivalists and Their Impact upon Religion in America* (Boston: Little, Brown and Company, 1958); and Catharine C. Cleveland, *The Great Revival in the West 1797–1805* (1916; reprint, Gloucester, MA: Peter Smith, 1959). Perhaps the only novel thing about the very first camp meetings was the camping itself. Methodist accounts from the period repeatedly speak of the novelty of widespread, planned camping by participants, but generally lack any other sense of novelty.

23. "Encampments" was an early term Asbury and others used for camp meetings in their nascent stage. See *JLFA* 2:368.

24. *Extracts of Letters,* 53-56. Quarterly meetings held as encampments in this region had begun, at least, in the previous summer. See pages 57-59 for an account of a late July 1802 quarterly meeting in Iredell County, North Carolina. The practice apparently extended to portions of Virginia in that same year. See pages 59-61 where the fall quarterly meeting near Rockingham, Virginia, was held for three days in the woods with several participants coming in wagons (a sign of camping).

25. Ibid., 70-76. Compare pages 68-70 where a participant in this meeting refers to it only as a camp meeting. The presiding elder's letter is very important in that it shows many of the features commonly seen in later camp meetings were already present in this very early one: clear organization of space, use of stages, use of trumpets to call people to worship, and family prayer meetings in the tents. Note also that many of the accounts reported the presence and activity of Baptists in these settings.

26. H. Smith, *Recollections and Reflections of an Old Itinerant* (New York: Lane & Tippett, 1848), 105-6. Compare the presiding elder's account of this same meeting in *Extracts of Letters,*

ings were being held in every region of Methodist activity, including Canada. An explicit camp meeting had been held in southern Virginia by early 1803.[27] That year saw camp meetings as well in western Virginia, Pennsylvania, and Maryland.[28] The expansion continued aggressively in the next year. By the end of 1804 camp meetings had been held in upstate New York, Connecticut, and Mississippi.[29] By the end of 1805 Massachusetts, Vermont, and New Hampshire had also seen camp meetings in their bounds.[30] Within a few years, camp meetings—both quarterly meetings held with a camping format and camp meetings in their own right—were a dominant fixture in American Methodism. From this time forward the dominance that "old-fashioned" quarterly meetings held began to slip as camp meetings moved to center stage. As one early itinerant noted, although quarterly meetings were "seasons of remarkable interest," camp meetings "presented more powerful attractions."[31]

This transition was a case of a younger sibling (the camp meeting) upstaging the older (quarterly meetings) since camp meetings are clearly clones of quarterly meetings. The remarkably quick stylizing of the order and routine for camp meetings naturally drew upon countless years of experience of holding quarterly meetings and thus, as others have pointed out, was "highly evocative of patterns" formed in quarterly meetings.[32]

Quarterly meetings' influence occurred on several levels. One involved the basic character of camp meetings: it seemed appropriate and familiar to assemble in the woods and hold a variety of worship services all day long for several days. The practice of distinguishing and then juxtaposing public and private services was also carried over

76-77. Note that members of Smith's circuit associated camping with trans-Appalachian Methodism, probably since Smith had just come from there. Note also that Smith's account accentuated the resistance as coming primarily from women: "Our females said, 'What! sleep in the woods: that will never do.' "

27. J. Lee, *A Short History of the Methodists, in the United States of America; Beginning in 1766, and Continued till 1809* (Baltimore: Magill & Clime, 1810; reprint, Rutland, VT: Academy Books, 1974), 289.

28. *Extracts of Letters*, 76-77, 83-84, 85-86, 91; *JLFA* 2:402.

29. Ibid., 99, 111; *JLFA* 2:469-70.

30. *JLFA* 2:474, 488.

31. Giles, *Pioneer*, 234. The continued interplay between the two types of meetings could continue to be quite important. Note that in Tennessee in the 1820s ([T. L. Douglass], "Account of the Work of God in the Nashville District," *MQR* 4 (1821): 191-95) quarterly meetings could still be occasions for continuation of the work of God but the main focus was clearly on camp meetings. In this instance, the quarterly meetings were used by Methodists to escalate their prayer activity in preparation for camp meetings.

32. Richey, *Early American Methodism*, 21.

from quarterly to camp meetings. Thus in camp meetings, like quarterly meetings, the most overt of the evangelizing exercises was placed next to the most intense of fellowship rituals with an expectation that the two would influence each other. Finally, the timing of camp meetings seems derived from previous quarterly meeting practices. The typical placement of camp meetings in a week, for instance, normally included Saturday and Sunday as the central days for the meeting. A very common pattern was a four-day camp meeting that began on Friday, reached its intensity over the weekend, and concluded on Monday. This was a short step from the common weekend-long quarterly meeting that included a Friday fast. Internally, organization of time seems related to the normal schedule for quarterly meetings. Camp meeting preaching was often appointed at the very hours as in its quarterly counterpart; Sunday morning usually included an act of private worship, most typically the love feast.

In these ways, camp meetings were essentially quarterly meetings held on a larger scale. That is why early Methodists so easily recognized, adopted, and fervently promoted camp meetings. Methodists distilled the essence of quarterly meetings, spread it over a longer period, and mixed in camping. Camp meetings were actually a "highly stylized recapitulation" or "ritual reenactment" of the nature of Methodism itself when gathered in an extended setting for worship and business—that is, quarterly meetings (and Annual Conferences).[33] Camp meetings gave Methodism a metaphor for itself, a mirror in which Methodists could perceive what they thought were the most grace-filled aspects of their fellowship and activity.[34]

Camp meetings went a step further, however. They were an opportunity for Methodists to divorce the business session—the conference, whether quarterly or annual—from the communal activities of worship and evangelism.[35] The holding of conference was incumbent for a quarterly meeting. The polity required it. Indeed, conference was officially the only reason to hold a quarterly meeting. At the polity level, conference *was* quarterly meeting. But camp meetings were a different species. Although many camp meetings were quarterly

---

33. Ibid., 24. It is astonishing how quickly a stylized form for holding camp meetings was created. Compare an 1802 Georgia camp meeting (*Extracts of Letters*, 70-71) to two 1819 meetings: one in Chesapeake Bay ([David Dailey], "Account of a Camp Meeting held on the Tangier Island in August 1819." Ms. St. George's United Methodist Church, Philadelphia, PA) and one in New York State (George Coles journal. Papers. United Methodist Church Archives-GCAH, Madison, NJ, 29 June 1819).

34. Richey, *Early American Methodism*, 21, 23-24, 30.

35. Ibid., 30.

meetings (with conference) held under the guise of camping, neither necessity nor requirement existed for this. There was no reason to hold conference in a camp meeting. That is why camp meetings are never mentioned in any *Discipline*, even though it was one of the most predominant institutions of nineteenth-century Methodism.

The ability to divorce business from worship and evangelism was even more evident in another gathering developed on analogy with quarterly meetings in the early nineteenth century: the "two days' meeting." A typical two days' meeting was everything that normally happened in a quarterly meeting except for the conference itself. It was a quarterly meeting that was not a quarterly meeting. The entire schedule was the same except for the omission of the business session.[36]

Two days' meetings arose about the same time as camp meetings and enjoyed similarly widespread adoption.[37] Most of the earliest references to these meetings derive from regions where the Second Great Awakening quickly and strongly emerged: Georgia, the Delmarva peninsula, and Kentucky.[38] That fact suggests that two days' meetings originated due to the revival; the excitement of the "work of God" provided occasion to schedule additional extended meetings, and desire to continue the "work" gave impetus. In some instances two days' meetings were called "extra" quarterly meetings, a term that lingered for a while.[39] The future bishop, John Emory,

---

36. See Benjamin McReynolds, Diary. Ts. Southern Historical Collection, University of North Carolina Library, Chapel Hill, NC, 31 May 1823; William Ormond journal. Papers. Special Collections Library, Duke University Library, Durham, NC, 12-13 October 1799; Marjorie Moran Holmes, "The Life and Diary of the Reverend John Jeremiah Jacob (1757–1839)" (master's thesis, Duke University, 1941), 310.

37. Two days' meetings also existed in longer versions: the three days' meeting (John Littlejohn, "Journal of John Littlejohn." Ts. Transcribed by Annie L. Winstead. Louisville Conference Historical Society, Louisville, KY. [Available on microfilm from Kentucky Wesleyan College, Owensboro, KY], 232; John Brooks, *The Life and Times of the Rev. John Brooks* [Nashville: Nashville Christian Advocate, 1848], 66; and Ormond journal, 12-14 November 1802) and the four days' meeting (Littlejohn journal, 203). It is not always clear whether these meetings involved widespread camping. If not, then a four days' meeting would essentially be an interesting variation of a camp meeting: one with no camping. However, in some cases, it is likely that "four days' meeting" was an early way of designating a camp meeting. See, for example, James B. Finley, *Sketches of Western Methodism: Biographical, Historical, and Miscellaneous*, ed. W. P. Strickland (Cincinnati: Methodist Book Concern, 1854; reprint, New York: Arno Press & The New York Times, 1969), 83, for a four days' meeting in Kentucky in August 1802. See also Littlejohn journal, 191.

38. For Georgia see Ormond journal, 12-13 October 1799; for Delmarva in 1800 see David Dailey, *Experience and Ministerial Labors of Rev. Thomas Smith, Late an Itinerant Preacher of the Gospel in the Methodist Episcopal Church* (New York: Lane & Tippett, 1848), 53, 64; and for 1803 Kentucky see Finley, *Sketches*, 83.

39. See especially the 1801–1802 entries in William Colbert, "A Journal of the Travels of William Colbert Methodist Preacher thro' parts of Maryland, Pennsylvania, New York, Delaware, and Virginia in 1790 to 1838." Ts. United Methodist Church Archives-GCAH, Madison,

reflecting on his own experience, noted that he "embraced religion, at a two days' meeting, then called an extra quarterly meeting" in 1806.[40]

While camp meetings provided ritual reenactments of the essential qualities of quarterly meetings, they also were clearly free to build upon this foundation. They evidenced an increasing complexity in ritualization that began to overshadow quarterly meetings liturgically. Even in the earliest camp meetings Methodists were markedly concerned about defining and preserving specific ritual practices.[41] Consequently, accounts of camp meetings often contain details about ritualized activities that are rarely found in quarterly meetings' accounts.

Many of these more complex rituals dealt with defining the assembly itself. Even before a single person had arrived to worship, great attention had often already been given to selecting, organizing, and creating the space. Standard patterns for arranging the worship space emerged with surprising quickness. Methodists' accounts of creating camp meeting spaces are quite specific in describing the distinctive worship environment at camp meeting as compared to accounts of

---

NJ, 4:14, 45, 77. Colbert used a similar term as far back as 1797 (2:141). See also Boehm journal, 2-3 October 1813. There was much fluidity in the terminology for extended meetings in the period. See, for example, the Ormond journal that speaks of "big meetings," "great meetings," "two days' meetings," "quarterly meetings," "three days' meetings," and, finally, "camp meetings" in the period between 1799 and 1802.

40. [Robert Emory], *The Life of the Rev. John Emory, D. D.* (New York: George Lane, 1841), 14. Some two days' meetings seem to have been planned and led predominantly by local preachers and not itinerants, although the reverse was true too; cf. John M'Lean, *Sketch of Rev. Philip Gatch* (Cincinnati: Swormstedt & Poe, 1854), 108. Indeed, the lack of a quarterly meeting conference meant that there was no official reason for any itinerant preachers to be present, whether preachers on the circuit or the presiding elder. Thus, like camp meetings, two days' meetings were never mentioned in the polity. In some instances the initiative of local preachers caused strained relationships with itinerant preachers, who tried to squelch these meetings. For instance, in an undated, unsigned handwritten account of the "state of religion" in the Edward Dromgoole papers (presumably written in the first person by Dromgoole), it was noted that "some of the Presiding Elders have discovered a disposition to check the locals having a two days meeting." The author of this sketch concluded by noting that Asbury himself, when he was alive, was frustrated too by presiding elders "trampling under foot" local preachers with respect to these meetings.

41. Compare Ann Taves, *Fits, Trances, and Visions: Experiencing Religion and Explaining Experience from Wesley to James* (Princeton, NJ: Princeton University Press, 1999), 114-17. She argues that camp meetings created "a new public time and place" for the use of the practices of the shout tradition to experience God. It was an institutionalization of the shout tradition, but one specifically outside of the formal structures of Methodism. Taves's assessment would explain some of the resistance camp meetings received, both within and without Methodism. It was not that the practices of the shout tradition were new, but that it made them much more visible and expected. Even within Methodism, with a growing body of "anti-shouters" in the early nineteenth century, the institutionalization of the shout tradition seemed unseemly to some.

quarterly meetings. Once gathered in the space, worshipers at camp meetings followed a complex, and apparently nearly universal, ritual for assembling that involved the blowing of trumpets. One or more trumpeters typically wandered through the campsite, signaling the time for an act of worship.[42] Such use of trumpets is virtually unknown at quarterly meetings, except for those held as camp meetings.

Camp meetings also evidence more complexity in the various rituals developed for the act of parting at the end of the meeting. These too were acts of defining the assembly, although they deal with facilitating its dissolution rather than its gathering. One excellent example occurred at the end of an 1806 Connecticut camp meeting:

> At length the last sermon was delivered and followed by exhortation, when the preachers, about twenty in number, drew up in a single line, and a procession was formed four deep, led by a preacher, in front of a number of little children singing hymns of praise and followed by hundreds who joined in the songs of Zion, marching round the encampment: at first they passed behind the line of ministers, until the children headed by the preacher came up to it again, when every person formed in procession shook hands with all the ministers successively.[43]

At least to the writer of this account, the ritual's meaning was clear: "souls filled with love are only parted in body, their minds are united in one" in Jesus Christ. The same writer offered other details about this sort of ritualized parting: some spectators did not participate, and sometimes the ritual itself was the catalyst for someone's conversion.[44]

The notion of a distinctively assembled community was accentuated by developing rules and regulations for the camp. In a sense these were

42. Francis Ward, *An Account of Three Camp-Meetings held by the Methodists, at Sharon, Litchfield County, Connecticut; at Rhinebeck, in Dutchess County; and at Petersburgh, In Rensselaer County, New-York State* (Brooklyn: Robinson & Little, 1806), 8. Compare Minton Thrift, *Memoir of the Rev. Jesse Lee. With Extracts from his Journals* (New York: Bangs & Mason, 1823), 311-12, where Lee complains about too much "ceremony and form" in the closing of an 1810 New Jersey camp meeting. Perhaps there were regional differences in the manner of parting.

43. For an excellent description of the practice see Brooks, *Life and Times*, 40. The use of trumpets can be dated very early in camp meetings. The earliest account I have found was at an 1802 Georgia camp meeting in *Extracts of Letters*, 70-71.

44. Ward, *Account of Three Camp-Meetings*, 19. See also pages 15-16. It is hard to tell how much of this sort of ritual was used in quarterly meetings not held as encampments. Again, quarterly meetings accounts are nearly silent, although it is clear the act of parting at quarterly meetings was often a very moving scene.

the "rubrics" of the assembly itself.[45] They were a regular feature of camp meeting organization early on, but seemed to have no place in quarterly meetings not held as encampments. In other words, part of the increased ritual complexity of camp meetings was the fact that the assembled community no longer just occurred but was created and regulated. Methodists employed the image of participation in an ordered city to describe salvation; well-regulated campgrounds gave concrete expression to this cornerstone of Methodist piety. Although assembling was an important act in previous quarterly meetings, camp meetings intensified the phenomenon by having the worship assembly actually live together for several days. In this and other ways early Methodists distilled the essence of their quarterly meetings and annually scheduled them as independent entities.[46] Although they did not mean to do so, they set in motion one contributing factor to the decline of quarterly meetings as liturgical festivals.

Camp meetings also represent a development beyond quarterly meetings in their even more aggressive form of liturgical pragmatism.

---

45. Like other features of the more complex ritualization of camp meetings, creation of a set of rules was a regular part of camp meetings from an early stage. An excellent example of a set of early rules was the one that William Chandler, presiding elder of the Delaware District, developed and read in an 1805 camp meeting (*Brief Account of the Work of God*, 16-17):

1. The travelling preachers, local preachers, and exhorters, are to give in their names at the preachers' tent; where they are to repair, each morning, at the sound of the morning trumpet, to receive their appointments for the day.
2. None of the men will be permitted to go beyond the limits of the tents, on the south side of the camp.
3. No person will be allowed to smoke, either the pipe or segars, upon the camp ground.
4. No persons are to come into the preachers & managers' tent, unless they have business there.
5. The men and women are to sit apart in the congregation.
6. Every person, who is not encamped on the ground, is requested to leave the camp by ten o'clock at night.
7. There must be no intermixture of the white & coloured people . . . the coloured people are to repair to the back court, the place prepared for them.
8. The order of the trumpets . . . (a schedule for services follows).
9. No person will be suffered to stand upon the seats.
10. The spiritual guard will attend, 1st to the seating of the congregation; 2dly, keeping the people from standing in the aisles; and, 3dly, to the order in the assembly during public worship.

46. It is interesting to note that when a summer/fall quarterly meeting was held as a camp meeting attendance among the local preachers, exhorters, stewards, and class leaders could increase dramatically. Compare the minutes for the August/September quarterly meetings beginning in 1806 in the Hockhocking (OH) circuit's "Book of Records." Ms. Ohio Wesleyan University Library, Delaware, OH. See also the records for the Fall Creek (IN) (Fall Creek Circuit [IN] Quarterly Meeting Conference records, 1828–1829. Ms. DePauw University Library, Greencastle, IN) and Honey Creek (IN) (Honey Creek Circuit [IN] Steward's Book, 1821–1829. Ms. DePauw University Library, Greencastle, IN) circuits. The result was that most official business in the circuit was done at these quarterly meetings, eclipsing the other three in the year.

Some pragmatic sensibility had been resident in American Methodism from the very beginning. Part of it was a Methodist tendency to assess the ever-increasing numbers as a sign of God's favor on the fledgling movement. With their rapid growth in the last quarter of the eighteenth century, Methodists could be giddy about the numeric "success" of grace.[47] The other part was a willingness to re-create those aspects of their ecclesial life that they saw as the most frequently effective occasions of grace. The official promotion of quarterly meetings as two-day festivals on a weekend format is itself an example of this nascent form of liturgical pragmatism. Naturally, Methodists gloated when they saw other ministers copying Methodist practices.[48]

While liturgical pragmatism is evidenced in American Methodism since its beginning, camp meetings represent a more intense stage of this sensibility. The manner in which they were named, promoted, spread, and supported indicates an aggressive use of this form by Methodists to extend the revival of the early nineteenth century. Before 1802 no one even used the term. By 1805 Methodists were holding camp meetings from Canada to Georgia to Mississippi. The intensity of Methodist rhetoric behind this promotion paralleled the love Methodists had for this form of successful "field fighting" or "fishing with a large net." Indeed, Methodists seemed enamored with how numerically successful camp meetings could be. The practice arose of counting the numbers on a daily basis, perhaps twice a day, and calculating the net results. The numbers were just confirmation for Bishop Asbury, an active promoter of camp meetings, that camp meetings represented an opportunity to "storm the devil's strongholds."[49]

Of course, the inherent danger in using numerical standards for assessing liturgical practices is that numbers can become self-validating and lead to less guarded forms of pragmatism. That appears to have been the case later in the nineteenth century; numerous examples can be found in the late–twentieth century as well. For the first several decades of American Methodism the pragmatism was seemingly held in check by a desire to maintain a strong countercultural stance, demonstrated by disciplinary exclusion of wayward members. With growing numbers, strict discipline was increasingly hard

47. See Wigger, *Taking Heaven by Storm*, 3, 197-200.
48. For an example see *Extracts of Letters*, 30-31.
49. *JLFA* 3:300.

to maintain. What remained was the use of numeric standards to gauge success. The result is a residual, fundamental liturgical pragmatism that presently characterizes the approaches to worship of many U.S. Protestants, including Methodists.

From Circuit to Stations

In 1824 an itinerant preacher, Overton Bernard, was sent by his bishop to serve in Edenton, North Carolina. Bernard had not been an itinerant for long, having been admitted on a trial basis during the 1822 Virginia Annual Conference and then ordained a deacon during its 1824 session. He went to Edenton with some trepidation. A self-identified "Uplander," Bernard worried about the preservation of his health in the North Carolina "lowlands."

But health concerns were not the only thing that troubled Bernard. Soon after his arrival in Edenton he noted his worries about the preaching appointments he was to meet regularly. Preferring to stay in residence in the city, Bernard tried to give himself a reason to appreciate the traveling required of him, but his rationalizations even left him unconvinced:

> There are four appointments in the country which it is expected I am to attend once in three weeks, which will form an agreeable excursion into the county, was it not that I shall have to go too often and loose too much time from study, and I somewhat fear the section of the country where those appointments are may not be very agreeable.[50]

Bernard's first round through these appointments, lasting five days and taking him twenty-five miles from Edenton, only confirmed his fears. To him the people looked "swarthy and unhealthy" and in some instances were "ignorant and uncouth in the extreme."[51] It is clear that his desire would have been to stay in the city where he could have time to study and meet his weekly responsibilities among more respectable people: preaching two or three times every Sunday, preaching every Wednesday night, and attending prayer meetings every Monday and Friday nights.[52]

50. Overton Bernard, Diary. Ms. Southern Historical Collection, University of North Carolina Library, Chapel Hill, NC, 12 April 1824.
51. Ibid., 17 April 1824.
52. According to the records for Edenton, Bernard was likely assisted by several local preachers, some of whom were elders and deacons.

Overton Bernard's ambivalence about traveling to preach and his desire to stay in pastoral residence reflect a major shift in Methodist ministry that took place progressively through the early nineteenth century.[53] This period witnessed a steady deterioration in active itinerancy as circuits were dissolved into stations and the number of preaching appointments to multiple places was regularly reduced. As this century progressed, the typical Methodist itinerant became increasingly like a parish minister in constant residence with a single congregation (or a few) under his care. Since the temporal rhythm of many early Methodist liturgical practices was determined by itinerancy, this fundamental shift from circuit to station affected all aspects of church life, even the rhythms of Methodist worship. For instance, with more pastors in residence the need to make use of quarterly meetings as special occasions for worship diminished.

The station was not an entirely new invention in early American Methodism. Since the beginning years of The Methodist Episcopal Church in the eighteenth century a few towns along the East Coast had been organized as stations. These earliest stations were, as one early itinerant stated it, essentially a whole city as one circuit. All the itinerant preachers in the city, along with the local preachers, rotated among the various preaching responsibilities throughout the city.[54] In 1790 New York for example, the journal of William Jessop, an itinerant preacher, shows a regular weekly round of preaching within the city itself by a variety of people, along with an occasional preaching appointment in Brooklyn, the "alms house," and the "two-mile stone."[55] By 1791 Baltimore; Fell's Point (a part of Baltimore); Philadelphia; Charleston, South Carolina; and even Annapolis, Maryland; Wilmington, Delaware; and Alexandria, Virginia, were stations.[56]

---

53. For a comparable nineteenth-century British perspective on the desirability of less active traveling for itinerants, see Richard Treffry, "An Address to the Young Ministers who were admitted into full connection with the Wesleyan-Methodist Conference," *MQR* 17 (1835): 291.

54. Daniel De Vinné, *Recollections of Fifty Years in the Ministry* (New York: Tibbals & Co., 1869), 34.

55. See the William Jessop journal beginning in October 1790 (Journal [1790–1791]. Ms. St. George's United Methodist Church, Philadelphia, PA). Jessop's journal sketches a rhythm of three Sunday preaching services, a Tuesday night preaching service, a Wednesday prayer meeting, a monthly love feast on a Thursday night, and a monthly Lord's Supper on the first Sunday of the month in one of the chapels. Similar liturgical rhythms are found in existing plans of stational preaching appointments.

56. According to George A. Phoebus, comp., *Beams of Light on Early Methodism in America* (New York: Phillips & Hunt; Cincinnati: Cranston & Stowe, 1887), Baltimore was turned into a station in 1788 (p. 85), Philadelphia seems a station in 1796 (pp. 217-31), Annapolis was already a station in 1789 (p. 104), and Alexandria was made a station in 1791. Careful attention to the *Minutes* of the annual conferences from this period reveals the other stations. To determine whether a listed

The proliferation of stations was one of two significant changes in the itinerant system in the nineteenth century. Stations began to be established with frequency around the turn of the century. By 1803 Norfolk, Virginia, was a station.[57] By 1805 at least fifteen cities in Georgia, North Carolina, South Carolina, and Virginia were stations. The phenomenon spread ever outward. By 1812 Lynchburg, Virginia, was a station. In the Genessee Conference the first two stations were formed about the same time: both Utica and Paris formed in 1815. Louisville, Kentucky, was a station by 1818 and the St. Augustine, Florida, mission was effectively a station by 1823.[58] By 1822, Connecticut, which probably had only one station (New Haven) ten years previous, contained three (New Haven, New London, and Middletown), and more were soon added (Hartford, Bridgeport).[59] This period had, as the report from the Committee of Safety cautioned the 1816 General Conference, "a general tendency to locality."[60]

This proliferation was not well received by some. As early as 1813 Bishop Asbury complained about the "growing evil of locality." In the same speech Asbury estimated that, out of seven hundred itinerants, about one hundred were in towns, cities, and "small rich circuits."[61]

appointment is a circuit or station I asked the following questions: (a) did the appointment bear the name of a city? (if so it was likely to be a station), (b) how many itinerants were appointed? (stations tend to have one or three or more; circuits usually two), and (c) how large was the membership? (other than the very large stations [Baltimore, Philadelphia, New York], stations tended to be smaller than an average circuit.)

57. From the *Minutes* of the annual conferences it appears that Norfolk might have been a station from the mid-1790s.

58. For documentation of this status see the following: March 1803 entries in the Ormond journal (Norfolk); 1805 letter in *JLFA* 3:306 (Georgia, North Carolina, South Carolina, Virginia); 1812 entries in the John Early journal ("Journal of Bishop John Early who lived Jan. 1, 1786–Nov. 5, 1873." Ts. Southern Historical Collection, University of North Carolina, Chapel Hill, NC) (Lynchburg); Zechariah Paddock, *Memoir of Rev. Benjamin G. Paddock, with Brief Notices of Early Ministerial Associates* (New York: Nelson & Phillips; Cincinnati: Hitchcock & Walden, 1875), 142 (Genessee Conference); M. M. Henckle, *The Life of Henry Bidleman Bascom, D.D., LL.D., Late Bishop of the Methodist Episcopal Church, South* (Louisville: Morton & Griswold, 1854), 113 (Louisville); and Joshua N. Glenn, "A Memorandum or Journal of the first part of my life up to the twenty third year of my age." Ms. on microfilm. Library of Congress, Washington, D.C., 149 (St. Augustine).

59. William Thacher, "A Sketch of the History and Present State of Methodism in Connecticut," *MQR* 5 (1822): 35.

60. *JGC*/1816, 1:157. The Committee also noted that "circuits have been formed, divided, and subdivided, on the principle of accommodation to local circumstances" so that circuits were reduced "almost exclusively to Sabbath appointments."

61. *JLFA* 3:475. Asbury's numbers are perhaps a little overstated. Review of *Minutes*/1813 reveals probably fewer than fifty true stations. Some of the probable newer stations include Augusta, Georgia; Columbia, South Carolina; Wilmington, North Carolina; Washington, D.C.; Pittsburgh, Pennsylvania; Brooklyn, New York; and Albany, New York. Even if Asbury's numbers were a little overstated for 1813, the number of stations grew steadily. Initially the *relative* number of stations seems not to have increased. Since this was a period of rapid growth for Methodism, new circuits were continually being added as well.

This episcopal complaint continued later in the century. In 1844 the bishops at General Conference warned of the impact of a "strong and increasing tendency to locality" so significant that "in some of the conferences little or nothing remains of the itinerant system."[62] Given the number of parsonages that were being built by the mid–nineteenth century, this certainly seemed to be the case. By one Methodist's reckoning at the time, about one parsonage was built every two days during years immediately prior to 1860.[63] Itinerants who had houses lost their need for horses. The trend toward stationing had grown so prominent that by the latter half of the century some Methodists were wondering whether, instead of being the most itinerant, they had "become the most localized of American Churches."[64]

The proliferation of stations early in the century was accentuated later in the century by a related development. The first stations were literally small circuits within a city. The multiple preaching appointments among all the city's congregations were shared by all the itinerants sent to the station, as well as the local preachers who lived there permanently.[65] By midcentury, however, there are signs of an increasing one-to-one association between an individual itinerant preacher and a specific congregation. As James Dixon, a visiting British Methodist, explained to his English readers in 1849, a "pure" itinerancy had been nearly abandoned in the towns and cities. Instead, Dixon said, the preachers were in stations, which he defined as "the appointment of a single minister to the pastoral charge of one society and congregation." According to Dixon, this stational practice had itinerants "literally confined to one congregation."[66]

---

62. *JGC*/1844, 2:157. The bishops also argued for a revival of the "primitive circuit system" in which circuits with multiple itinerants were more predominant than stations and in which presiding elders could spend "a Sabbath at each quarterly meeting for the year." See also Richey, *The Methodist Conference in America*, 115-16. At that same General Conference, the report of the Committee on Itinerancy reveals similar concerns. The Committee suggested (2:115) that a presiding elder should not be "a mere business man" who can hold efficient business meetings but should be someone who could take the lead "in the more important religious exercises appropriated to a quarterly meeting occasion." The Committee likewise suggested that every quarterly meeting should be a protracted meeting and that presiding elders should spend several days at each meeting.

63. Abel Stevens, "Methodism: Suggestions Appropriate to Its Present Condition," *MQR* 42 (1860): 134. Stevens also estimated that during this time period 970 churches had been built.

64. David Sherman, "Ministerial Transfers," *MQR* 52 (1870): 236.

65. See these various stational plans for preaching appointments: New York in 1831–1832 (Seaman, Annals of New York Methodism, 480-81); Cincinnati in 1833–1834 (John Wigger, "Holy, 'Knock-'em-down' Preachers," *Christian History* 14.1 [n.d.], 24; Philadelphia in 1822–1823 (Ezekiel Cooper papers); Philadelphia in 1826–1827 (St. George's United Methodist Church, Philadelphia, PA); and Baltimore in 1831–1832 (United Methodist Historical Society, Lovely Lane Museum, Baltimore, MD).

66. James Dixon, *Personal Narrative of a Tour Through a Part of the United States and Canada,* 2nd ed. (New York: Lane & Scott, 1849), 274, 276. Dixon's statement, although indicating the general

Within stations the quarterly meetings assumed a role different from the one they had within circuits. The emphasis was much less on the festive gathering of the Methodist people, and others, scattered across a circuit. Instead these quarterly meetings were more restricted to being quarterly meeting *conferences,* or business sessions. Accordingly, the scope of the meetings was restricted in two ways. First, the business meetings became detached from the typical weekend format and occupied only a part of one day. Second, their liturgical dimensions were abbreviated as the quarterly meeting conference became somewhat autonomous. Thus William Colbert's descriptions of quarterly meeting days in 1805 Philadelphia show an abbreviated pattern: a part-day business session for the members of the conference, held on the first Monday of a month, perhaps followed by an evening love feast for the members in general.[67] Colbert's descriptions tend to be short and sometimes matter-of-fact about the whole day, particularly as compared to some of his descriptions of quarterly meetings in circuits. As the century progressed and the trend toward the establishment of one-to-one association between minister and congregation progressed, the abbreviation of quarterly meetings became more pronounced. Quarterly meeting conferences were no longer held for an entire city but strictly for a single congregation.

The proliferation and development of stations in the nineteenth century certainly had an effect on the way Methodists worshiped, both at and outside of quarterly meetings. One immediate difference for a typical Methodist would have been greater, more frequent access to the variety of Methodist worship services.[68] In a station, every congregation would have had preaching two or three times each Sunday Additional preaching services and prayer meetings were commonly scheduled for weeknights. The Lord's Supper was administered on a

---

direction for all Methodism, should be modified somewhat for the midsection of the country where this trend seems slower to have been adopted. Compare the statement about midcentury Illinois and Iowa in Rev. Dr. [?] Wheeler, "Our Methodist Local Preachers," *MQR* 64 (1882): 241.

67. See, for example, Colbert journal 5:87, 105. There are some indications that this Monday night love feast was not even connected to the quarterly meeting but was a regular part of the monthly liturgical rhythms in this city (cf. Colbert journal 5:93, 119, and 139). Note that the quarterly meeting conferences in Philadelphia continued to be regularly held on Mondays twenty-five years later. See the records for 22 June 1829 to 2 January 1843 in "Minutes of the Quarterly Conferences of St. George's Charge." Ms., St. George's United Methodist Church, Philadelphia, PA.

68. For examples of the liturgical rhythms of stations see Phoebus, *Beams of Light,* 105 and 124; Jessop journal, October 1790 and following; Glenn journal, entries for 1823; [Tobias Spicer], *Autobiography of Rev. Tobias Spicer: Containing Incidents and Observations; also Some Account of his Visit to England* (New York: Lane & Scott, 1852), 71; and Colbert journal 5:67-120.

regular monthly basis within any congregation, often with different congregations having the sacrament on a different Sunday of the month. Love feasts perhaps had a similar rhythm; at a minimum, their administration was not necessarily tied to quarterly meetings. The more frequent celebration of love feasts and other rites meant that preachers with the necessary ecclesial authority were more likely to be in relatively permanent residence. Methodists in a station were no longer dependent upon the quarterly encounter with the presiding elder for sacraments and love feast.[69] The more regular weekly and monthly liturgical rhythms of stations meant that they need not expect their quarterly meetings to be exceptional liturgical festivals.

With an active itinerancy and a preponderance of circuits, early Methodists lived in a form of self-imposed diaspora. They belonged intimately to something spread across space—the Connection—and this directly influenced the temporal rhythms for their worship activities. How Methodists related to space determined how they related to liturgical time. Emergence and use of quarterly meetings as great liturgical festivals created one set of Methodist self-understandings; one that emphasized their relationship connectionally. As stations proliferated and individual congregations gained greater one-to-one correspondence with a minister, Methodists developed a new relationship to space and thus earlier rhythms of worship changed, including those associated with quarterly meetings.[70] This change in how Methodists related to space and time as reflected in quarterly meetings did not go unnoticed in the nineteenth century. As Orange Scott described the situation in 1835, because Methodists' "circuits are made so small that they (quarterly meetings) are held in almost every neighborhood," attendance at the meetings had dropped. According to Scott, the decline in interest in quarterly meeting was "the natural consequence of cutting up the work into small circuits and stations."

---

69. In looking at shifts in early liturgical rhythms one must also consider the increasing number of local or located preachers who were ordained. The original intent was for ordination to have been strictly limited to itinerants (see Lester Ruth, "A Reconsideration of the Frequency of the Eucharist in Early American Methodism," *Methodist History* 34.1 [October 1995]: 52-56). This original plan changed. In 1788 the *Discipline* (p. 6) allowed local preachers to be ordained as deacons. In 1812 the *Discipline* (p. 75) allowed local deacons to be ordained as elders. Moreover, of the 213 itinerants who located through 1799, 105 had been ordained as elders and 71 as deacons. (Some were ordained subsequent to their locating.) See Edwin Schell, "Methodist Travelling Preachers in America 1773–1799," *Methodist History* 2 (1964): 51-67. The general impact was an ever increasing number of preachers ordained to a residential ministry through the nineteenth century.

70. See the similar assessment in Russell Richey, "Itineracy in Early Methodism," in *Send Me?: The Itinerary in Crisis*, ed. Donald E. Messer (Nashville: Abingdon, 1991), 34-35.

He reasoned that Methodists likely felt no compulsion to attend a meeting of a station or church to which they were not connected. In Scott's mind this factor resulted as well in a decreasing propensity for Methodists to attend their own quarterly meetings.[71] The circuit that Methodists once sought in quarterly meetings could now be scheduled by station Methodists in their own congregations.

Indeed, the changing liturgical role of quarterly meetings meant that they were now sometimes viewed as an interruption in the normal rhythms of Methodist worship. For example, the joint quarterly meeting conference for Bridgeport and Stratford, Connecticut, had to pass a resolution so that the worship of some of the congregations under its purview would not conflict with that of the quarterly meeting. Surely a tension caused by increasing parish consciousness was behind its 1840 resolution:

> Resolved by this conference that when the quarterly meetings are held in Stratford it is expedient to close the Church in Bridgeport during the time of holding the usual Morning service and that the Church be invited to attend the lovefeast & morning service at Stratford and contrawise when the quarterly meetings are held in Bridgeport.[72]

Such a resolution imploring American Methodists to interrupt their local weekly liturgical rhythms and to make a pilgrimage to quarterly meetings would have been unnecessary a half century before.

While the complete disintegration of quarterly meetings as liturgical event proceeded slowly in places, it did steadily proceed. The quarterly meeting for Stratford, Connecticut, is helpful for identifying the several stages of this decline. Through the middle part of the nineteenth century many of its quarterly meetings continued on a weekend format with multiple preaching services, love feast, and sacrament. However, the quarterly meeting itself began to itinerate: certain parts

---

71. Scott, "Quarterly Meetings," 8. Note that Scott had spent his ministry up to 1835 in New England. See Lucius C. Matlack, *The Life of Rev. Orange Scott* (New York: C. Prindle and the author; 1847; reprint, Freeport, NY Books for Libraries Press, 1971). Scott also complained that people had grown indifferent not only to attending quarterly meeting worship on Saturday but also to the early Sunday morning love feast, thus indicating that the two-day, weekend format was still continuing in some places. See Richey's similar assessment of Scott in *Conference,* 115 and 262 n. 37. Though these trends are clear, they did not occur at the same time everywhere. Compare the description of liturgically full 1830s quarterly meetings, seemingly in upstate New York, by one itinerant (James Erwin, *Reminiscences of Early Circuit Life* [Toledo, OH: Spear & Johnson, 1884], 14-17). However, by the end of the nineteenth century this itinerant too was noting that "our congregations are now more local. We cannot bring the tribes together (at a quarterly meeting) as in olden times."

72. Stratford Circuit records, 9 July 1840, p. 135. Bridgeport and Stratford were adjacent towns.

of the weekend would be held at Stratford and other parts at one of the few other preaching appointments that made up the station.[73] These Connecticut Methodists no longer had to travel to the quarterly meeting; the quarterly meeting traveled to them! Another stage seems to have emerged by the 1870s: the quarterly meeting conference became an isolated event tucked into an opportune moment in the parish's life. Worship dimensions were abbreviated sharply, limited to opening "religious exercises." Thus Stratford's December 1870 meeting was held at the parsonage and opened with "devotional exercise." Its November 1875 meeting, held on a Friday evening, opened simply with a prayer by the presiding elder. Its May 1884 meeting was held at the close of the regular Wednesday evening prayer meeting in the prayer meeting room of the church.[74]

While these quarterly meeting conferences were important administrative meetings here and elsewhere, they no longer played any role as great liturgical festivals. The prominent Methodist historian Abel Stevens noted the change midway through the nineteenth century, describing a quarterly meeting of a previous era: "Formerly its exercises were largely, mostly indeed spiritual . . . (it was) a great religious festival."[75] But those days and those events were past. While a fuller form of quarterly meetings continued in some places, particularly in active circuits,[76] nineteenth-century Methodism had discovered another way to be church.

---

73. See the Stratford records for the 1860s, pp. 205-43.

74. Ibid., 10 December 1870 (p. 248); 12 November 1875 (p. 275); "Record Book of the Quarterly Conference of the Methodist Episcopal Church, Stratford, Connecticut, 1885–1899," 7 May 1884 (p. 2). For comparable descriptions in other stations, see the diary in the Charles A. Merrill Papers, March 10, 1856 Ms. United Methodist Church Archives-GCAH, Madison, NJ; and especially the Bishop William Burt diary, 12 December 1883 (p. 86), United Methodist Church Archives-GCAH, Madison, NJ.

75. Abel Stevens, *The Centenary of American Methodism* (New York: Carlton & Porter, 1865), 111-12.

76. For evidence of continued use of the two-day format in Texas see the Walter S. South diaries. Ts. United Methodist Church Archives-GCAH, Madison, NJ; for Utah, see the J. D. Gillilan Collection. Ms. United Methodist Church Archives-GCAH, Madison, NJ; and for New Jersey, see [Rebecca Turner], "Excerpts from Rebecca Turner's Diary," in *The History of Bethel Methodist Episcopal Church, Gloucester County, New Jersey, 1945*, comp. Mrs. Walter Aborn Simpson (n.p., 1945), 135-48. Even in these accounts of continued two-day quarterly meetings there seems a routine state to the meetings, given the matter-of-fact way they are usually described. Subsequent history only saw the continued accentuation of the trend toward an abbreviated quarterly meeting. See Richey, *The Methodist Conference in America* for a more detailed history of later quarterly meetings. In summary, the administrative tasks for quarterly meetings continued to increase as they became occasions for extensive reports on a wide variety of parish life. The liturgical dimension has tended to be minimal, often including only some initial devotion, or perhaps attachment for a fuller service that preceded. Among some Methodists the quarterly rhythm too has been lost, as the meetings have become annual affairs. In United Methodism, for instance, the yearly charge conference is the descendant of the quarterly conference, which, as we have seen, is the descendant of the quarterly meeting conference or quarterly meeting.

Conclusion

In several ways the original quarterly meetings, starting in England in the late 1740s, were simply business meetings. Stewards responsible for the circuits' finances were selected, the class meeting leaders had their class papers reviewed, and the current bills were paid. Their originator, John Bennet, was pleased with their usefulness and reported the same to John Wesley.[77]

But based on his reports of these early meetings, Bennet was also excited about their other dimensions. Surely it was something more than paying bills that caused Bennet to exult in his letter to Wesley, "The Lord did bless our Meeting in a very extraordinary Manner." The cause seems indicated in his next statement: "After Business was ended we sang a Hymn, several of the Brethren pray'd, and I gave a short Exhortation."[78] Indeed, Bennet's accounts stressed the liturgical dimensions of these earliest meetings as in the case of a 1749 spring meeting where the business was "over in good Time" and several stayed the night and held a service the next day.[79]

It does not appear that quarterly meetings were originally intended to be occasions for deep fellowship and exuberant worship. Their purpose was for administration. Bennet had not aspired for quarterly meetings to become times for intense fellowship and worship. But given the nature of eighteenth-century Methodism, those seeds were present in the earliest quarterly meetings. As British Methodism developed in the eighteenth century, those seeds began to germinate.

Full bloom and harvest came in America. For the first quarter century of American Methodism, the purpose of quarterly meetings expanded to include dimensions beyond administration. Ask an early American Methodist what a quarterly meeting was about and she or he would likely discuss the fellowship and liturgical dimensions first of all; the business was important, but it was only a part. Their experience of revival in these settings only deepened this conviction.

A time came when the harvest was over, however. Somewhat ironically, business again became the dominant theme as quarterly meetings evolved through the nineteenth century, responding to changes

---

77. Frederick Hunter and Frank Baker, "The Origin of the Methodist Quarterly Meeting," *London Quarterly and Holborn Review* (January 1949): 30-32.

78. John Bennet, Letter to John Wesley (22 October 1748), *Works* 26:336. Bennet's letter is actually addressed to his London steward, William Briggs. The contents of the letter, however, show that Wesley was the ultimate recipient.

79. Hunter and Baker, "Origin," 30-32.

in Methodism as a whole. Worship and fellowship became only residual fruit—a mere vestige of their former quarterly meeting status—as
administration moved once more to the forefront. Indeed, the administration had become complex enough, with a variety of reports from
Sunday school, missionary, and other endeavors, that little room was
left for worship and fellowship.[80]

If quarterly meetings were windows into the basic nature of early
Methodism, then their nineteenth-century evolution reveals a church
emerging into its institutional maturity. In finding other ways to be
church, Methodism also developed new patterns for its worship life.

---

80. Compare the similar assessment in Richey, *The Methodist Conference in America*, 116, 166, as
he describes the fracturing of what had been integrated strands in early Methodism: fraternity,
revival, business. Richey rightly notes that Methodists found outlets for fellowship and worship
other than quarterly meetings.

Epilogue

The evolution of worship in early American Methodist quarterly meetings is perhaps one of the deepest ironies in the history of eighteenth-century worship. What began as a straightforward borrowing of an administrative idea and name from British Quakers—a group not known for its liturgical exuberance—became one of the loudest, liveliest occasions for worship in one of the fastest growing "popular" American denominations in the early republic, The Methodist Episcopal Church.[1] That this administrative plagiarism from the Quakers would become one of the seeds out of which camp meetings arose only compounds the irony. A short time frame makes the situation even more remarkable: The shift from Quaker administrative idea to occasion for Methodist raucous worship occurred in about a quarter of a century, and the development to camp meeting occurred just twenty-five years later.

In the late 1740s, British Methodism was still in its infancy; its administrative polity was still in flux. One itinerant preacher at the time, John Bennet, noticed a helpful idea used by the Quakers: quarterly administrative meetings known simply as "quarterly meetings."

---

1. For an accounting of the numbers of American Methodists between the years 1770 and 1820, a period that has been called a "virtual miracle of growth," see John H. Wigger, *Taking Heaven by Storm: Methodism and the Rise of Popular Christianity in America* (New York: Oxford University Press, 1998), 3-7.

In 1748 Bennet began to schedule some of the same for his and adjoining circuits. These and other early Methodist quarterly meetings must have served some useful purpose because a decade later they were a standard part of Methodist polity. Here monies were gathered, bills and salaries paid, and licenses for local preaching and exhorting issued, among other regular matters. And something else began to happen. By the 1760s, if not before, accounts of British Methodist quarterly meetings sometimes include another important detail: sizable numbers, more than those who were required for administration, had gathered for worship.

When Methodist founder John Wesley began to send preachers to the American colonies in the late 1760s and early 1770s, they brought this form of quarterly meeting with them. The accounts from the time describe quarterly meetings in a format recognizable on both sides of the Atlantic: typically quarterly meetings were one-day affairs where a business meeting was surrounded by a standard fare of Methodist liturgical activity. Most commonly mentioned were preaching services, love feasts, and occasional watch night services. Tuesday was a very common day to hold the meeting. Even in this nascent stage, quarterly meetings were already an important setting for American Methodist worship.

A revival in southern Virginia in 1776 sparked even greater development of quarterly meetings as settings for worship and accelerated the shift away from their Quaker origins. From this year forward American Methodist quarterly meetings began to be held as multiple-day events for worship and evangelism. Before long many were being scheduled over weekends to facilitate attendance for Methodists and non-Methodists alike across racial groups. Making the most of this additional time, quarterly meetings came to include almost every kind of worship service or ritual from the rich variety of Methodist practices. Multiple preaching services were supplemented by love feasts, prayer meetings, watch nights, and (eventually) the Lord's Supper, baptisms, weddings, and funerals. By the time of the establishment of The Methodist Episcopal Church in 1784, quarterly meetings had become "great festivals" to which hundreds, even thousands, flocked.

The development of quarterly meetings into great worship festivals is explained in part by the context of eighteenth-century America and the nature of Methodist polity. For many regions in eighteenth-century America, particularly those where quarterly meetings first gained festival status, community was defined more by event than by space. The nature of Methodist church life would have only accentuated this tendency since, unlike modern Methodism, most Methodists lived on circuits with no minister in residence. Methodists belonged not so much to a parish or congregation as to the Connection. Quarterly meetings provided the opportunity for the circuit to assemble as a worshiping community. When The Methodist Episcopal Church was organized, it appears that its leaders relied upon this already existing phenomenon as they ordained enough preachers to at least be able to provide sacraments and pastoral rites in these settings.

Quarterly meetings' festival status was not permanent. A series of factors in the nineteenth century eventually eroded their liturgical role. For one thing, the decline of active itinerancy by ordained Methodist preachers meant an ever increasing growth of congregations with ministers in residence and also a greater sense of identification with a particular parish. There was less occasion and motivation to assemble for quarterly meetings. They eventually regained their original purpose: to serve as business meetings only, surviving in that role among many branches of twentieth-century Methodism.

Great festivals for worship and evangelism were not lost in nineteenth-century Methodism, however. American Methodists distilled what they saw as the essential aspects of their quarterly meetings and standardized them as camp meetings right after the turn of the century. With the standardization came active promotion. Camp meetings quickly became a widespread part of Methodist life and evangelistic efforts. Having been spawned from quarterly meetings, this new type of protracted meeting eventually upstaged quarterly meetings as settings for worship, leaving the latter increasingly restricted to administration.

By their own descriptions, early Methodists were sometimes staggered by their sense of a gracious God in their midst during quarterly meeting worship. The awe extended to appreciating the nature of themselves as a liturgical fellowship. Being much better theological poets than systematicians, American Methodists developed a complex set of metaphors, images, and catchphrases to describe their worship so graced by the God of salvation. The most basic was a word used to describe being inwardly moved: the "melting" of a human heart. Methodists were quite confident that during worship God often melted a heart by an affective experience of grace. This was their way of expressing and endorsing a long-standing Christian theological claim: people can experience God's grace when they worship.

Their experience of Methodist fellowship as liturgical assembly only strengthened this conviction. Their claims about the nature of this liturgical fellowship seem almost unbelievable at times. After one love feast, for example, the only thing that seemed suitable to one participant was to refer to his experience as some sort of preliminary participation in heaven itself. According to this Methodist, the difference between the liturgical fellowship experienced here and that experienced in heaven is more about quantity than quality.[2] Another worshiper simply said, "The love, joy and power which we felt exceeds what human language can fully express."[3]

These testimonies from early Methodists contradict the conclusions of much recent scholarship on early Methodist worship. Many scholars view the early period of American Methodist worship as a time of liturgical impoverishment. Like some sort of prodigal, American Methodism is often portrayed as squandering the rich liturgical and sacramental heritage that John Wesley had bequeathed to it. The previous chapters have tried to show that—in contrast to this modern portrayal—early Methodist worship had an amazing complexity and richness. It offered a greater variety of services than is experienced by the average modern Methodist. It provoked a greater intensity. It manifested a greater sense of liturgical assembly than is evident in modern forms of Methodism. And early Methodists had a more sophisticated vocabulary (even if not a precise or balanced one) to describe the gracious presence of God in worship.

How could scholars have missed this richness, charging early American Methodists with liturgical poverty? Their inaccurate conclusions reflect problems in their historical method. One of the most central problems has been their tendency to constrict the analysis of American Methodist liturgical history to the study of liturgical texts. For the early period, this results in primary attention been devoted to a comparative study of Wesley's *Sunday Service* (a revision of the Church of England's *Book of Common Prayer* that he prepared in 1784 and sent over for use in the newly established American church) and the revision of materials adopted from this resource by the American Methodists in 1792. Cast in this comparative isolation, the 1792 revision (perhaps better called a reduction) is almost inevitably going to

---

2. William Watters, *A Short Account of the Christian Experience, and Ministereal Labours, of William Watters* (Alexandria: S. Snowden, 1806), 75-76.

3. Ezekiel Cooper, "A brief account of the work of God," in George A. Phoebus, comp., *Beams of Light on Early Methodism in America* (New York: Phillips & Hunt; Cincinnati: Cranston & Stowe, 1887), 95.

be judged as a liturgical step backward, since the Americans set aside large parts of what Wesley had recommended to them.

But to portray the history in this manner is to skew it by avoiding a more central issue: What were the existing conditions in American Methodism for the reception and use of the *Sunday Service*? In reality the *Sunday Service*—its rites and its assumed liturgical rhythms—had to be grafted onto an already functioning set of Methodist ritual patterns; it did not arrive in America to be inscribed upon an ecclesiastical clean slate. By 1784 American Methodism had been operating for some time with a much loved set of liturgical practices as a group of United Societies (to use the original Methodist terminology). For example, two-day, weekend quarterly meetings were already a well-established liturgical setting for American Methodists by this time. They were deeply convinced that a history of God's blessing validated their forms of ministerial itinerancy and connectional worship. They could not be expected simply to set these aside. The real question for them was how to fit the "extras" (including the *Sunday Service*), which they received with ecclesiastical organization, into how they already worshiped as a societal movement.

There is a further liability to focusing primarily on liturgical texts in telling the history of a group's worship: changes in texts—or the lack thereof—do not necessarily parallel important changes in liturgical practice and piety. This discontinuity can be readily demonstrated in American Methodism. For example, the text for the Lord's Supper remained fairly stable from 1792 until the mid-nineteenth century. But during this same period major changes were taking place in the typical liturgical practices of American Methodists. In particular, the setting and constituency of eucharistic observance were dramatically influenced by the growth in numbers and the "settling" of Methodist clergy. In reality, the second decade of the nineteenth century, with its proliferation of stations, its ordination of local preachers as elders, and its tendency toward itinerants locating close to one congregation, is probably a more critical time of liturgical transformations than was 1792.

To be sure, no modern scholar has based an analysis of American Methodist worship solely on liturgical texts. They have turned to other Methodist writings to portray the setting in which these texts were used. But here a second methodological problem has served to misguide their analysis: they have tended to limit too narrowly the scope of other Methodist writings used. Liturgical historians must go beyond reliance upon the writings of John Wesley, Francis Asbury,

213

and Peter Cartwright—as important as these men were. Methodism was not coterminous with Wesley even in his own lifetime. Asbury's journal shows the itinerant pattern of a bishop (bishops traveled actively too!), at least after 1784, and thus is not that useful for ascertaining the liturgical rhythms of the average circuit. In addition, even when Asbury's journal describes a worship event, it is not necessarily a full description, either through simple omission or through later editing.[4] Cartwright is too late and too western to assess what is the most critical period and region for early American Methodist worship: the mid-Atlantic states in the last quarter of the eighteenth century. An adequate portrayal of early American Methodist worship requires that major attention be devoted to the writings of Methodists like John Littlejohn, Ezekiel Cooper, Richard Allen, Henry Boehm, Catherine Livingston Garrettson, William Colbert, and Benjamin Lakin, since these writings describe worship in average circuits and stations. Cooper, Boehm, and Colbert are particularly crucial sources.

One further methodological caution needs to be mentioned. However broad the range of materials we consult, scholars of Methodist worship must be careful not to allow modern sensibilities—particularly those derived from recent liturgical renewal movements—to skew their appreciation for early Methodism in its own right. Take for example the question of whether early American Methodists maintained the strong eucharistic piety they inherited from John Wesley. Many recent scholarly appraisals have framed this question in terms of the issue of frequency: Does the typical frequency of sacramental administration and reception in early Methodism reflect a devaluation of the Lord's Supper? Using a liturgical criterion that sets weekly communion as the norm, and noting that this frequency was not common for them, these scholars have portrayed early American Methodists as a group for whom the sacrament did not hold a central position in its liturgical life or piety. In at least one often-cited study, Francis Asbury has been portrayed as the main culprit for this lamentable decline since Asbury's journal seemingly reflects a eucharistic frequency less than what Wesley had modeled himself and what Wesley had supposedly instructed to be the practice in the American church in 1784.[5]

4. By using the writings of other Methodists, I have found numerous examples where Asbury was present at services including a celebration of the Lord's Supper but his journal fails to mention the sacrament.

5. William Nash Wade, "A History of Public Worship in the Methodist Episcopal Church and Methodist Episcopal Church, South, from 1784 to 1905" (Ph.D. diss., Notre Dame, 1981).

But this whole sort of portrayal imposes a false standard upon early Methodists. How would early American Methodists have known that weekly celebration of the Lord's Supper was a liturgical norm? Where could they have looked in the American religious landscape in the late–eighteenth century and seen an example of weekly communion? Even Wesley's personal practices and his instructions attached to the *Sunday Service* for elders to administer weekly are not conclusive proof that Americans should have known this standard was some sort of norm. Wesley's clear intent was that ordination be linked to active itinerancy, which means—because itinerancy involves regular absence of the minister—that Wesley did not construct a strict model of weekly sacramental reception for American Methodism.[6]

Early American Methodists would likely be startled by the accusations that they did not value the Lord's Supper, or that it did not hold a central place in their piety. They regularly scheduled it for one of their most important and greatly anticipated settings for worship, the quarterly meeting. In that setting they frequently linked it to one of their most loved rituals, the love feast, and thus surrounded the sacrament with the most intense, enjoyable fellowship context imaginable. That is why—in contrast to common scholarly portrayals— these Methodists found it hard to find words that could begin to describe their experience of God in the sacrament.

Forcing modern sensibilities upon early Methodism has an additional danger: the failure to realize that many of the things about which liturgical scholars complain have their roots in John and Charles Wesley themselves. The affective, experiential nature of American Methodist liturgical piety, for example, is harmonious with the Wesleys and related strands of eighteenth-century evangelicalism, and not a discontinuity. Consider how often a knowledge of God or of salvation is rooted in feeling in the Wesleys' hymns and journal accounts. Similarly, the aggressive evangelical zeal of American Methodists was not self-created. All they had to do was to look at the polity that John Wesley had so carefully crafted to see his clear instruction on a preacher's main responsibility: "save as many souls as you can."[7] In light of Wesley's own evangelistic concern, liturgical

---

6. See Lester Ruth, "Reconsideration of the Frequency of the Eucharist in Early American Methodism," *Methodist History* 34.1 (October 1995): 49-57, for more details and for a more thorough critique of Wade.

7. The passage is from the British polity documents called the "Large Minutes" (Q. 26) and was carried over into the American *Disciplines*. See *Works* (Jackson) 8:310.

historians should be less surprised that American Methodists could begin to think about counting numbers and assessing worship's pragmatic use. The difference between the Wesleys and early American Methodism is more a matter of balance than of basic substance: the Wesleys' broader historical knowledge, greater theological sophistication, and stronger commitment to Anglican churchmanship provided them a more balanced context for the intense form of evangelical, affective "experimental religion" that was shared by all Methodists.

Yet even if early American Methodist worship was not "impoverished," it is not beyond critique. Some critique can be based precisely on the American deficiency in those balancing factors found in the Wesleys. Do the Americans show too exclusive a reliance on affective, experiential categories for worship and salvation, for instance? It is obvious that an emphasis on "experimental religion" was at the center of their piety; Bishop Coke once reported that a student at Cokesbury College had been expelled for ridiculing "experimental religion."[8] And it is clear that this emphasis holds a potential danger of luring the American Methodists to lose the balance between the cosmic, objective dimensions of salvation (God was in Christ reconciling the world) and the personal dimensions (I am reconciled to God in Christ). Part of the genius of the hymns of Charles Wesley is the way that they maintain this balance.[9] By contrast, the personal dimension threatens at times to move the other dimension to the margins in American Methodist piety. The essential form of sacred history recounted at their most intense times of liturgical fellowship was personal testimony, not direct exposition of Scripture.

The root tension here concerns religious and liturgical epistemology: What can one still know as true about God's work in Christ, particularly in worship, if feelings are providing no information or assurance? Is there no salvation if the individual has felt nothing? Can there be true knowledge of God's grace apart from inward feeling? In worship, these questions are especially crucial regarding the sacraments. Do sacraments do anything if no feelings are aroused? Without a balance to their emphasis on affective experience, early American Methodists seem inclined to answer in the negative. The

---

8. Thomas Coke, *Extracts of the journals of the Rev. Dr. Coke's five visits to America* (London: G. Paramore, 1793), 111.

9. See Teresa Berger, *Theology in Hymns? A Study of the Relationship of Doxology and Theology According to a Collection of Hymns for the Use of the People Called Methodists (1780)*, trans. Timothy E. Kimbrough (Nashville: Kingswood, 1995), 108-32.

trajectory from this way of thinking lives on in continuing Methodist discussions about baptismal regeneration and in a present eucharistic piety that overemphasizes the Lord's Supper as a private experience.

Similarly, the transferal of Wesley's evangelistic zeal to an American community that lacked the balances of his historical and theological knowledge resulted in the cultivation of a liturgical pragmatism that still characterizes many American Protestant liturgical traditions. As evidenced by the early Methodists, Americans tend to ascertain what "works" in worship by counting numbers. Although the liturgical pragmatism of early Methodism is less developed than that of mid–nineteenth century figures like Charles Grandison Finney, they clearly were motivated, at least in part, by numerical standards of success as they modified their liturgical acts in order to facilitate the experiencing of grace.[10] And they showed no qualms about standardizing and replicating those features, or about gloating when they saw ministers in other denominations do the same. Both the evolution of quarterly meetings into weekend festivals and the subsequent spin-off of independent camp meetings are examples of this nascent liturgical pragmatism. As Asbury said in defending camp meetings, "they have never been tried without success."[11]

More often than not, this sort of liturgical "success" in America has been measured by the number of converts gained. Perhaps this fascination with numbers and their use to validate liturgical practices are among the enduring legacies of early American Methodism. It was common for Methodists to understand the increased number of converts, adherents, and members as positive evidence of God's activity among them.[12] American Methodists understood their phenomenal growth during the early period as an indication of God's favor. On a large scale, numerical growth after the establishment of The Methodist Episcopal Church demonstrated that God approved of separation from the Church of England. On a smaller scale, they were convinced that an increase in any given locale was the "Lord's doing."[13] This same correspondence was used to justify various liturgical practices and innovations. For example, the journal of Methodist

---

10. Russell E. Richey, *Early American Methodism* (Bloomington: Indiana University Press, 1991), 28.

11. *JLFA* 3:251.

12. See Kenneth E. Rowe, "Counting the Converts: Progress Reports as Church History," in *Rethinking Methodist History*, ed. Russell E. Richey and Kenneth E. Rowe (Nashville: Kingswood, 1985), 11-17.

13. See Ruth, "A Little Heaven Below," 221-22 for examples.

preacher Henry Boehm fastidiously records the numbers of "conversions" and "sanctifications" every morning and evening for early camp meetings.[14]

The inherent danger of equating growth in numbers with divine favor is that numbers can become self-validating and lead to unrestrained, unguarded pragmatism in liturgical matters. Initially, this tendency was held in check by a desire to maintain a strong countercultural ethos within Methodist societies, demonstrated by disciplinary exclusion of wayward members. As Bishop Coke once advocated while explaining a numeric decrease one year in New Jersey, "Rotten members, be they ever so numerous, must be lopped off" lest Methodists become like all other people.[15] Whatever the pruning that went on, Methodism grew rapidly during Asbury's era, and tensions accompanied this growth. Already in 1810, while reflecting on the increase of numbers that the camp meetings he had championed were providing, Asbury could worry that "we monopolize religion in some places, all together; as if the offence of the cross was ceasing."[16] With the continuing growth through the nineteenth century, American Methodism's disciplinary rigor subsided, allowing a less restrained pragmatic liturgical perspective to permeate the church. Again, my critique centers on the tendency to rely too heavily on experiential categories—such as the number of people who testify to a transformative experience during worship—to assess the liturgy itself.

If there are some troubling tendencies rooted in early American Methodist worship that would have benefited from the greater breadth of Wesley's liturgical approach, there are others that appear to result from the plurality of voices that were present in the American church. Early American Methodism was a hybrid institution, and the careful listener will hear it articulate its self-understanding in at least four major "languages": a popular "evangelical" language, a Wesleyan "societal" language, an Anglican "episcopal" language, and a "republican" language.[17] As others have noted, the interplay of these languages was not always harmonious. With respect to worship, the evangelical and societal languages formed an uneasy merger with the episcopal. The latter is what rooted early Methodist worship in broad catholic liturgical traditions. But the

---

14. See Boehm journal, 13-17 June 1806 and 8-12 August 1806.
15. Coke, *Extracts*, 113.
16. *JLFA* 3:429.
17. Richey, *Early American Methodism*, 82-97.

evangelical and societal languages are what made Methodist worship distinctly Methodist and thus could not be dropped without loss of identity. As such, the episcopal language could never find pure expression in Methodist worship. The evangelical and societal languages gave Methodists a certain accent when they spoke of things that belonged to long-standing Western liturgical traditions.

At times the accent was so strong that the result sounds garbled or confusing to outside hearers more used to a clearer "speaking" of liturgical traditions. The tension formed in using affective terms as the main, perhaps even sole, way to assess the Divine Presence in worship and sacraments, notwithstanding the more direct affirmations of the Articles of Religion, is one example. Another is the fusion of societal categories about ministry (assistant, itinerant preacher, local preacher, conference membership, location) with the Anglican-derived categories (bishop, elder, deacon). Specifically, the initial restriction of ordination to itinerant preachers created an uneasy merger of societal and episcopal polities. The typical early Methodist only saw an itinerant preacher—who might or might not have been ordained—once every two weeks. This might have seemed a bit long to wait for a funeral or a baptism. Not surprisingly, within a few years local preachers were made eligible for ordination as deacons and, eventually, as elders. Also not surprising was the way in which the early *Disciplines* continually revised assignment of responsibility for certain societal liturgical practices (watch nights, love feasts) to various categories of ministers. In 1785 these were the responsibilities of an assistant (the original polity assignment); in 1787 they were assigned to deacons; and by 1798 they were given to "those who had charge of a circuit," whether elder, deacon, or unordained preacher. These shifts reflect a clash of understandings of Christians' orders derived from different sources. More broadly, it shows American Methodism's particular liturgical "accent" caused by the fusion of societal polity and worship with traditional ecclesiastical notions. Some of these language tensions have never died. American Methodists still struggle, for instance, with deciding what categories of preachers/pastors are eligible for ordination/conference membership and whether ordination is strictly necessary for administering sacraments.

It is exactly at these points of liturgical tension that a study of early American Methodism is most helpful. If, as some have suggested, Methodism is a uniquely "superb window" to understand the

American religious experience,[18] then it seems incumbent upon anyone who wishes to sketch out the history of worship in this country to take Methodism seriously on its own terms. Although its worship may be critiqued, it should still be appreciated as its own form of popular American religiosity. This appreciation provides insight into what apparently are characteristics of popular American liturgical sensibilities more generally. Given the amazing growth of early Methodism, it is probably safe to say that it helped move certain aspects of these sensibilities from the periphery of American church life to the center.[19]

The residual effects of the character of early Methodist worship upon current expressions of American worship remain evident. Understanding these traits is a good way to understand the nature of some basic themes in American religiosity, particularly with respect to liturgical piety. As in early Methodism, many Americans come to Sunday morning worship still expecting to sense God's presence as assessed by affective, experiential categories.[20] Should anyone be surprised about the use of testimonies as an especially potent form of sacred history in some liturgical circles, even in some now considered the most innovative? Should anyone be surprised that exuberant liturgical participation has been a constant of American popular religiosity, often at the point where new expressions of this religiosity are being birthed? Similarly, a liturgical pragmatism reminiscent of early Methodism is still rampant among many American Christians. Creation and promotion of liturgical practices using numbers to evaluate the "success" of a given liturgical style continues in countless churches.

There are several implications in considering Methodism for the writing of liturgical history. For one thing liturgical historians would

---

18. Nathan O. Hatch, "The Puzzle of American Methodism," *Church History* 63 (1994): 186.

19. The numbers are indeed staggering: in 1775 Methodism made up only 2 percent of total American church membership; seventy-five years later it was 34 percent (Wigger, *Taking Heaven by Storm*, 3, 197-200).

On page 3, Wigger writes of Methodism's increase as nearly miraculous: "Between 1770 and 1820 American Methodists achieved a virtual miracle of growth, rising from fewer than 1,000 members to more than 250,000. In 1775 fewer than one out of every 800 Americans was a Methodist; by 1812 Methodists number one out of every 36 Americans. By 1830 membership stood at nearly half a million. At midcentury, American Methodism was nearly half again as large as any other Protestant body, and almost ten times the size of the Congregationalists, America's largest denomination in 1776."

20. For examples of this approach's strong advocacy, see Sally Morgenthaler, *Worship Evangelism: Inviting Unbelievers into the Presence of God* (Grand Rapids: Zondervan, 1995), 97; and Terry Wardle, *Exalt Him! Designing Dynamic Worship Services* (Camp Hill, PA: Christian Publications, 1988), 20.

do well to consider dropping the use of geographic designations like "frontier" to explain basic aspects of popular American liturgical piety. Their widespread nature as part of the rapidly expanding Methodist movement and their continued resilience in modern forms of popular religiosity hint that there is something more fundamentally American about this liturgical perspective than association with a geographic context long since past. Nathan Hatch's suggestion regarding the usefulness of Methodist history generally seems well-heeded by liturgists specifically: "The story of Methodism tells us much more about American religion as it actually unfolded, not great, not sophisticated, not awe inspiring, but what it is."[21]

In addition, commentators concerned with the displacement of long-standing liturgical traditions by "contemporary" styles in our own days of the late-twentieth century can take comfort in the history presented here. Early Methodists were accused of the same type of pragmatism that advocates of "seeker" services face today. Yet, as we have seen, services with an explicitly evangelical purpose mediated grace to many and furthered the mission of the churches. The debates between "traditionalists" and "pragmatists" have long raged on American soil. The threat to the integrity of Christian worship is no greater today than at other times—regardless of the strident rhetoric on both sides.

Specific consideration of the nature of early Methodist worship at quarterly meetings might have some direct contributions to make to current liturgical studies. If nothing else, early Methodism should reawaken modern scholars to some liturgical categories that have had great prominence in the past, among Methodists and others, but tend to be overlooked today. One important example is the use of "private" and "public" designations for describing particular modes of worship. The use of these terms by early Methodism recalls for us that throughout church history not all worship has been open to everyone. In fact, access to the most crucial symbolic liturgies has often been closely guarded. The reasons offered, whether by Methodists or others, have theological and experiential substance. In the midst of all the current discussions about relating evangelism to worship, perhaps the public/private categories are an important dynamic that needs to be reintroduced into the conversation. We need to remember that liturgical tradition offers up suggestions not only

---

21. Hatch, "Puzzle of American Methodism," 189.

about prayer texts and orders of worship but also about a variety of modes for including the unbaptized or nonmember in worship.

There is at least one other place where modern liturgical scholars might benefit from consideration of early American Methodist liturgical practices. The interplay between public and private worship in early Methodism provides a concrete example of the argument in recent sacramental theologies that the sacramental efficacy of liturgical rites must be rooted first in the sacramentality of the liturgical community. What these theologies explore in sophisticated theological jargon was for early Methodists a regularly experienced reality that they described in poetic, biblically inspired speech. "Enter, and find that God is here" one hymn said about joining Methodists in fellowship.[22] Statements of early Methodists resound with bold affirmation regarding the sacramental quality of their worshiping fellowship. Time and again they spoke of the efficacious revelation of God, God's love, Jesus Christ, and other ultimate aspirations of human hope in the midst of their worship. For early Methodists, quarterly meeting worship satisfied the most profound longings for the things of God. "The saints struck my mind with the deepest views of heaven, and the love of God," exclaimed one at a quarterly meeting. Another exults, "I was in a little heaven below."[23]

22. *Pocket Hymn-book* (1786), 191.
23. R. Garrettson, "An Account of the Revival of the Work of God at Petersburg, in Virginia." *AM* 13 (1790): 302; Watters, *Short Account*, 75-76.

Sermon Outlines[1]

Outline 1:

Luke 15 2 This man receiveth Sinners
First I shall show you that all come under the character here advanced, sinner
Secd This man's authority for receiveing sinner
Thirdly The times, or conditions on which he receives sinners and the blessing that shall accrue to those that are receiv'd by him
Fourth Apply[2]

Outline 2:

Sunday 10. Sister Ellises Amos 4-12-Prepare to meet thy God O Israel
Prosecution, first how come Man first to be Unprepar'd by the fall and transgression of Adam,
Secondly, whats the condescention of our Lord toward fallen Creations?
First the gift of his only Son Jesus Christ, to Redeem us from the Curse of his Law.

---

1. Original spelling, punctuation, and format have been retained unless specified otherwise.
2. Philip Gatch, Sermon Outline Book. Papers. Ohio Wesleyan University Library, Delaware, OH, 14.

Thirdly, what's Imploy'd in being prepar'd to meet the Tremendous God

first Repentance whereby we forsake Sin and faith in our Lord Jesus Christ

Second being Crucified to the world and the Things of the world having power and Dominion over Sin purified Soul and Spirit-for without Holiness no Man Shall see the Lord

Fourthly, what is the blessed Effect of being prepard?

First it is life it is health it is peace and Joy in this present world, and then and there of Everlasting Life

Fifthly what is the Consequence of those when the Lord shall come that's found wanting? they shall be consum'd, bound hand and foot and cast into outer Darkness, where there shall be weeping and wailing and gnashing of Teeth forever and ever[3]

Outline 3:

Job 19-25 I know that my Redeemer liveth

Intro who Job was, or of what family I shall not enquire However it is thought that he lived in a very period of the word, many years before Moses the supposed author of this book, but it is evident that he was a man of sorrows and acquainted with grief, stripped of his earthly comforts, children, honours, and substance, yea his own familiar friends added to his grief. The wife of his Bosom made herself strainge unto him his body was afflicted with some boils from head to foot, but in the midst of all he had this to comfort him I know that my Redeemer liveth that those words may be rendered profitable to us I shall in the

I place show the necessity for a Redeemer

/1/ we are involved in debt more than 1,000 talents

/2/ we are poor and not able to pay one

We must say forgive &c Matt 6-12

/3/ Imprisoned in darkness (sin) bound in unbelief Rom 7-24

/4/ Kept under a severe master viz the Devil Rom 6-16

/5/ Employed a laborious Servitude the drudgery of the devil

3. Entry for Sunday, 10 February 1788, in memorandum book in James Meacham Papers. Ms. Special Collections Library, Duke University Library, Durham, NC. Note that the formatting for this outline has been changed from the original. Originally in paragraph form, the divisions have been highlighted here by separation.

/6/ Taskmasters over them the world the flesh hurrying them

II Who this redeemer is how he has discharged the office and what he redeems those from, who put their trust in him

/1/ Who this Redeemer is viz L-J-Christ a person of infinite dignity Almighty

/2/ how he has discharged the office of a Redeemer

/1/ taking our curse in hand

/2/ becoming our near kinsman taking upon him our nature

/3/ keeping that Law which we had broken

/4/ suffered death the penalty due to sin so that we were bought with a price

III What he redeems his people from

/1/ the curse of a broken law

/2/ from the bondage of sin

/3/ from the guilt of sin

/4/ from the love and remains of sin Titus 2-14

/5/ from the fiars of death and hell I Cor 15 54, 55

IIII Show the certainty believers may have that Christ is their Redeemer

I know that my Redeemer &c

/1/ they know it by faith Rom 5-1 John 3-18

/2/ they know by the witness of the Spirit R 8-16

/3/ they know it by change wrought in the soul

/4/ that he liveth in heaven as their advocate Heb 7-25

/5/ in the heart by faith the hope of glory Col 1 27

Apply the subject

/1/ to sinners by showing them their miserable condition

/2/ to Christians by showing them their privalage viz to be redeemed from all sin and to know it[4]

---

4. John Price, Sermon Book. Ms. St. George's United Methodist Church, Philadelphia, PA.

Exhortations from the George A. Reed Manuscript Papers[1]

Exhortation 1:

Seek the Lord while he may be found
How many are deceived
Seek him in his works of providence
in his word here we learn that he can save the sinner
Seek him in the means of grace
Religious society—prayer private—P.M. [prayer meeting?]—C Meeting [Camp Meeting?]—preaching—love feast—the ordinances of God's house—
But has man ability to seek God—what do you mean by ability do you mean independant power if so I say no—but if you mean power under God to seek I say he has or why exhort David to seek the Lord—Perhaps you may suppose that I am doing away with the office of the H.S. [Holy Spirit] not so it is the S that quickens and sanctifies but I would be doing injustice to the cause of my maker if I were to close without offering salvation through J.C. [Jesus Christ] now some suppose that they have nothing to do but to render a tacit acknowledgement to the truth of the Script to live moral life and they shall be saved but shurley such forget the purity of the God they have

---

1. Original spelling, punctuation, and format have been retained.

to deal with—the holiness of his law—the deep corruption of the human heart—the condemnation of sin—and that the holy God has said without holiness no man shall see God

I would here like to close but notwithstanding there is no pleasure in preaching damnation it is a part of our commission—and we hold up the threatnings of God against the sinner

Exhortation 2:

O Sinner hear the word of the Lord: "Cry aloud, & spare not; lift up thy voice like a trumpet (saith ye Prophet), and show my people their transgressions, & ye house of Jacob their sins. (Isa 58.1.)" . . . The wrath of God is revealed from Heaven ag^t. all ungodliness and unrighteousness of men. (Rom 1.18)" . . . God will bring every word into judgment, with every secret thing, whether it be good or evil (Eccl. 12.14). . . . "Whatsoever a man soweth, that shall he reap. (Gal. 6.7.). . . ." Not every one that saith, unto me, Lord, Lord shall enter into ye kingdom of Heaven (Mat 7.21.) By nature we are ye children of wrath (Eph 2.3.) and as helpless as we are guilty: no more able to deliver ourselves from ye dominion of sin, than y^e "Ethiopian" to "change his skin, or ye Leopard his spots" (Jer. 13.23.) . . . however moral and virtuous, you must be "born again," as well as ye worst of others, or "not see ye kingdom of God (Jno. 3.3) You must "put on ye new man wch after God is created in righteousness & true holiness" (Eph 4.24) . . . while you are in a state of nature, and not "renewed in ye spirit of *your* mind" (Eph. 4.23) you are exposed to everlasting ruin, without a way to escape; . . . your doom is for ever fixed, unless your condition on earth be quite altered. "If any man have not ye spirit of Christ, he is none of his" (Rom. 8.9.) . . . If we do not feel ye power of Xt. in our hearts; if we are not washed from ye guilt of sin by his blood, & delivered from ye dominion of it by "his Spirit dwelling in us" (Rom 8.11.), so y^t we truly experience "a death unto sin, & a new birth unto righteousness," Xts dying & rising again avails us nothing . . . Let all impenitent sinners know, . . . they are going to hell together, & y^t every soul of them will perish if they repent not, . . . they are blind, & see not where they are going; . . . they are enemies to God, & hate his ways & people, but are true slaves to sin & Satan; . . . they are dead to God & all goodness: Yes . . . that by actual & original transgression, they have brought upon themselves his curse & condemnation: . . . it is not all they can do, will save them from everlasting wrath: If they get not an interest in Xt, they must be consumed for ever.

Early Hymns Emphasizing Shouting[1]

Hymn 1:

The way to praise the God above
Is first to feel his pardoning love
Then time and Talents always give
To God, while he shall let us live

Seek not the form, but feel the power
Stand always catch the streaming shower
of grace and glory from above
Drink, praise, & shout redeeming love[2]

Hymn 2:

Yea children of zion, that's aiming for glory,
Inlisted with Jesus to fight against Sin:
Lo! Canaan's bright borders are now just before You,
Tho' Jordan's proud billows are rolling between

---

1. Original spelling, punctuation, and format have been retained.
2. Entry for 1 February 1806 in Nathaniel Mills, Journal. Ms. United Methodist Historical Society, Lovely Lane Museum, Baltimore, MD.

Then Thousands have cross'd it and now are in heaven:
A shouting and praising the great One in Seven
And I hope my Saviour will bring us all over,
To the land of sweet Canaan for ever to dwell.

This makes my heart merry, it fills me with glory,
That toiling and labouring with me will be o'er,
At the feet of My saviour I'll tell the glad story,
When Sin, pain, and sorrow, can touch us no more,
Be bold and Courageous and fear not the devil,
Tho' he should speak of you all manner of evil,
altho' hell enrages, yet Jesus engages
To bring us all shouting to Canaan's bright shore.[3]

Hymn 3: "My Saviour's Name I'll Gladly Sing"

My Saviour's name I'll gladly sing-*Halle-hallelujah*-
He is my Captain, friend & King-*Halle-hallelujah*
Where'er I go his name I'll bless-*Halle-hallelujah*
And shout among the Methodist-*O glory Hallelujah*

The Devil's Camps I'll bid adieu,
And Zions pleasant way pursue;
O Sinners turn, repent and list,
And fight like valiant Methodist.

I'm not asham'd to own the Lord,
Nor to defend his holy word;
My soul has often been refresh'd
Among the shouting Methodist.

As good a church, as can be found,
Their doctrine is so pure and sound,
One reason which I give for this,
The Devil hates the Methodist.

The World, the Devil, and Tom Pain,
Have tried their force, but all in vain,

---

3. Undated, unsigned hymn in a book of sermon outlines found in the George A. Reed Papers.

They can't prevail—the reason is,
The Lord defends the Methodist.

If Satan could them all destroy,
The troops of Hell would shout for joy;
I'll pray that God would them increase
And fill the world with Methodist.

They pray, they sing, they preach the best,
And do the Devil, most molest;
If Satan had his cursed way,
He'd kill and damn them all to-day.

They are despis'd by Satan's train,
Because they shout and preach so plain;
I'm bound to march to endless bliss,
And die a shouting Methodist.

The Saint of every sect I love,
And hope to meet their souls above;
But yet for all, I must confess,
I do prefer the Methodist.

There's many of a different name,
That's followers of the bleeding Lamb;
But most of them were brought to peace,
By the despised Methodist.

We shout too much for sinners here,
But when in Heaven we do appear,
Our shouts shall make the Heavens ring,
When all the Saints shall join to sing.[4]

Hymn 4: "Christians Shouting"

My God my heart with love inflam'd
That I may in thy holy name

4. Henry Bradford, Hymnbook. Ms. Southern Historical Collection, University of North Carolina Library, Chapel Hill, NC; see also Stith Mead, *A General Selection of the Newest and Most Admired Hymns and Spiritual Songs, Now in Use (1807 original edition).* The second edition revised, corrected, enlarged, and published by permission of the Virginia Conference held at Raleigh (NC) (Lynchburg: Jacob Haas, 1811), for a different version.

Aloud with songs of praise rejoice
While I have breath to raise my voice
Then will I shout then will I sing
And make the heavenly arches ring
I'll sing and shout for evermore
On that eternal happy shore

O hope of glory Jesus come
And make my heart thy constant home
For the short remnant of my days
I want to sing and shout thy praise
Incessantly I want to pray,
And live rejoicing every day
And to give thanks in every thing
And sing and shout and shout and sing

When on my dying bed I lay
Lord give me strength to sing and pray
And praise thee with my latest breath
Untill my tongue is still'd by death
Then brothers, sisters shouting come
My body follow to the Tomb
And as you march the solemn road
Loud sing and shout the praise of God.

Then you below and I above
We'll sing and shout the God we love
Untill that great tremendous day
When he shall call our slumbering clay
Then from our dusty beds we'll spring
And shout O death! where is thy sting?
O grave where is thy victory
We'll shout thro all eternity[5]

Hymn 5:

1. O! how I have longed for the coming of God
I sought him by praying and searching his word

5. Ms. hymnal entitled "Spiritual Songs" in Edward Dromgoole Papers. Southern Historical Collection, University of North Carolina Library, Chapel Hill, NC. [Available on microfilm from

In watching and fasting my soul was oppress'd
Nor would I give over till Jesus had blessed.

2. The tokens of mercy at length did appear
According to promise he answered my prayer
And glory is opening in floods on my soul
Salvation from Zion is beginning to role

3. The news of his mercy is spreading abroad
And sinners comes crying and praying to God
Their mourning and praying is heard very loud
And many have found favour in Jesuses love

4. There's more my dear Jesus that falls at thy feet
Oppress'd with a burden enormously great
O! raise them dear Jesus to tell of thy love
May they shout Hallelujah like the angels above

5. We wait for his Chariot it seems to draw near
O Come my dear Saviour let glory appear
We long to be singing and shouting above
With angels overwhelmed in Jesuses love

6. Shout all the creation below and above
Ascribing salvation to Jesuses love
Break forth into singing ye trees of the wood
For Jesus is bringing lost sinners to God.

7. I'll sing and I'll shout and shout and I'll sing
O! God make the nations with praises to ring
With loud acclamations of Jesuses love
And carry us all to the City above[6]

University of North Carolina.]; for another version of the same hymn see Richard Allen, *A Collection of Hymns and Spiritual Songs* (Philadelphia: T. L. Plowman, 1801; reprint, Nashville: A.M.E.C. Sunday School Union, 1987), 10-11.

6. Hymn signed by H. Bradford, 21 September 1803 in Henry Bradford, Hymnbook; another version of the hymn had previously been published in Allen, *Collection of Hymns,* 58.

Prayers from the George A. Reed Manuscript Papers[1]

Prayer 1:

Almighty & most merciful God, unto thee all hearts are open, & all desires are know, for there is nothing that is hid from thy sight. We pray thee to look compassionately upon us who have assembled this morning in thy house to worship thee—Grant us the all powerful aid of thy Holy Spirit, that we may wait before thee in spirit and in truth.

We extol thy holy name for thy merciful kindness manifested to us thy unworthy servants.

We Bless, we praise, we magnify thy name that when man had forfitted thy favour, & thus destroyed all his hopes of happiness—Thou dist not leave him in his lost estate—but sent salvation to him.

We adore thee for thy infinite mercy to us, in the gift of thy only begotten Son, for thy blessed word (which thou hast given to us) teaches that thou dist give him to become the atoning sacrifice for the sins of the human race—and for the hope of glory, which is founded in our belief of the fact that thou art now in Christ Jesus reconciling the world unto thyself, not imputing our trespasses unto us.

We acknowledge that we are unworthy of the least of thy favours, by reason of our sins—And rejoice that thou hast laid help upon one

---

1. Original spelling, punctuation, and format have been retained.

who is Mighty to save & strong to deliver, for his sake blot out our sins and establish us in thy favour & the faith of the Gospel.

O that we may all be enabled to forsake every means by which we may have been seeking to justify ourselves before thee, save that righteousness that is found in & through Jesus Christ our only saviour.

Lord bless thy professing children through the world, this day, o that they may realize that being justified by faith they have peace with God.

May thy ministering servants be sustained by thy power and wherever thy word may be preached, make it the means of bringing many from nature's darkness to the light of truth that converteth the soul.

We commend unto thee thy servant the pastor of this Church, Be thou his comfort & support through all the scenes and trial he may pass through—protect him & his from harm, and soon restore him to this the people of his charge, blessed with that degree of health and reliance on thee, as may be necessary to make him a blessing to thy Church.

And now O Lord our God, we pray that thou will for thy own name's sake, bless us individually and collectively, as thou seest we need. Cleanse thou us from all things that may have a tendency to impede the progress, or prevent the reception of truth—for the believing portion of this congregation, we pray that thou wouldst establish our faith—confirm our hope, and perfect us in love.

For the impenitent that their eyes may be opened to see the nature, the guilt, and final consequences of sin, and that they may be induced to ground the weapons of Rebellion, and except of the terms of reconciliation proposed in the Gospel & be saved by grace through faith in Christ Jesus.

And thy servant to declare thy truth. Lord we allways stands in [need?] of thy assistance but never more than on the present occasion—and though the word may be sown in weekness—make it the power of God unto the salvation of those who hear.

Guide us by thy spirit through life and afterwards receive us to glory—and unto thee 3 [in?] one God who is the Lord—be praise, honor & dominion henceforth and ever more. Amen.

Prayer 2:

Holy, holy, holy lord God Almighty, which art, and wast, and art to come.

—

Thou art the Father of light, with whom is no variableness or shadow of turning, and from whom proceedeth every good & perfect gift.

—

We therefore come to thee believing, that thou art, and that thou art the powerful and bountiful rewarder of them that diligently seek thee.

—

Who can utter the mighty acts of the Lord? who can show forth all his praise?

—

Who is a God like unto thee, glorious in holiness, fearful in praises, doing wonders.

—

As the heaven is high above the earth, so are thy thoughts above our thoughts, and thy ways above our ways.

—

Thou art God, and changest not; therefore is it that we are not consumed

—

Thou art a God at hand, and a God afar off; none can hide himself in secret places that thou canst not see him, for thou fillest heaven & earth.

—

Thine eyes are in every place beholding the [bad?] and the good: they run to and fro through the earth, that thou mayest show thyself strong on the behalf of those whose hearts are upright with thee.

—

O the depth of the wisdom and knoledge of God! how unsearchable are his judgments, and his ways past finding out.

—

In thy hand is the soul of every living thing, and the breath of all mankind.

—

All power is thine both in heaven and in earth.

—

Holy and revered is thy name; and we give thanks at the remembrance of thy holiness.

—

Righteous art thou, O God, when we plead with thee; and [we?] wilt be justified when thou speakest, and clean when thou judgest.

—

Thou art good, and thy mercy endureth for ever. Thy loving is great towards us, and thy truth endureth to all generations.

—

Thou hast appointed us a great high-priest, in whose name we may come boldly to a throne of grace, that we may find mercy & grace to help in time of need.

—

What is man that thou art thus mindful of him, and the son of man that thou visitest him, and dost thus magnify him.

—

O our God! we are ashamed, and blush to lift up our faces before thee, our God; for our iniquities are increased over our head, and our trespass is grown up unto the heavens. To us belong shame and confusion of face, because we have sinned against thee.

—

If thou, Lord, shouldst mark iniquities, O Lord, who should stand! But there is forgiveness with thee, that thou mayest be feared; with thee there is mercy, yea, with our God there is plentious redemtion, and he shall redeem Israel from all his iniquity.

Examples of Love Feast Testimonies[1]

All that had obtained peace with God, and all who were seeking it, were invited, and the barn was nearly full. As few present had ever been in a love-feast, Mr. Mair explained to us its nature and design, namely, to take a little bread and water, not as a sacrament, but in token of our Christian love, in imitation of a primitive usage, and then humbly and briefly to declare the great things the Lord had done for them in having had mercy on them.

Mr. James Sterling, of Burlington, West Jersey, was the first who spoke, and the plain and simple narrative of his Christian experience was very affecting to many. After him rose one of the new converts, a Mr. Egbert, and said, "I was standing in my door, and saw a man at a distance, well mounted on horseback, and as he drew near I had thoughts of hailing him, to inquire the news; but he forestalled me by turning into my yard and saying to me, 'Pray, sir, can you tell me the way to heaven?' 'The way to heaven, sir! we all *hope* to get to heaven, and there are *many ways* that men take.' 'Ah! but,' said the stranger, 'I want to know the best way,' 'Alight, sir, if you please; I should like to hear you talk about the way you deem the best. When I was a boy I

1. Account by Thomas Ware, an early itinerant, of the testimonies given at a 1780 quarterly meeting love feast in *Sketches of the Life and Travels of Rev. Thomas Ware, who has been an Itinerant Methodist Preacher for More than Fifty Years* (New York: Lane & Sandford, 1842), 63-69. Original spelling, punctuation, and format have been retained.

used to hear my mother talk about the way to heaven, and I am under an impression you must know the way.' He did alight, and I was soon convinced the judgment I had formed of the stranger was true. My doors were opened, and my neighbours invited to come and see and hear a man who could and would, I verily believed, tell us the best way to heaven. And it was not long before myself, my wife, and several of my family, together with many of my neighbours, were well assured we were in the way, for we had peace with God, and with one another, and did ardently long and fervently pray for the peace and salvation of all men. 'Tell me, friends,' said he, 'is not this the way to heaven?'

"It is true, many of us were for a time greatly alarmed and troubled. We communed together, and said, It is a doubtful case if God will have mercy on us, and forgive us our sins; and if he does, it must be after we have passed through long and deep repentance. But our missionary, to whom we jointly made known our unbelieving fears, said to us, 'Cheer up, my friends, ye are not far from the kingdom of God. Can any of you be a greater sinner than Saul of Tarsus? and how long did it take him to repent? Three days were all. The Philippian jailer, too, in the same hour in which he was convicted, was baptized, rejoicing in God, with all his house. 'Come,' said he, 'let us have faith in God, remembering the saying of Christ, *Ye believe in God, believe also in me.* Come, let us go down upon our knees and claim the merit of his death for the remission of sins, and he will do it—look to yourselves, each man, God is here.' Instantly one who was, I thought, the greatest sinner in the house except myself, fell to the floor as one dead, and we thought he was dead; but he was not literally dead, for there he sits with as significant a smile as any one present'." Here the youth of whom he spoke uttered the word *glory,* with a look and tone of voice that ran through the audience like an electric shock, and for a time interrupted the speaker; but he soon resumed his narrative, by saying, "The preacher bid us not be alarmed—we must all *die* to *live.* Instantly I caught him in my arms and exclaimed, The guilt I *felt,* and the vengeance I *feared,* are gone, and now I know heaven is not far off; but here, and there, and wherever *Jesus* manifests himself, is *heaven'.*" Here his powers of speech failed, and he sat down and wept, and there was not, I think, one dry eye in the barn.

A German spoke next, and if I could tell what he said as told by him, it would be worth a place in any man's memory. But this I cannot do. He, however, spoke to the following import:—"When de preacher did come to mine house, and did say, 'Peace be on dis habitation;·I am come, fader, to see if in dese troublesome times I can find any in your parts dat does know de way to dat country where war, sorrow, and crying is no more; and of whom could I inquire so properly as of one to whom God has given many days?' When he did say dis, I was angry, and did try to say to him, Go out of mine house; but I could not speak, but did tremble, and when mine anger was gone I did say, I does fear I does not know de way to dat goodist place, but mine wife does know; sit down, and I will call her. Just den mine wife did come in, and de stranger did say, 'Dis, fader, is, I presume, yourn wife, of whom you say she does know de way to a better country, de way to heaven. Dear woman, will you tell it me?' After mine wife did look at de stranger one minutes, she did say, *I do know Jesus*, and is not he de way? De stranger did den fall on his knees and tank God for bringing him to mine house, where dere was one dat did know de way to heaven; he did den pray for me and mine children, dat we might be like mine wife, and all go to heaven togeder. Mine wife did den pray in Dutch, and some of mine children did fall on deir knees, and I did fall on mine, and when she did pray no more de preacher did pray again, and mine oldest daughter did cry so loud.

"From dat time I did seek de Lord, and did fear he would not hear me, for I had made de heart of mine wife so sorry when I did tell her she was mad. But de preacher did show me so many promises dat I did tell mine wife if she would forgive me, and fast and pray wid me all day and all night, I did hope de Lord would forgive me. Dis did please mine wife, but she did say, We must do all in de name of de Lord Jesus. About de middle of de night I did tell mine wife I should not live till morning, mine distress was too great. But she did say, Mine husband, God will not let you die; and just as de day did break, mine heart did break, and tears did run so fast, and I did say, Mine wife, I does now believe mine God will bless me, and she did say, Amen, amen, come, Lord Jesus. Just den mine oldest daughter, who had been praying all night, did come in and did fall on mine neck, and said, O mine fader, Jesus has blessed me. And den joy did come into mine heart, and we have gone on rejoicing in de Lord ever since. Great fear did fall on mine neighbours, and mine barn would not hold all de peoples dat does come to learn de way to heaven." His looks, his tears, and his broken English, kept the people in tears, mingled with smiles, and even laughter, not with lightness, but joy, for they believed every word he said.

241

After him, one got up and said, For months previous to the coming of Mr. Mairs into their place, he was one of the most wretched of men. He had heard of the Methodists, and the wonderful works done among them, and joined in ascribing it all to the devil. At length a fear fell on him; he thought he should die and be lost. He lost all relish for food, and sleep departed from him. His friends thought him mad; but his own conclusions was, that he was a reprobate, having been brought up a Calvinist; and he was tempted to shoot himself, that he might know the worst. He at length resolved he would hear the Methodists; and when he came, the barn was full; there was, however, room at the door, where he could see the preacher, and hear well. He was soon convinced he was no reprobate, and felt a heart to beg of God to forgive him for ever harbouring a thought that he, the kind Parent of all, had reprobated any of his children. And listening, he at length understood the cause of his wretchedness; it was guilt, from which Jesus came to save us. The people all around him being in tears, and hearing one in the barn cry, Glory to Jesus, hardly what he did, he drew his hat from under his arm, and swinging it over his head, began to huzza with might and main. The preacher saw him and knew he was not in sport, for the tears were flowing down his face, and smiling, said, "Young man, thou art not far from the kingdom of God; but rather say, Hallelujah, the Lord God omnipotent reigneth." Several others spoke, and more would have spoken, had not a general cry arisen when the doors were thrown open that all might come in and see the way that God sometimes works.

American Sacramental Hymns[1]

Hymn 1:

Here round thy table Lord we meet
And neal before thy face
With reverence worship at thy feet
Our refuge is thy grace

Thy body broken for our sin
Upon the Cursed tree
When we behold the bread and wine
With eyes of faith we see

Those streams of blood gush from thy side
Thy hands in purple gore
While cruel Jews thy pains deride
And mock almighty powr

Earth trembles when her maker dies
The sun witholds her light
The flinty rocks rend with surprise
All trembling at the Light

---

1. Original spelling, punctuation, and format have been retained.

He rose to Heven to plead our cause
The Bread of life he gives
Our Souls by love he gently draws
In Heven our Jesus lives

Lord fead our souls with living bread
Wash us and make us clean
For Jesus is our Living head
He doth our souls redeem

The wine of consolation give
Thy healing Blood apply
Make us anew and we shall live
And reign with God on high[2]

Hymn 2:

We meet our Saviour at the feast
His Blood was shed for us
Our faith and love Lord now increase
And raise us from the dust

Thou Jesus who didst tast the gaul
That we might drink the wine
Thy Blood was spilt for us for all
Our heart to the incline

Our souls by faith in Raptures gaze
Upon the bleeding Lamb
We round thy table sing thy praise
Thy Dieing love proclaim

But when we rise to worlds of love
In shineing robes of white
To praise our God who reings above
In uncreated light

With holy Angles joyn the train
And this the glorious song

---

2. Hymn 47, simply entitled "Sacramental" in Ebenezer Hills, Hymnal. Ms. Ezekiel Cooper Papers. Garrett-Evangelical Theological Seminary Library, Evanston, IL.

The Lamb is worthy that was slain
To him all praise belong[3]

Hymn 3:

Jesus once for Sinners slain,
From the dead was rais'd again;
And in Heaven is now sat down,
With his Father on his Throne.

There he reigns a King supreme,
We shall also reign with him;
Feeble Souls be not dismay'd,
Trust in his Almighty aid.

He has made an end of Sin,
And his Blood has wash'd us clean;
Fear not, He is ever near,
Now, e'en now He's with us here.

Thus assembling we by Faith,
Till He come, shew forth His Death;
Of His Body, Bread's the Sign,
And we drink His Blood in Wine.

Bread thus broken, aptly shows
How His Body God did bruise;
When the Grape's rich Blood we see,
Lord we then remember thee.

Saints on Earth, and Saints above,
Celebrate his dying Love,
And let every ransom'd Soul,
Sound His praise from Pole to Pole.[4]

Hymn 4:

1 When David found a feast,
Of soul-reviving grace;

---

3. Hymn 48 in Ebenezer Hills, Hymnal.

4. *Extracts of Letters, Containing Some Account of the Work of God Since the Year 1800 Written by the Preachers and Members of the Methodist Episcopal Church, to their Bishops* (Barnard, VT: Joseph Dix, 1812), 120.

He wanted all to come and taste,
Yea, all the human race.

2 He found it precious food,
And wanted all to share;
To come and taste that God was good,
He has enough to spare.

3 And all who truly know
The love of Jesus Christ,
Will find a banquet here below,
Of precious food the best.

4 Fruits of his dying love,
To sinners freely given;
And all who come, shall fully prove
An antepast of heaven.

5 O come, on Christ believe,
And taste this precious food;
You from his fulness may receive
All that is truly good.[5]

Hymn 5:

Behold the suffering Son of God,
Press'd down with sheaves a pond'rous load;
His hands, his feet, his gushing side,
Exceed bold Jordan's swelling tide.
Ye scarlet sinners now draw nigh,
Whose sins are of the deepest dye;
Baptize your souls in this rich flood,
Fresh springing from a dying God.

Behold the dying Jesus rise,
With flaming troops above the skies;
He tramples Hell beneath his feet,
And takes his Mediatorial seat.

---

5. Hymn 84 based on Psalm 34:8 in Enoch Mudge, *The American Camp-Meeting Hymn Book. Containing a Variety of Original Hymns, Suitable to be Used at Camp-Meetings; and at Other Times in Private and Social Devotion* (Boston: Burdakin, 1818), 100.

Ten thousand thousand in a band,
Around the throne adoring stand;
They had the conqu'ring prince of war,
And gaze upon each glorious scar.

His fame shall sound from pole to pole;
His grace shall flow from soul to soul;
Ten thousands shall his love proclaim,
And infants learn to lisp his name,
His blood we'll drink, his flesh we'd eat,
His gospel shall adorn our feet;
His righteousness shall us entwine,
In garments of salvation shine.

Each soldier bold, with sword in hand,
Fight valiantly for Canaan's land;
With helmet, breast plate and the shield,
We'll force the pow'rs of Hell to yield.
Your general brave has gone before,
Hark! don't you hear his trumpets roar?
Come on, come on, ye little band,
You soon will gain fair Canaan's land.

We soon shall stand where Moses stood,
From Pisgah's top cross Jordan's flood;
With eagle's wings, outstrip the wind,
And leave its raging waves behind.
We'd meet on that delightful shore,
And then the promis'd land explore;
Meanwhile redeeming grace admire,
In praises sweet the golden lyre.[6]

---

6. Stanzas 8-12 in Richard A. Humphrey, comp., *History and Hymns of John Adam Granade: Holston's Pilgrim-Preacher-Poet* (n.p.: Commission on Archives and History, Holston Annual Conference, The United Methodist Church, 1991), 87-88.

Select Bibliography

Unpublished Primary Material from Individuals

Ayres, Robert. "The Journal of Robert Ayres." Ts. United Methodist Church Archives-GCAH, Madison, NJ.

Bangs, Nathan. Journal. Ms. Nathan Bangs papers. United Methodist Church Archives-GCAH, Madison, NJ.

Bennet, John. Journal. Ms. The John Rylands University Library, University of Manchester, England.

Bernard, Overton. Diary. Ms. Southern Historical Collection, University of North Carolina Library, Chapel Hill, NC.

Boehm, Henry. Journal. Ms. Henry Boehm Papers, United Methodist Church Archives-GCAH, Madison, NJ. [Microfilm copy at Iliff Theological Seminary, Denver, CO.]

Bradford, Henry. Hymnbook. Ms. Southern Historical Collection, University of North Carolina Library, Chapel Hill, NC.

Coker, Daniel. Journal. Ms. on microfilm. The Peter Force Collection Series 8 and 9. Ms. 17137, The Library of Congress Manuscript Division, Washington, D.C.

Colbert, William. "A Journal of the Travels of William Colbert Methodist Preacher thro' parts of Maryland, Pennsylvania, New York, Delaware, and Virginia in 1790 to 1838." Ts. United Methodist Church Archives-GCAH, Madison, NJ.

Coles, George. Papers. United Methodist Church Archives-GCAH, Madison, NJ.

Collins, John. Diary. Ms. St. George's United Methodist Church, Philadelphia, PA.

Cooper, Ezekiel. "A brief account of the work of God in Baltimore: written by E. C. in an Epistle to Bishop Asbury." Ts. Barratt's Chapel & Museum, Frederica, DE.

———. Papers. Garrett-Evangelical Theological Seminary Library, Evanston, IL.

Cooper, Samuel. Diary. Ms. DePauw University Library, Greencastle, IN.

[Dailey, David]. "Account of a Camp Meeting held on the Tangier Island in August 1819." Ms. St. George's United Methodist Church, Philadelphia, PA. [No author is listed but the account is stored with the Dailey diary and apparently is in the same hand.]

———. Diary. Ms. St. George's United Methodist Church, Philadelphia, PA.

Deem, John Campbell. Autobiography. Ms. Ohio Wesleyan University Library, Delaware, OH.

Doub, Peter. Diary. Ms. William Clark Doub Papers. Special Collections Library, Duke University Library, Durham, NC.

Dromgoole, Edward. Papers. Southern Historical Collection, University of North Carolina Library, Chapel Hill, NC. [Available on microfilm from the University of North Carolina.]

Duke, William. "The Journal of William Duke 1774–1776." Ts. United Methodist Historical Society, Lovely Lane Museum, Baltimore, MD.

Early, John. "Journal of Bishop John Early who lived Jan. 1, 1786–Nov. 5, 1873." Ts. Southern Historical Collection, University of North Carolina, Chapel Hill, NC.

Fidler, Daniel. Papers. Ms. United Methodist Church Archives-GCAH, Madison, NJ.

Fidler, Noah. "Journal of Noah Fidler." Ts. Transcribed by Annie L. Winstead. The Upper Room Devotional Library and Museum, Nashville, TN.

Garrettson, Catherine Livingston. Papers. United Methodist Church Archives-GCAH, Madison, NJ.

Gatch, Philip. Papers. Ohio Wesleyan University Library, Delaware, OH.

Glenn, Joshua N. "A Memorandum or Journal of the first part of my life up to the twenty third year of my age." Ms. on microfilm. Library of Congress, Washington, D.C.

Grant, Daniel. Letters. David Campbell Papers, Special Collections Library, Duke University Library, Durham, NC.

Greene, Myles. Journal. Ms. Special Collections Library, Duke University Library, Durham, NC.

Haskins, Thomas. "The Journal of Thomas Haskins (1760–1816)." Ts. Transcribed by Louise Stahl. Indiana State University, Terre Haute, IN.

Hills, Ebenezer. Hymnal. Ms. Ezekiel Cooper Papers. Garrett-Evangelical Theological Seminary Library, Evanston, IL.

Hollaway, Mary. Letter to John Pearce, 9 July 1810. Newby Larkin Papers. Special Collections Library, Duke University Library, Durham, NC.

Jessop, William. Journal (1788). Ms. United Methodist Church Archives-GCAH, Madison, NJ.

———. Journal (1790–1791). Ms. St. George's United Methodist Church, Philadelphia, PA. [A much later, abbreviated handwritten copy of this journal can be found at Garrett-Evangelical Theological Seminary Library, Evanston, IL.]

Kilburn, David. Journal. Ms. United Methodist Church Archives-GCAH, Madison, NJ.

Lakin, Benjamin. Journal. Ms. on microfilm. Washington University Library, St. Louis, MO. Some of Lakin's journal can be found in William Warren Sweet, *The Methodists* (Chicago: University of Chicago Press, 1946).

Littlejohn, John. "Journal of John Littlejohn." Ts. Transcribed by Annie L. Winstead. Louisville Conference Historical Society, Louisville, KY. [Available on microfilm from Kentucky Wesleyan College, Owensboro, KY.]

McReynolds, Benjamin. Diary. Ts. Southern Historical Collection, University of North Carolina Library, Chapel Hill, NC.

Mann, Thomas. Journal. Ms. Special Collections Library, Duke University Library, Durham, NC.

Matthias, John B. Journal. Ms. John B. Matthias Papers, United Methodist Church Archives-GCAH, Madison, NJ.

Meacham, James. Journal. Ms. Special Collections Library, Duke University Library, Durham, NC.

Mills, Nathaniel. Journal. Ms. United Methodist Historical Society, Lovely Lane Museum, Baltimore, MD.

Norman, Jeremiah. Journal. Ms. Stephen Beauregard Weeks Papers. Southern Historical Collection, University of North Carolina, Chapel Hill, NC.

Ormond, William. Papers. Special Collections Library, Duke University Library, Durham, NC.

Owen, Thomas. Letter to John Owen, 8 November 1800. David Campbell Papers. Special Collections Library, Duke University Library, Durham, NC.

Price, John. Sermon book. Ms. St. George's United Methodist Church, Philadelphia, PA.

Rankin, Thomas. "The Diary of Reverend Thomas Rankin." Ts. Garrett-Evangelical Theological Seminary Library, Evanston, IL.

Reed, George A. Papers. Special Collections Library, Duke University Library, Durham, NC.

Reed, Nelson. "Diary of Rev. Nelson Reed." Ts. United Methodist Historical Society, Lovely Lane Museum, Baltimore, MD.

Reiley, James. "Life of James Reiley." Ts. United Methodist Historical Society, Lovely Lane Museum, Baltimore, MD.

Tees, Francis, comp. "Book of Antiquities." St. George's United Methodist Church, Philadelphia, PA.

Thacher, William. Letter to Robert Emory, 14 December 1840. United Methodist Church Archives-GCAH, Madison, NJ.

Thompson, Amos G. Letter to Henry Waters, 26 August 1787. Amos G. Thompson papers. United Methodist Church Archives-GCAH, Madison, NJ.

Wallcut, Thomas. Letter to James Freeman, 31 October 1789. Thomas Wallcut papers. American Antiquarian Society, Worcester, MA.

Watts, James. Journal. Ms. United Methodist Historical Society, Lovely Lane Museum, Baltimore, MD.

Whatcoat, Richard. Journal. Ts. Garrett-Evangelical Theological Seminary Library, Evanston, IL.

Wilson, Norval. Diary. Ms. Special Collections Library, Duke University Library, Durham, NC.

Wrenshall, John. Autobiography. Ms. United Methodist Church Archives-GCAH, Madison, NJ.

Unpublished Primary Material from Circuits and Stations

(listed by circuit or station; title provided if available)

Accomack Circuit (VA) Quarterly Meeting Conference records, 1804–1825. Ms. Cokesbury United Methodist Church, Onancock, VA.

Baltimore Circuit (MD) Steward's Book, 1794–1815. Ms. United Methodist Historical Society, Lovely Lane Museum, Baltimore, MD.

Baltimore City Station (MD) Records. Ms. on microfilm. Maryland State Archives, Annapolis, MD.

Berkley Circuit (MD) Steward's Book. Ms. United Methodist Historical Society, Lovely Lane Museum, Baltimore, MD.

Bertie Circuit et al. (NC) Recording Steward's Book, 1817–1822. Special Collections Library, Duke University Library, Durham, NC.

Camden Circuit (NC) Quarterly Meeting Conference records. Ms. Stephen Beauregard Weeks Papers, Southern Historical Collection, University of North Carolina, Chapel Hill, NC.

Cumberland Circuit (NJ). "Quarterly Conference Minutes Cumberland Circuit (NJ) 1816–1820." Ts. Commission on Archives and History of the Southern New Jersey Annual Conference, The United Methodist Church, Pennington, NJ.

Durham (CT) Methodist Episcopal Church Records, 1816–1847. Ms. United Methodist Church Archives-GCAH, Madison, NJ.

Edenton (NC) Quarterly Meeting Conference records. Ms. on microfilm. Southern Historical Collection, University of North Carolina, Chapel Hill, NC.

Fairfeald Circuit (OH). "Steward's Book for Fairfeald Circuit (OH) of the Methodist Episcopal Church." Ms. Ohio Wesleyan University Library, Delaware, OH.

Fall Creek Circuit (IN) Quarterly Meeting Conference records, 1828–1829. Ms. DePauw University Library, Greencastle, IN.

Frederick Circuit (MD). "Proceedings of the Quarterly Conferences held in Frederick Circuit Commencing on the 14th Day of December 1805." Ms. photocopy. Wesley Theological Seminary, Washington, D.C.

Greensville Circuit (VA). Steward's Book, 1798–1805. Ms. Edward Dromgoole Papers. Southern Historical Collection, University of North Carolina Library, Chapel Hill, NC.

Harford Circuit (MD) Quarterly Meeting Conference records, 1799–1830. Ms. United Methodist Historical Society, Lovely Lane Museum, Baltimore, MD.

Hockhocking Circuit (OH). "Book of Records." Ms. Ohio Wesleyan University Library, Delaware, OH.

Hockhocking Circuit (OH) Steward's Book, 1805–1815. Ms. Ohio Wesleyan University Library, Delaware, OH.

Honey Creek Circuit (IN) Steward's Book, 1821–1829. Ms. DePauw University Library, Greencastle, IN.

Lawrenceburg Circuit (IN) Steward's Book, 1828–1829. Ms. DePauw University Library, Greencastle, IN.

Madison Circuit (KY) Quarterly Meeting Conference records, 1810–1825. Ms. Kentucky Wesleyan College Library, Owensboro, KY.

Milford Circuit (OH). Report of Committee of 2nd Conference. Ms., Philip Gatch Papers, Ohio Wesleyan University, Delaware, Ohio.

New Haven (OH) Class Meeting Records for 1806, 1808, and 1811. Ms. Ohio Wesleyan University Library, Delaware, OH.

New Mills Circuit (NJ). "Steward's Book for the New Mills Circuit (NJ)." Ts. Commission on Archives and History of the Southern New Jersey Annual Conference, The United Methodist Church, Pennington, NJ. (Original in the Ocean County Historical Society, Toms River, New Jersey.)

New River Circuit (NC). "Recording Steward's Book for New River-Trent-Newport & Trent & Newport Circuits VA & NC Conferences Commencing 1815." Ms. Special Collections Library, Duke University Library, Durham, NC.

Paint Creek Circuit (OH) Quarterly Meeting Conference records, 1811–1815. Ms. Ohio Wesleyan University Library, Delaware, OH.

Patoka Circuit (IN). "Journal of Patoka Circuit (IN)." Ms. DePauw University Library, Greencastle, IN.

Petersburg (VA). Allin Archer Account book for Petersburg, VA, 1819–1850s. Ms. Fletcher H. Archer Papers. Special Collections Library, Duke University Library, Durham, NC.

Philadelphia. "[Constitution for the] United Societies 1801." Ms. dated 18 August 1801. In Francis Tees's "Book of Antiquities." St. George's United Methodist Church, Philadelphia, PA.

———. "Minutes of the Quarterly Conferences of St. George's Charge." Ms. St. George's United Methodist Church, Philadelphia, PA.

Pompey Circuit (NY). "Journal of Pompey Circuit, March 25, 1809, to March 12, 1814." In Religion on the American Frontier 1783–1840. Vol. 4, The Methodists. Edited by William Warren Smith. Chicago: University of Chicago Press, 1946.

Rocky River Circuit (SC) Quarterly Meeting Conference records, 1807–1819. Ms. Special Collections Library, Duke University Library, Durham, NC.

Salem Circuit (NJ). "The Proceedings of the Quarterly Meeting 1789. Copied from the Original Stewards Book for Salem Circuit (NJ) 1789." Ts. Commission on Archives and History of the Southern New Jersey Annual Conference, The United Methodist Church, Pennington, NJ.

Silver Creek Circuit (IN). "Collection and Distribution of Money." 1809–1820. Ms. DePauw University Library, Greencastle, IN.

Silver Creek Circuit (IN) Quarterly Meeting Conference records, 1809–1825. Ms. DePauw University Library, Greencastle, IN. (Partly reprinted in *Religion on the American Frontier 1783–1840*. Vol. 4, *The Methodists*. Edited by William Warren Smith. Chicago: University of Chicago Press, 1946.)

Stratford Circuit and Station (CT). Quarterly Meeting Conference records. Ms. Stratford United Methodist Church, Stratford, CT, 1813–1899.

Tar River Circuit (NC) Quarterly Meeting Conference records, 6-7 July 1800 (addressed to John Howell, Steward). Ms. William Ormond Papers, Special Collections Library, Duke University Library, Durham, NC.

Union and Mad River Circuits (OH) Quarterly Meeting Conference records, 1807–1814. Ms. Ohio Wesleyan University Library, Delaware, OH.

Wilmington (DE). "A Journal of Quarterly Conference of Asbury Church (Wilmington, DE)." Ms. Barratt's Chapel & Museum, Frederica, DE.

Published Primary Material

[Adams, John]. *The Life of "Reformation" John Adams, an Elder of the Methodist Episcopal Church*. Vol. 1. Edited by Enoch George Adams. Boston: George C. Rand, 1853.

[Adams, William]. "A short account of the Life and Death of William Adams, A youth of Virginia. Drawn up by a friend, personally acquainted with the deceased." *AM* 12 (1789): 80-92.

Allen, B[everly]. "Some Account of the Work of God in America." *AM* 15 (1792): 403-8.

Allen, J[ohn?]. "A short Account of the Revival of the Work of GOD, at Manchester, &c." *AM* 13 (1790): 279.

Allen, Richard. *A Collection of Hymns and Spiritual Songs*. Philadelphia: T. L. Plowman, 1801; reprint, Nashville: A.M.E.C. Sunday School Union, 1987.

———. *The Life Experience and Gospel Labors of the Rt. Rev. Richard Allen*. New York: Abingdon, 1960.

Asbury, Francis. *The Journal and Letters of Francis Asbury*. 3 vols. Edited by Elmer T. Clark. London: Epworth; Nashville: Abingdon, 1958.

Bangs, Heman. *The Autobiography and Journal of Rev. Heman Bangs*. New York: Tibbals & Son, 1872.

Bangs, John. *Auto-biography of Rev. John Bangs, of the New-York Annual Conference*. New York: printed for the author, 1846.

Bangs, Nathan. *A History of the Methodist Episcopal Church*. Vol. 1. 3rd ed. New York: Mason and Lane, 1840.

———. "Memoir of Rev. J. B. Matthias." John B. Matthias Papers. United Methodist Church Archives-GCAH, Madison, NJ.

Boyd, Robert. *Personal Memoirs: Together With a Discussion upon the Hardships and Sufferings of Itinerant Life; and also a Discourse upon the Pastoral Relation*. Cincinnati: Methodist Book Concern, 1868.

Boyd, William K. "A Journal and Travel of James Meacham." *Annual Publication of Historical Papers of the Historical Society of Trinity College* 9 (1912): 66-95; 10 (1914): 87-102.

Brooks, John. *The Life and Times of the Rev. John Brooks.* Nashville: Nashville Christian Advocate, 1848.

Brown, George. *Recollections of Itinerant Life: Including Early Reminiscences.* Cincinnati: Carroll & Co., 1866.

[Bruce, Philip]. "An extract of a letter from Philip Bruce, elder of the Methodist Episcopal church, to Bishop Coke, dated Portsmouth, Virginia, March 25, 1788." *AM* 13 (1790): 563-64.

Brunson, Alfred. *A Western Pioneer: or, Incidents of the Life and Times of Rev. Alfred Brunson, A.M., D.D., Embracing a Period of over Seventy Years.* Cincinnati: Hitchcock & Walden; New York: Carlton & Lanahan, 1872; reprint, New York: Arno Press, 1975.

Bull, Robert J. "John Wesley Bond's Reminiscences of Francis Asbury." *Methodist History* 4.1 (October 1965): 3-32.

Camp-meetings Described and Exposed; and "Strange Things" Stated. N.p., ca. 1825.

Capers, William. "Letter to the Editors" (Georgia, 17 September 1819). *MQR* 2 (1819): 476-77.

Cartwright, Peter. *Autobiography of Peter Cartwright.* Edited by W. P. Strickland. New York: Hunt & Eaton; Cincinnati: Cranston & Curts, 1856.

[Chandler, William]. *A Brief Account of the Work of God on the Delaware District, Since the Sitting of Conference, in May, 1805; in Which is Included an Account of the Camp-Meeting, Held in the State of Delaware, July 25, &c. in a Letter to Francis Asbury.* Dover: 1805.

Chase, Abner. *Recollections of the Past.* New York: Joseph Longkin, 1848.

[Clark, Laban]. *Laban Clark: Autobiography about his early life from 1778–1804: Circuit Rider for the Methodist Episcopal Church.* Edited by E. Farley Sharp. Rutland, VT: Academy Books, 1987.

Coke, Thomas. Letter to Samuel Seabury, Philadelphia, 14 May 1791. In *A Letter to a Methodist.* 4th ed. Baltimore: George Lycett, 1869.

———. *Extracts of the journals of the Rev. Dr. Coke's five visits to America.* London: G. Paramore, 1793.

Coker, Daniel. *Journal of Daniel Coker, A Descendant of Africa, From the Time of Leaving New York in the Ship Elizabeth, Capt. Sebor. on a Voyage for Sherbro, In Africa.* Baltimore: Edward J. Coale, 1820; reprint, Nendeln/Leichtenstein: Kraus Reprint, 1970.

Coles, George. *My First Seven Years in America.* New York: Carlton & Porter, 1852.

Cooper, Ezekiel. "An Account of the Work of God at Baltimore, in a Letter to ———." *AM* 13 (1790): 409-11.

———. Letter to Thomas Coke, Philadelphia, 7 September 1801. *MQR* 1 (1802): 423-26.

[Cox, Philip]. "Extract of a Letter from Mr. Phillip Cox, dated Brunswick-County, Virginia." *AM* 11 (1788): 486-87.

———. "An Extract of a Letter from Philip Cox, Elder of the Methodist-Episcopal Church in America (then Preacher) to Bishop Coke, dated, Sussex-county, Virginia, July 1787." *AM* 13 (1790): 91-95.

Crowell, Seth. *The Journal of Seth Crowell; containing an Account of His Travels as a Methodist Preacher for Twelve Years.* New York: J. C. Totten, 1813.

Crowther, Jonathan. *A True and Complete Portraiture of Methodism.* New York: J. C. Totten, 1813.

Dailey, David. *Experience and Ministerial Labors of Rev. Thomas Smith, Late an Itinerant*

Preacher of the Gospel in the Methodist Episcopal Church. New York: Lane & Tippett, 1848.

De Vinné, Daniel. *Recollections of Fifty Years in the Ministry.* New York: Tibbals & Co., 1869.

Dixon, James. *Personal Narrative of a Tour Through a Part of the United States and Canada.* New York: Lane & Scott, 1849.

[Douglass, T. L.]. "Account of the Work of God in the Nashville District." *MQR* 4 (1821): 191-95.

Dow, Lorenzo. *Extracts from Original Letters, to the Methodist Bishops, Mostly from their Preachers and Members, in North America: Giving an Account of the Work of God, Since the Year 1800. Prefaced with a Short History of the Spread and Increase of the Methodists; with a Sketch of the Camp Meetings.* Liverpool, 1806.

Edwards, John Ellis. *Life of Rev. John Wesley Childs: For Twenty-Three Years an Itinerant Methodist Minister.* Richmond and Louisville: John Early, 1852.

[Emory, Robert?]. *The Life of the Rev. John Emory, D. D.* New York: George Lane, 1841.

Everett, Joseph. "An Account of the most remarkable Occurrences of the Life of Joseph Everett. [In a Letter to Bishop Asbury]." *AM* 13 (1790): 601-11.

Extracts of Letters, Containing some Account of the Work of God since the Year 1800. New York: J. C. Totten, 1805; reprint, Barnard, VT: Joseph Dix, 1812.

Ffirth, John. *Experience and Gospel Labors of the Rev. Benjamin Abbott; to which is annexed a Narrative of his Life and Death.* New York: Carlton & Phillips, 1853.

Finley, James B. *Autobiography of Rev. James B. Finley; or, Pioneer Life in the West.* Edited by W. P. Strickland. Cincinnati: Methodist Book Concern, 1853.

———. "Extract of a letter from the Rev. J. B. Finley, to the Editors, dated Mount-Plesant, June 30, 1819." *MQR* 2 (1819): 308-11.

———. *Sketches of Western Methodism: Biographical, Historical, and Miscellaneous.* Edited by W. P. Strickland. Cincinnati: Methodist Book Concern, 1854; reprint, New York: Arno Press and The New York Times, 1969.

Fletcher, Miram. *The Methodist; Or, Incidents and Characters from Life in the Baltimore Conference.* New York: Derby & Jackson (1859): 1:129, 142.

Gaddis, Maxwell Pierson. *Foot-Prints of an Itinerant.* Cincinnati: Methodist Book Concern, 1856.

Gannaway, Robertson. "Autobiography of Rev. Robertson Gannaway." *Virginia Magazine of History and Biography* 37 (1929): 316-22; 38 (1930): 137-44.

Garrettson, R. "An Account of the Revival of the Work of God at Petersburg, in Virginia." *AM* 13 (1790): 300-307.

Gifford, Carolyn De Swarte, ed. *The Nineteenth-Century American Methodist Itinerant Preacher's Wife.* New York: Garland Publishing, 1987.

Giles, Charles. *Pioneer: A Narrative of the Nativity, Experience, Travels, and Ministerial Labours of Rev. Charles Giles.* New York: G. Lane & P. P. Sandford, 1844.

[Hagerty, John]. "An extract of a letter from John Hagerty, Elder of the Methodist Episcopal Church in America, to Bishop Asbury, dated Annapolis, February 17, 1789." *AM* 13 (1790): 355-57.

Hall, B. M. *The Life of Rev. John Clark.* New York: Carlton & Porter, 1856.

[Haw, James]. "An extract of a letter from James Haw, elder of the Methodist Episcopal church in America, to Bishop Asbury: written from Cumberland near Kentucke, about the beginning of the year 1789." *AM* 13 (1790): 202-4.

Henckle, M. M. *The Life of Henry Bidleman Bascom, D.D., LL.D., Late Bishop of the Methodist Episcopal Church, South.* Louisville: Morton & Griswold, 1854.

Hibbard, Billy. *Memoirs of the Life and Travels of B. Hibbard, Minister of the Gospel, Containing an Account of his Experience of Religion; and of his Call to and Labours in the Ministry, for Nearly Thirty Years.* New York: Totten, 1825.

Hobart, Chauncey. *Recollections of My Life. Fifty Years of Itinerancy in the Northwest*. Red Wing, MN: Red Wing Printing Co., 1885.

Hodges, Graham Russell, ed. *Black Itinerants of the Gospel: The Narratives of John Jea and George White*. Madison, WI: Madison House Publishers, 1993.

Holmes, Marjorie Moran. "The Life and Diary of the Reverend John Jeremiah Jacob (1757–1839)." Master's thesis, Duke University, 1941.

Horton, James P. *A Narrative of the Early Life, Remarkable Conversion, and Spiritual Labours of James P. Horton, Who has been a Member of the Methodist Episcopal Church Upward of Forty Years*. N.p.: Printed for the author, 1839.

Hudson, John B. *Narrative of the Christian Experience, Travels and Labors of John B. Hudson, a Local Elder of the Methodist Episcopal Church*. Rochester, NY: William Alling, 1838.

Humphrey, Richard A., comp. *History and Hymns of John Adam Granade: Holston's Pilgrim-Preacher-Poet*. N.p.: Commission on Archives and History, Holston Annual Conference, The United Methodist Church, 1991.

Jarratt, Devereux. *A Brief Narrative of the Revival of Religion in Virginia in a Letter to a Friend*. 3rd. ed. London: J. Paramore, 1786.

———. *The Life of the Reverend Devereux Jarratt*. Baltimore: Warner & Hanna, 1806.

[Jenkins, James]. *Experience, Labours, and Sufferings of Rev. James Jenkins, of the South Carolina Conference*. N.p.: Printed for the author, 1842.

Keith, William. *The Experience of William Keith. [Written by Himself.] Together with Some Observations Conclusive of Divine Influence on the Mind of Man*. Utica: Seward, 1806.

Landon, S. *Fifty Years in the Itinerant Ministry*. New York: Tibbals & Co., 1868.

Lee, Jesse. *A Short Account of the Life and Death of the Rev. John Lee, a Methodist Minister in the United States of America*. Baltimore: John West Butler, 1805.

———. *A Short History of the Methodists, in the United States of America; Beginning in 1766, and Continued till 1809*. Baltimore: Magill & Clime, 1810; reprint, Rutland, VT: Academy Books, 1974.

Lee, Leroy M. *The Life and Times of the Rev. Jesse Lee*. Richmond: John Early, 1848.

Lewis, David. *Recollections of a Superannuate: or, Sketches of Life, Labor, and Experience in the Methodist Itinerancy*. Edited by S. M. Merrill. Cincinnati: Methodist Book Concern, 1857.

M'Clintock, John, ed. *Sketches of Eminent Methodist Ministers*. New York: Carlton & Phillips, 1854.

[M'Gee, John]. "Commencement of the Great Revival of Religion in Kentucky and Tennessee, in 1799, In a Letter to the Rev. Thomas L. Douglass." *MQR* 4 (1821): 189-91.

M'Lean, John. *Sketch of Rev. Philip Gatch*. Cincinnati: Swormstedt & Poe, 1854.

[Maffitt, John N.]. *Tears of Contrition; or Sketches of the Life of John N. Maffitt: With Religious and Moral Reflections*. New London, CT: Samuel Green, 1821.

Matlack, Lucius C. *The Life of Rev. Orange Scott*. Freeport, NY: Books for Libraries Press, 1971.

[Maynard, Sampson]. *The Experience of Sampson Maynard, Local Preacher of the Methodist Episcopal Church*. New York: Printed for the author, by Wm. C. Taylor, 1828.

Mead, Stith. *A General Selection of the Newest and Most Admired Hymns and Spiritual Songs, Now in Use*. The second edition revised corrected and enlarged, and published by permission of the Virginia Conference held at Raleigh (N.C.). 1807. Reprint, Lynchburg: Jacob Haas, 1811.

Morrell, Thomas. *The Journals of the Rev. Thomas Morrell*. Edited by Michael J. McKay. Madison, NJ: Historical Society, Northern New Jersey Conference, The United Methodist Church, 1984.

Morris, Thomas A. *Miscellany: Consisting of Essays, Biographical Sketches, and Notes of Travel.* Cincinnati: L. Swormstedt & A. Poe, 1854.

Mudge, Enoch. *The American Camp-Meeting Hymn Book. Containing a Variety of Original Hymns, Suitable to be Used at Camp-Meetings; and at Other Times in Private and Social Devotion.* Boston: Burdakin, 1818.

Myles, William. *A Chronological History of the People called Methodists.* London, 1813.

Newell, Ebenezer Francis. *Life and Observations of Rev. E. F. Newell, who has been more than Forty Years an Itinerant Minister in the Methodist Episcopal Church.* Worcester, MA: C. W. Ainsworth, 1847.

Osborn, Elbert. *Passages in the Life and Ministry of Elbert Osborn, an Itinerant Minister of the Methodist Episcopal Church, illustrating the Providence and Grace of God.* New York: published for the author, 1847–1850.

Paddock, Zechariah. *Memoir of Rev. Benjamin G. Paddock, with Brief Notices of Early Ministerial Associates.* New York: Nelson & Phillips; Cincinnati: Hitchcock & Walden, 1875.

Paine, Robert. *Life and Times of William M'Kendree, Bishop of the Methodist Episcopal Church.* Nashville: Publishing House of the Methodist Episcopal Church, South, 1885.

[Pawson, John]. *The Letters of John Pawson (Methodist Itinerant, 1762–1806).* Vol. 1. Edited by John C. Bowmer and John A. Vickers. World Methodist Historical Society, 1994.

Peaslee, Reuben. *The Experience, Christian and Ministerial of Mr. Reuben Peaslee.* Haverhill, MA: Burrill & Tileston, 1816.

Peck, George. *Early Methodism within the bounds of the old Genesee Conference from 1788 to 1828: or, The first forty years of Wesleyan evangelism in northern Pennsylvania, central and western New York, and Canada. Containing sketches of interesting localities, exciting scenes, and prominent actors.* New York: Carlton & Porter, 1860.

———. *The Life and Times of Rev. George Peck, D.D.* New York: Nelson & Phillips, 1874.

———, ed. *Sketches & Incidents; or, a Budget from the Saddle-bags of a Superannuated Itinerant.* New York: Lane & Scott, 1850.

Phoebus, George A., comp. *Beams of Light on Early Methodism in America.* New York: Phillips & Hunt; Cincinnati: Cranston & Stowe, 1887.

Phoebus, William. *Memoirs of the Rev. Richard Whatcoat, Late Bishop of the Methodist Episcopal Church.* New York: Joseph Allen, 1828.

Pilmore, Joseph. *The Journal of Joseph Pilmore.* Edited by Frederick E. Maser and Howard T. Maag. Philadelphia: Message Publishing Co. for the Historical Society of the Philadelphia Annual Conference of The United Methodist Church, 1969.

A Pocket Hymn-book, designed as a Constant Companion for the Pious. Collected from Various Authors. 5th ed. New York: W. Ross, 1786.

———. 23rd ed. Philadelphia: Henry Tuckniss, 1800.

Seaman, Samuel A. *Annals of New York Methodism being a History of the Methodist Episcopal Church in the City of New York from A. D. 1766 to A. D. 1890.* New York: Hunt & Eaton; Cincinnati: Cranston & Stowe, 1892.

Sigston, James. *Memoir of the Life and Ministry of Mr. William Bramwell, Lately an Itinerant Methodist Preacher; with Extracts from his Interesting and Extensive Correspondence.* 6th American ed. New York: Lane & Scott, 1849.

Simpson, Robert Drew, ed. *American Methodist Pioneer: The Life and Journals of The Rev. Freeborn Garrettson.* Rutland, VT: Academy Books, 1984.

Smith, George G. *The Life and Letters of James Osgood Andrew.* Nashville: Southern Methodist Publishing House, 1882.

Smith, Henry. *Recollections and Reflections of an Old Itinerant.* New York: Lane & Tippett, 1848.

257

[Smith, John]. "The Journal of John Smith, Methodist Circuit Rider, of his Work on the Greenbrier Circuit, (West) Virginia and Virginia." *The Journal of the Greenbrier Historical Society* 1.4 (October 1966): 11-54.

[Sneath, Richard]. "Diary." In *The History of Bethel Methodist Episcopal Church Gloucester County New Jersey 1945.* Compiled by Mrs. Walter Aborn Simpson. N.p., 1945.

Snelling, Joseph. *Life of Rev. Joseph Snelling, Being a Sketch of His Christian Experience and Labors in the Ministry.* Boston: John M'Leish, 1847.

[Spicer, Tobias]. *Autobiography of Rev. Tobias Spicer: Containing Incidents and Observations; also Some Account of his Visit to England.* New York: Lane & Scott, 1852.

Steele, David L., ed. "The Autobiography of the Reverend John Young, 1747–1837." *Methodist History* 13.1 (October 1974): 17-40.

Stevens, Abel. *Life and Times of Nathan Bangs, D.D.* New York: Carlton & Porter, 1863.

———. *Memorials of the Early Progress of Methodism in the Eastern States.* Boston: C. H. Pierce and Co., 1852.

Stevenson, Edward. *Biographical Sketch of the Rev. Valentine Cook, A.M. with an Appendix, Containing his Discourse on Baptism.* Nashville: published for the author, 1858.

Stewart, John. *Highways and Hedges; or, Fifty Years of Western Methodism.* Cincinnati: Hitchcock & Walden; New York: Carlton & Lanahan, 1870.

Stokes, Ellwood H. *A Pilgrim's Foot-Prints, or Passages in the Life of Rev. John Hancock, of East Madison, N.J., who Labored for 50 Years as a Local Minister in the Church of Jesus Christ.* New York: Dix & Edwards, 1855.

Strickland, W. P. *The Life of Jacob Gruber.* New York: Carlton & Porter, 1860.

[Swain, Richard]. *Journal of Rev. Richard Swain.* Edited and transcribed by Robert Bevis Steelman. Rutland, VT: Academy Books, 1977.

Sweet, William Warren. *Religion on the American Frontier 1783–1840.* Vol. 4, *The Methodists.* Chicago: University of Chicago Press, 1946.

Telford, John, ed. *Wesley's Veterans.* 7 vols. London: Charles H. Kelly, 1914.

Thrift, Minton. *Memoir of the Rev. Jesse Lee. With Extracts from his Journals.* New York: Bangs & Mason, 1823.

Todd, Robert W. *Methodism of the Peninsula; or, Sketches of Notable Characters and Events in the History of Methodism in the Maryland and Delaware Peninsula.* Philadelphia: Methodist Episcopal Book Rooms, 1886.

[Travis, Joseph]. *Autobiography of the Rev. Joseph Travis, A.M.* Edited by Thomas O. Summers. Nashville: Stevenson & Evans, 1856.

Trollope, Frances. *Domestic Manners of the Americans.* 5th ed. New York: Dodd, Mead & Co., 1927.

[Turner, Rebecca]. "Excerpts from Rebecca Turner's Diary." In *The History of Bethel Methodist Episcopal Church Gloucester County New Jersey 1945.* Compiled by Mrs. Walter Aborn Simpson. N.p., 1945.

[Valton, John]. *The Life and Labours of the Late Rev. John Valton.* Edited by Joseph Sutcliffe. New York: Mason & Lane, 1837.

Wakeley, J. B. *The Heroes of Methodism, containing Sketches of Eminent Methodist Ministers, and Characteristic Anecdotes of their Personal History.* New York: Carlton & Porter, 1857.

———. *Lost Chapters Recovered from the Early History of American Methodism.* New York: Carlton & Porter, 1858.

———. *The Patriarch of One Hundred Years; Being Reminiscences, Historical and Biographical of Rev. Henry Boehm.* New York: Nelson & Phillips, 1875; reprint, n.p.: Abram W. Sangrey, 1982.

Wallace, Adam. *The Parson of the Islands: A Biography of the Late Rev. Joshua Thomas,* with Sketches of Many of his Contemporaries and an Account of the Origin of Methodism on the Islands of the Chesapeake and Eastern Shores of Maryland and Virginia. Philadelphia: Office of the Methodist Home Journal, 1872.

Ward, Francis. *An Account of Three Camp-Meetings held by the Methodists, at Sharon, Litchfield County, Connecticut; at Rhinebeck, in Dutchess County; and at Petersburgh, In Rensselaer County, New-York State.* Brooklyn: Robinson & Little, 1806.

Ware, Thomas. "The Christmas Conference of 1784." *MQR* 14 (1832): 96-104.

———. *Sketches of the Life and Travels of Rev. Thomas Ware, who has been an Itinerant Methodist Preacher for More than Fifty Years.* New York: Lane & Sandford, 1842.

[Watson, James V.]. *Tales and Takings, Sketches and Incidents, from the Itinerant and Editorial Budget of Rev. James V. Watson.* New York: Carlton & Porter, 1857.

[Watson, John Fanning]. *Methodist Error.* Trenton: D. & E. Fenton, 1819.

Watters, William. *A Short Account of the Christian Experience, and Ministereal Labours, of William Watters.* Alexandria: S. Snowden, 1806.

Wesley, John. *John Wesley's Sunday Service of the Methodists in North America.* Introduced by James F. White. Nashville: United Methodist Publishing House, 1984. (This is a partial reprint of the original 1784 London edition.)

Wightman, William M. *Life of William Capers, D.D., One of the Bishops of the Methodist Episcopal church, South; Including an Autobiography.* Nashville: Southern Methodist Publishing House, 1858.

Willson, Shipley Wells, and Ebenezer Ireson, ed. *The Methodist Preacher: or Monthly Sermons from Living Ministers.* Vols. 1 and 2 for 1830 and 1831. 2nd. ed. Boston: C. D. Strong, 1832.

[Woolsey, Elijah]. *The Supernumerary; or, Lights and Shadows of Itinerancy. Compiled from Papers of Rev. Elijah Woolsey.* Compiled by George Coles. New York: Lane & Tippett, 1845.

Wright, John F. *Sketches of the Life and Labors of James Quinn, who was Nearly Half a Century a Minister of the Gospel in the Methodist Episcopal Church.* Cincinnati: Methodist Book Concern, 1851.

[Young, Dan.] *Autobiography of Dan Young, A New England Preacher of the Olden Time.* Edited by W. P. Strickland. New York: Carlton & Porter, 1860.

[Young, Jacob]. *Autobiography of a Pioneer: or, the Nativity, Experience, Travels, and Ministerial Labors of Rev. Jacob Young, with Incidents, Observations, and Reflections.* Cincinnati: Swormstedt & Poe, 1857.

Secondary Material

Baker, Frank. *Methodism and the Love-Feast.* London: Epworth, 1957.

Barratt, Thomas H. "The Place of the Lord's Supper in Early Methodism." *London Quarterly Review* 140 (July 1923): 56-73.

Bedell, Kenneth B. *Worship in the Methodist Tradition.* Nashville: Tidings, 1976.

Berger, Teresa. *Theology in Hymns? A Study of the Relationship of Doxology and Theology According to a Collection of Hymns for the Use of the People Called Methodists (1780).* Translated by Timothy E. Kimbrough. Nashville: Kingswood, 1995.

Bishop, John. *Methodist Worship in Relation to Free Church Worship.* New York: Scholars Studies Press, Inc., 1975.

Borgen, Ole E. *John Wesley on the Sacraments.* Nashville: Abingdon, 1972.

Bowmer, John C. "A Converting Ordinance and the Open Table." *Proceedings of the Wesley Historical Society* 34 (1964): 109-13.

———. *The Lord's Supper in Methodism 1791–1960.* London: Epworth, 1961.

————. *The Sacraments of the Lord's Supper in Early Methodism*. Westminster: Dacre Press, 1951.

Brown, Earl Kent. "Liturgy Today: Historical Perspectives on Methodist Worship." *Religion in Life* 39 (spring 1970): 28-34.

Bucke, Emory Stevens. "American Methodism and the Love Feast." *Methodist History* 1 (July 1963): 8-13.

Burdon, Adrian. *The Preaching Service—The Glory of the Methodists: A Study of the piety, ethos and development of the Methodist Preaching Service*. Alcuin/GROW Liturgical Study, no. 17. Bramcote: Grove Books Limited, 1991.

Church, Leslie F. *The Early Methodist People*. New York: Philosophical Library, 1949.

————. *More about the Early Methodist People*. London: Epworth, 1949.

Felton, Gayle Carlton. *This Gift of Water: the Practice and Theology of Baptism among Methodists in America*. Nashville: Abingdon, 1992.

Hatch, Nathan O. *The Democratization of American Christianity*. New Haven: Yale University Press, 1989.

Heyrman, Christine Leigh. *Southern Cross: The Beginnings of the Bible Belt*. New York: Knopf, 1997.

Hohenstein, Charles R. "The Revisions of the Rites of Baptism in the Methodist Episcopal Church, 1784–1939." Ph.D. diss., University of Notre Dame, 1990.

Hood, Fred. "Community and the Rhetoric of 'Freedom': Early American Methodist Worship," *Methodist History* 9.1 (October 1970): 13-25.

Hudson, Winthrop S. "Shouting Methodists." *Encounter* 29 (1968): 73-84.

Hunter, Frederick, and Frank Baker. "The Origin of the Methodist Quarterly Meeting." *London Quarterly and Holborn Review* (January 1949): 28-37.

Isaac, Rhys. *The Transformation of Virginia 1740–1790*. Chapel Hill: University of North Carolina Press, 1982.

Johnson, Charles Albert. *The Frontier Campmeeting*. Dallas: SMU Press, 1955.

Johnson, Richard O. "The Development of the Love Feast in Early American Methodism." *Methodist History* 19.2 (January 1981): 67-83.

Johnson, Todd E. "The Sermons of Francis Asbury: Reconstruction and Analysis." *Methodist History* 33.3 (April 1995): 149-61.

Rattenbury, J. Ernest. *The Eucharistic Hymns of John and Charles Wesley*. London: Epworth, 1948; reprint with updated grammar, Cleveland: OSL Publications, 1990.

Richey, Russell E. *Early American Methodism*. Bloomington: Indiana University Press, 1991.

————. *The Methodist Conference in America: A History*. Nashville: Kingswood, 1996.

Ruth, Lester. " 'A Little Heaven Below': Quarterly Meetings as Seasons of Grace in Early American Methodism." Ph.D. diss., University of Notre Dame, 1996.

————. "A Little Heaven Below: The Love Feast and Lord's Supper in Early American Methodism." *Wesleyan Theological Journal* 32.2 (fall 1997): 59-79.

————. "A Reconsideration of the Frequency of the Eucharist in Early American Methodism." *Methodist History* 34.1 (October 1995): 47-58.

Sanders, Paul S. "An Appraisal of John Wesley's Sacramentalism in the Evolution of Early American Methodism." Th.D. diss., Union Theological Seminary, 1954.

————. "The Sacraments in Early American Methodism." *Church History* 26.4 (December 1957): 355-71. Reprinted in *Perspectives on Early American Methodism: Interpretive Essays*. Edited by Russell E. Richey, Kenneth E. Rowe, and Jean Miller Schmidt. Nashville: Kingswood, 1993.

Schmidt, Leigh E. *Holy Fairs: Scottish Communions and American Revivals in the Early Modern Period*. Princeton: Princeton University Press, 1989.

Senn, Frank. *Christian Liturgy: Catholic and Evangelical*. Minneapolis: Fortress, 1997.

Stockton, C. R., "The Origin and Development of Extra-liturgical Worship in Eighteenth Century Methodism." D.Phil. diss., Oxford University, 1969.

Taves, Ann. *Fits, Trances, and Visions: Experiencing Religion and Explaining Experience from Wesley to James.* Princeton, NJ: Princeton University Press, 1999.

————. "Knowing Through the Body: Dissociative Religious Experience in the African- and British-American Methodist Traditions." *The Journal of Religion* 73 (1993): 200-222.

Tigert, Jno. J. *A Constitutional History of American Episcopal Methodism.* 2nd ed. Nashville: Publishing House of the Methodist Episcopal Church, South, 1904.

Voigt, Edwin E. *Methodist Worship in the Church Universal.* Nashville: Graded Press, 1965.

Wade, William Nash. "A History of Public Worship in the Methodist Episcopal Church and Methodist Episcopal Church, South, from 1784 to 1905." Ph.D. diss., University of Notre Dame, 1981.

Westerfield Tucker, Karen. " 'In Thankful Verse Proclaim': English Eucharistic Hymns of the Seventeenth and Eighteenth Centuries." *Studia Liturgica* 26 (1996): 238-53.

————. " 'Till Death Us Do Part': The Rites of Marriage and Burial Prepared by John Wesley and Their Development in the Methodist Episcopal Church, 1784–1939." Ph.D. diss., University of Notre Dame, 1992.

White, James F. *Protestant Worship: Traditions in Transition.* Louisville: Westminster/John Knox, 1989.

Wigger, John H. "Holy, 'Knock-'em-down' Preachers," *Christian History* 14.1 [n.d.], 24.

————. *Taking Heaven by Storm: Methodism and the Rise of Popular Christianity in America.* New York: Oxford University Press, 1998.

Index